Uncovering Texas Politics
in the 21st Century

Uncovering Texas Politics in the 21st Century

Eric Lopez

Marcus Stadelmann

Robert E. Sterken Jr.

The University of Texas at Tyler

PRESS

Tyler, Texas

The University of Texas at Tyler

Michael Tidwell, President
Amir Mirmiran, Provost
Neil Gray, Dean, College of Arts and Sciences

UT Tyler Press

Publisher: Lucas Roebuck, Vice President for Marketing
Production Supervisor: Olivia Paek, Agency Director
Content Coordination: Colleen Swain, Associate Provost for Undergraduate and Online Education
Author Liaison: Ashley Bill, Executive Director of Academic Success
Editorial Support: Emily Battle, Senior Editorial Specialist
Design: Matt Snyder

ISBN-13
978-1-7333299-1-0

UT Tyler Press
3900 University Blvd.
Tyler, Texas 75799
www.uttyler.edu/press

Table of Contents

Dear Student:

This is a great time to live in Texas! Arguably the most influential state in the Union, Texas is an economic, cultural, and educational leader worthy of study. Understanding the dynamic politics of Texas is a great introduction to political science. Through the study of political science, students gain insight into their civic rights and responsibilities, empowering them to impactfully participate in the democratic process.

At UT Tyler, we believe that providing access to knowledge regardless of means is an important part of a healthy society. That is why UT Tyler Press is providing the electronic version of Uncovering Texas Politics in the 21st Century free of charge to Texas students, and the print version at cost. The rising cost of higher education should not be a barrier to achievement; this free textbook initiative is one way we are working to lower the cost of higher education.

The creation of this textbook is funded in part by a grant from the University of Texas System in support of our Open Educational Resources (OER) initiative to make college more affordable by providing free access to course materials. I extend our deepest gratitude to UT System for sharing our passion for student success through affordable education.

Uncovering Texas Politics in the 21st Century is authored by three UT Tyler professors, and their high level of expertise and dedication to student learning is evident throughout every chapter.

Dr. Eric Lopez is a specialist in American politics, the federal court system, and the development of Constitutional law. Dr. Marcus Stadelmann is chair of the Department of History and Political Science and teaches comparative politics and international relations. Dr. Robert E. Sterken Jr. is a Senior Fulbright Scholar who has taught politics around the world, most recently in Burma/Myanmar, Thailand, and Cambodia.

On behalf of UT Tyler Press and President Michael Tidwell, I congratulate Drs. Lopez, Stadelmann, and Sterken on an excellent textbook, and I again thank UT System for their critical support of this OER project. We hope you find this textbook illuminating and relevant as you progress in your academic career.

All the best,

Dr. Amir Mirmiran
Provost, UT Tyler

uttyler.edu

1

The People in Texas

Texas Demographics

Political Culture and Ideology
in a Diverse State

Chapter 1

A State of Diversity:
Demographics, Culture, and the Struggle for Identity

TEXAS! What images, stereotypes, and ideas come to mind when you think of the Lone Star State? Do you think of the rugged men who fought at the Alamo or of pickup trucks that proudly display "Come and Take It" bumper stickers? Do you think of barbecue, boots, and sad country music at the Houston Livestock Show and Rodeo? Do you see Texas as the land of oilfields, cowboys, and hardworking super-patriotic people who defy all governmental authority?

Whether you have lived in Texas all your life or just arrived from Vietnam, you likely picture Texans as rugged and rowdy people with a fierce streak of individualism. To some extent, these images of Texas are based on reality, but an entirely different picture is woven into these old stereotypes of Texas culture. The cowboy image of Texas was always unidimensional and incomplete; it is now far outdated.

In Austin, Dallas, El Paso, Houston, Lubbock, Mineola, Nacogdoches, San Antonio, and Tyler today you will find a cowboy or two driving a pickup truck, but you will also find poets, high-tech business leaders, edgy musicians, super-star athletes, aerospace engineers, fine artists, celebrated professors, and

FIGURE 1.1 Capitol building in Austin, Texas.

uttyler.edu

FIGURE 1.2

Top 10 Languages Other than English Spoken in Texas Households, 2017

Of the 25 million people in Texas five years or older, 65 percent speak only English at home. The rest speak more than 160 languages combined.

Language	Number of Speakers
Spanish	7,498,255
Vietnamese	214,373
Chinese *(incl. Mandarin, Cantonese)*	164,449
Tagalog *(incl. Filipino)*	82,851
Urdu	77,847
Arabic	77,686
Hindi	73,089
French	69,428
German	62,527
Korean	56,064

Source: The American Community Survey 2017[1]

even world-renowned chefs, all living within a widely diverse set of cultures, languages, people, and foods from every corner of the earth. The stereotypical image of Texas embodies a single state of mind and a specific way of life—a monoculture—but this image badly needs an update!

The People in Texas

Today, Texas is home to immigrants from all over the world. More than 165 languages are spoken across the state. Of the estimated 29 million people living in Texas in 2019, about 65% speak only English. A very large majority—almost 85%—of those who speak another language speak Spanish **(Figure 1.2)**. It might be surprising that Vietnamese is the third most common language in Texas. The number of Chinese, Urdu, Arabic and Hindi speakers has risen significantly since 2010.

All this diversity is shaping and reshaping the culture and identity of Texas. In this chapter we will discover not only who makes up the Texas population, but how the diverse population of communities of native Texans, settlers, and immigrants combine to share and govern the state. The diverse population in Texas continues to evolve and is changing the **political culture** across the state and in doing so creating tensions and challenges for Texans.

Political culture: the set of attitudes, norms, and values that provide the underlying assumptions and rules that govern a society.

First Texans

All Texans are immigrants because no humans used to live in the land today known as Texas.[2] Although exact dates are lost, we do know there were no native Texans—people migrated to this region of the world. Tens of thousands of years ago, long before humans began recording history, a land bridge connected the continents of Asia and Alaska. On that land bridge, the first human immigrants made their way to North America. When these early humans entered Texas, they had hundreds of thousands of years of evolution and social development behind them. These early people were hunters, cooked with fire, wore fur garments, and made tools of flint and bones. These early immigrants eventually settled in the Valley of Mexico, far south of Texas. In Mexico, a long succession of Aztec, Mayan, Toltec, and other people farmed and grew into a complex and large society. These people developed immense cities, a written form of communication, complex mathematics, and remarkably accurate astronomy. They worked with silver, gold, and copper to create beautiful art. Over time, farmers in the Mexican valley began to settle and plant their corn, moving northward. Around 1000 CE, these Mexican (Pueblo) people expanded into the high plains of Texas and then into the Rio Grande Valley.

Indigenous People

Hundreds of groups of native people with various languages, customs, and beliefs lived on the land that became Texas for at least eleven thousand years before Europeans arrived. Long before Europeans migrated to Texas, the land was inhabited by descendants of ancient immigrants from Asia and then from Mexico. Over time, the region of Texas became home to many immigrant tribes—today we call them *Native Americans*. Among these Native Americans were the Caddo people who lived near the Red River in Northeast Texas near present-day Nacogdoches (as well as in Arkansas, Louisiana, and Oklahoma).

The Caddo people lived in large complex societies and were known for cultivating corn and for beautiful ceramics. The Apache people lived farther south and as far west as Big Bend. While the Caddo were farming, the Apache lived off herds of roaming buffalo. From the rainy woods of East Texas to the humid Gulf Coast and to the arid plains of West Texas, the native peoples established complex societies, advanced agricultural practices, and organized spiritual ceremonies and rituals.

By the late 17th century, Spanish and French explorers were racing to plant flags across the region that became Texas. The Native Americans and the land in North America meant new labor, natural resources, power, and new sources of wealth for Europeans. In 1685, René Robert Cavelier and Sieur de La Salle established the first European settlement in Texas.

French

Though ill-fated, La Salle's Texas settlement gave the French a claim to parts of Texas. By early February in 1685, La Salle had established a colony of about

uttyler.edu

FIGURE 1.3

Ethnolinguistic Distribution of Native Texans, 1500 and 1776

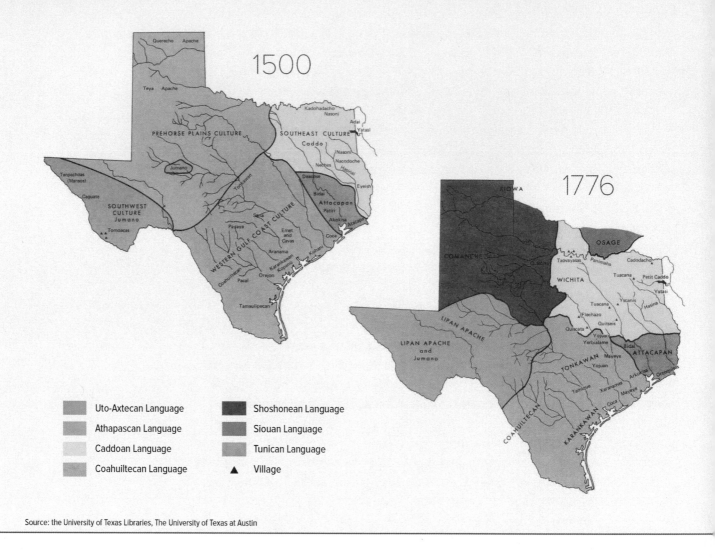

Uto-Axtecan Language
Athapascan Language
Caddoan Language
Coahuiltecan Language

Shoshonean Language
Siouan Language
Tunican Language
▲ Village

Source: the University of Texas Libraries, The University of Texas at Austin

two hundred French men, women, and children at Matagorda Bay in Spanish-claimed territory. The French established trade among the Caddo in East Texas and in 1817, and the French pirate Jean Laffite set up a "republic" on Galveston Island. A year later, Laffite's Galveston settlement had grown to more than one thousand French people. The French, like nearly all immigrants who came to Texas, came in search of better lives, and so contributed much French culture to Texas.

The U.S. census of 1860 indicates that there were about two thousand French-born people in Texas. By 1930, the U.S. census showed over ten thousand people of French nationality in the state. Every year on July 14th, many Texans celebrate Bastille Day (a celebration of the uprising that began in the French Revolution). French settlements were abandoned because of food shortages and threats from Spanish authorities. The Spanish worried the

French would ally with the Native Americans to take over the northern Mexico silver mines, so they sent troops to push out the French.

Spanish

Spanish migrants came seeking gold and silver in a land they thought held the fountain of youth. In the 1530s and 1540s, Cabeza de Vaca, Vasquez de Coronado, and Luis de Moscoso Alvarado mapped the area and established missions and military outposts along the Texas coast and throughout eastern and northern Texas. Over the next two hundred years, the mission and military outposts administered and controlled the region under Spanish rule. The Spanish conquest in the Americas was not about colonizing or settling on the land. Spain tightly regulated emigration, and those who did settle did not expect to live off the land. Rather, they would extract raw resources and labor from the native population. The brutal Spanish conquest was destructive to the native societies. Beginning with Columbus's second voyage, the Spanish enslaved alarming numbers of Native Americans to work in gold and silver mines. By 1520, entire Caribbean islands had been depopulated and the inhabitants moved to gold mines in what is now the Dominican Republic. Tens of thousands of native Americans were worked to death, even after the Spanish monarchy outlawed slavery. The Spanish colonial system envisioned a new society with a paternalistic Spanish–Native culture in which they would rule, care for, reshape, and profit from the native people and the land.

This paternalistic approach gave enormous power and responsibility to the Catholic missionary priests and Catholic Church leaders. The Church would attempt to spread Christianity and to be the teachers and law-givers across the Spanish colonies. The Church would bring "civilization" to what they saw as "heathen" people. The Spanish people thought saving the souls of heathens was a very important duty because they believed their religion was the only true path to salvation. For more than a thousand years, however, the native people the Spanish encountered had their own long-cherished and deeply held religious traditions. Interestingly, the Caddo and Pueblo people were open to the teachings of the Catholic priests, so the Spanish thought that was a willing acceptance of Catholicism. By the early 1600s, they began reporting to Spain that many native people had been converted to Christianity. The native people saw things differently, as they had no intention of letting Christianity take the place of their own religion. The Caddo and Pueblo people would accept and even attend Christian practices, but they did not want nor intend to stop their own practices. The Spanish then demanded that the native people stop practicing their own religion. They banned native ceremonies, burned their religious icons, and destroyed their places of worship. The Spanish became increasingly brutal, and tensions reached a breaking point in 1675 when 47 Pueblo religious leaders were imprisoned in Santa Fe for practicing their native religion. The Spanish publicly flogged and then hung three religious leaders. The Pueblo people called for war, and on August 10th, 1680, thousands of Pueblo warriors descended on the Spanish, killing hundreds and specifically targeting Catholic priests. Religious conflicts with the Spanish and

>> The Spanish colonial system envisioned a new society with a paternalistic Spanish-Native culture in which they would rule, care for, reshape, and profit from the native people and the land.

uttyler.edu

the diseases they brought to Texas greatly diminished the Pueblo and Caddo societies and the numbers of Native Americans. The Spanish empire would become even more brutal and oppressive, thriving for hundreds of years and reshaping the area's religion, social structure, culture, and land.

Today, much in Texas is shaped by the Spanish. Hundreds of towns, cities, counties, and geographic features across the state have Spanish names. The Texas legal system is still influenced by a Spanish approach to law and justice. Spanish crops, foods, drinks, livestock and farming techniques are still very much part of the culture across Texas. A very large number of Catholics live in Texas, and the Spanish mission architecture still dominates much of the state—especially in Central and West Texas. After a series of revolts, the United Mexican States (Mexico) won independence from Spain in 1821. A few years later, the Texas revolution began with the battle of Gonzales in October 1835.

Tejanos

The Texas revolution from Mexico ended with the battle of San Jacinto on April 21, 1836, but over the next decade a tangled series of conflicts over the next decade—including the United States-Mexican War (1846–1848)—resulted in the United States acquiring about half of Mexico's territory. Many Mexican Texans, called Tejanos, lived far and wide across the newly acquired territory. The Spanish adjective *Tejano* (or *Tejana*) denotes a Texan of Mexican descent. *Tex-Mex* is a recently coined adjective related to, but not synonymous with, Tejano.

Anglo migrants in Texas clashed with the Tejanos, and the two groups struggled for power and to maintain their place in the region. Stephen F. Austin, an early settler who lived in East Texas, organized a small group of men called *rangers* to protect the Anglo immigrants and their property.[3] In 1835, Texas lawmakers formally instituted Austin's men as the Texas Rangers. The Texas Rangers worked to ensure that the Anglo immigrants flourished in their new land, but their success came at the expense of groups they considered enemies and of groups they used for labor. Austin's men battled Tejano landowners and the indigenous people, including the Caddo and the Apache. The Texas Rangers targeted the *Indian warrior* and the Mexican *vaquero* as enemies of white supremacy.

Some Tejanos resisted the newest Texas immigrants with violence. By the summer of 1859, Juan Nepomuceno Cortina had come to hate the Texas Rangers and the Anglo judges whom he accused of expropriating land from Tejanos who were unfamiliar with the U.S. judicial system. On July 13, 1859, Cortina saw the Brownsville Marshal, Robert Shears, brutally beat and then arrest a Tejano who Cortina once employed. Cortina shot Marshal Shears and rode out of Brownsville with the Tejano prisoner. A couple of months later on September 28, 1859, Cortina rode back into Brownsville, this time with some eighty men. Cortina and his men raced through the streets shouting, "Death to the Americans!" and "Viva Mexico!" They seized control of the town and shot and killed five men, including the city jailer. Cortina described the Anglo immigrants as "wild beasts" and "vampire guises of men" who murdered Tejanos.

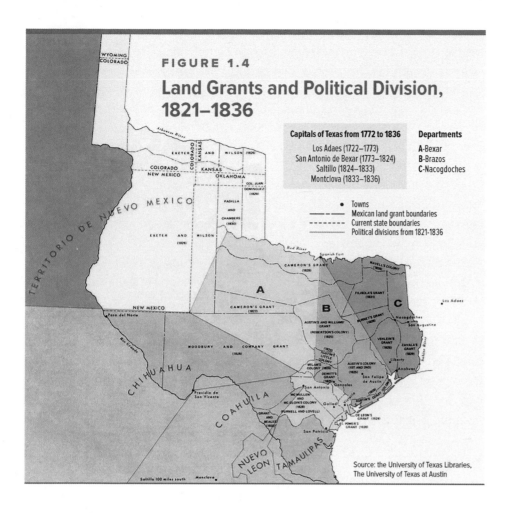

FIGURE 1.4

Land Grants and Political Division, 1821–1836

Capitals of Texas from 1772 to 1836

Los Adaes (1722–1773)
San Antonio de Bexar (1773–1824)
Saltillo (1824–1833)
Montclova (1833–1836)

Departments

A-Bexar
B-Brazos
C-Nacogdoches

- Towns
— · — · Mexican land grant boundaries
———— Current state boundaries
- - - - Political divisions from 1821-1836

Source: the University of Texas Libraries,
The University of Texas at Austin

Cortina's stand for the Tejanos would earn him an honored spot in Texas music. A genre of *border ballads* is sung by ethnic Mexicans to honor those who stand up to discrimination, colonization, and injustice. The Tejanos also brought cultural influence in language, literature, art, music, and food to their new state.

Anglos

The Spanish who ruled Texas in the 1790s were very concerned about Anglos from the United States migrating into the territory. Anglos rapidly expanded throughout the United States in the late 1700s and early 1800s, threatening Spanish and, later, Mexican control over Texas. Some Anglos were fugitives and others were wandering entrepreneurs looking for riches, but most were subsistence farmers moving into East Texas for the rich rain-soaked soil. The Spanish were concerned about these American squatters moving into East Texas without authorization, and they focused on Americans who came into Texas to steal Texas's natural resources and sell them in the United States.

One enterprising American, Philip Nolan (who immigrated to the United States from Ireland), was well known to Spanish authorities by 1785. In October of 1800, Nolan presented a map he made of Texas and a bold plan to Baron de Carondelet, the governor of Louisiana, to travel to Texas, capture wild horses, and sell them to a Louisiana regiment. The illegal plan was approved, and

Nolan set out on his fourth expedition into Spanish Texas with about twenty heavily armed men and a few slaves to capture horses. Near the Brazos River, in the present-day Waco area, Nolan and his men built a small fortification and corrals for the horses. By March of 1801, Nolan had managed to round up around three hundred horses. Spanish authorities had been looking for Nolan, and the Governor of Texas, Juan Bautista de Elguezabal, issued an order to "put Nolan out of the way" if he ever returned to Texas.[4] On the night of March 21, 1801, a full company of Spanish soldiers from Nacogdoches, under Spanish commander Miguel Francisco Músquiz, surrounded Nolan's camp and attacked just before sunrise the next morning. Nolan was shot and killed. The men accompanying Nolan were captured and led to Nacogdoches, where they were held in the Old Stone Fort (which still stands on the campus of Stephen F. Austin State University). Then, they were taken to Mexico. Nolan is recognized as the first of many Anglo migrants who eventually took Texas from Spanish and Mexican rule. Because of the surge in illegal Anglo immigration (immigrants like Nolan), the Spanish authorities in Texas decreed laws in the 1830s to stop further immigration into Texas. Eventually, both the illegal Anglo immigrants and the Tejanos called for independence for Texas. Following the Texas Revolution, the relationship between the Tejanos and the Anglos devolved into a violent power struggle as the Anglos—now the majority—seized land from the Tejanos.[5]

Africans

The first Africans in Texas were slaves. Records show that the Spanish held African people as slaves in Mexico as early as the 1520s. A slave named Estevanico is thought to be the first person from Africa to arrive in Texas, but his migration was not voluntary. In 1528, Estevanico was a slave in a group of about eighty Spanish explorers who survived a shipwreck and washed ashore at Galveston Island. Estevanico was also the first non-Native to visit the Pueblo lands in Mexico, where he served as guide for other Spanish expeditions to the region.

Hundreds of thousands of Africans and native Americans were enslaved during the Spanish empire's roughly three hundred years in Mexico. Later, Anglo settlers from the United States brought slaves with them as well. Stephen F. Austin's Rangers used to preserve slave-based agriculture by violently policing African men and women. The Rangers tracked and punished enslaved people trying to cross the Rio Grande into Mexico and to freedom. By the time of the Texas Revolution in 1836, there were about five thousand African slaves in Texas.[6] By 1850, about thirty-nine thousand slaves were abused to support the agrarian economy. Even after slavery was outlawed by the Spanish and then by the Mexican and U.S. governments, people profited from the enterprise by deploying legal terms and frameworks to continue the practice.

After the Civil War, the Texas legislature enacted a series of *Black Codes* that restricted the civil rights and freedoms of former slaves and continued slavery by adopting laws that nullified the intentions of the Thirteenth Amendment, such as convict leasing and vagrancy laws. After Mexico outlawed slavery,

Mexicans used the *convict leasing* tactic to enslave native Texans. After the U.S. Civil War, Anglo Texans employed the same tactic to continue using slave labor for profit. These laws also created a violent and new form of slavery that has again recently come to light.

In February 2018 in Sugarland, Texas (a suburb of Houston), a backhoe operator was preparing ground for the construction of a new school when he saw something in the dirt. From his tractor seat, it looked like he had uncovered human bones. Bioarchaeologist Dr. Catrina Banks Whitley was immediately called to the site. By June 2018, the remains of 95 bodies—94 men and one woman—had been exhumed. These 95 people recall a violent system of social control from one of the darkest times in Texas's history.

Sugarland, Texas has long been the home of the Imperial Sugar Company, and sugarcane farming prior to the American Civil War relied heavily on slave labor. After the South's defeat in the Civil War and the abolition of slavery, sugar plantations could no longer rely on slave labor. Most sugar plantations in south Texas went bankrupt, but not the Imperial Sugar Company. After the Civil War, Texas leaders and the Imperial Sugar Company turned to a different form of slavery called *convict leasing*. In the unmarked graves uncovered in Sugarland were the bodies of black Americans targeted and arrested for offenses such as vagrancy, flirting with a white woman, or accusations of petty theft. African Americans, many who had been slaves, were arrested and jailed for Jim Crow laws meant to control blacks and "keep them in their place." The African-American people unearthed in Sugarland were convicts who were "leased" to the Imperial Sugar Company. Being arrested and sent to prison in Texas was a horrible and constant fear for African Americans. The 95 people exhumed in Sugarland were among the over thirty-five hundred leased convicts who died in Texas between 1866 and 1912.

In November 2016, thousands of Texans gathered in Austin in front of the Capitol to celebrate the unveiling of a 27-foot-high and 32-foot-wide monument. The monument depicts 48 slaves and marks Juneteenth—June 19, 1865—the day Union troops arrived in Texas to free all Texas slaves. The monument includes other major social, political, and cultural state icons from years later. At the unveiling, Texas Governor Greg Abbott said the monument recognizes moments in Texas history that have long needed acknowledgment. Governor Abbott said, "To know where we are going in life, we have to understand where it is that we have come from. The triumphs, the tragedies, the lessons that we learn along the way. They are a legacy for the generations that are to come forward in the future. But chapters have been missing from the story of Texas. That changes today."[7]

》 By 1850, about thirty-nine thousand slaves were abused to support the agrarian economy. Even after slavery was outlawed by the Spanish and then by the Mexican and U.S. governments, people profited from the enterprise by deploying legal terms and frameworks to continue the practice.

Vietnamese

In 2019, the third most common language in Texas was Vietnamese. The U.S. government began its involvement in Vietnam in 1950 with military aid for the French. In the Vietnam war, U.S. armed forces and South Vietnam fought against the North Vietnamese Army and the Vietcong. U.S. involvement in the war included hundreds of thousands of U.S. soldiers, large-scale aerial

FIGURE 1.5

Population in Growing States, 2010–2017

	2010 Population	2017 Population	Numeric Change 2010–2017	Percent Change 2010–2017
United States	308,745,538	325,719,178	16,973,640	5.5%
Texas	**25,145,561**	**28,304,596**	**3,159,035**	**12.6%**
California	37,253,956	39,536,653	2,282,697	6.1%
Florida	18,801,310	20,984,400	2,183,090	11.6%
Georgia	9,687,653	10,429,379	741,726	7.7%
North Carolina	9,535,483	10,273,419	737,936	7.7%
Washington	6,724,540	7,405,743	681,203	10.1%
Arizona	6,392,017	7,016,270	624,253	9.8%
Colorado	5,029,196	5,607,154	577,958	11.5%

Source: the U.S. Census Bureau's 2000 and 2010 Census Count, 2017 Population Estimates

bombardment, and the use of napalm over North and South Vietnam that killed millions of civilians and hundreds of thousands of soldiers and almost totally destroyed the small Southeast Asian country.[8] The fall of Saigon on April 30, 1975 marked the end of the Vietnam War and the capture of Saigon by North Vietnamese forces. After Saigon's fall, hundreds of thousands of Vietnamese refugees came to the United States. In the late 1970s and early 1980s, many of those refugees made their way to Texas. In 2019, Houston was home to more than eighty thousand Vietnamese—the largest population outside of California.

In 2018, because of its quickly growing Vietnamese population, Tarrant County (Fort Worth) joined a list of Texas counties required to provide election materials in Vietnamese. The Voting Rights Act, passed in 1965, prohibits state and local governments from passing laws or policies that deny American citizens the equal right to vote. Part of the Voting Rights Act requires states to provide registration, voting notices, forms, instructions, assistance, and other materials or information relating to the electoral process, including ballots, in languages of applicable minority groups in addition to English.[9] In 2018, Tarrant County, the third-largest county in Texas, joined Harris County (Houston), the largest, in translating voting materials into Vietnamese and providing interpreters for Vietnamese-speaking voters.

Like the Houston Astros and Texas Rangers baseball teams, the Livestock Show and Rodeo, and the NASA space center, Vietnamese people are now part Texas's identity![10] Vietnamese Texans have infused new culture and ideas into the existing Texan population—many speak Vietnamese, celebrate the Lunar New Year, and practice Buddhism. On Houston's Bellaire Boulevard—the main street of the district known as Little Saigon—street signs appear in Vietnamese and English. Every decently sized Texas city now has a Pho noodle shop. Pots of piquant shrimp bubbling in Vietnamese and Cajun spices and other Mexican, Vietnamese, and Texan fusions have given Texas a diverse and spicy new menu.

Texas Demographics

In February 2018, the U.S. Citizenship and Immigration Services changed its mission statement to eliminate a passage that describes the United States as "a nation of immigrants."[11] Yet, Texas is a state made entirely of immigrants, becoming one of the most diverse populations in the United States. In 2018, an estimated twenty-nine million people lived in Texas, a substantial increase from about twenty-five million in 2010. The metropolitan areas of Dallas and Houston ranked 4th and 6th in overall population out of all U.S. metropolitan areas. The Dallas metropolitan area (including Dallas, Fort Worth, and Arlington) is home to about seven and a half million people. The Houston metropolitan area (including the Woodlands and Sugarland) is home to another seven million people. Texas has three cities with more than one million people: Dallas, Houston, and San Antonio. In addition, El Paso, Fort Worth, and Austin, each have over five hundred thousand people. Texas' population is expected to double by 2050 to 54.4 million people.

Texas's Hispanic population is on pace to become the largest group in the state by 2022, given that it increased from 9.7 million in 2010 to 11.1 million in 2017, according to census population estimates. Meanwhile, the state's white population increased by about 458,000 people.

Urban Texans

The vast majority (83%) of land in Texas is rural, meaning it is farmed, ranched, or forested. However, Texas is losing rural lands faster than any other state, and the metropolitan areas of Texas have seen exploding growth. According to the Texas A&M Institute of Renewable Natural Resources survey, Texas lost about one million acres of open-space lands between 1997 and 2012.[12] Texas suburbs are still the state's fastest-growing areas. In 1910, only 24% of the Texas population resided in urban areas, and 76% of Texans lived in rural areas. By 2010, the urban share of Texas population had risen to 85% with just 15% living in rural areas.[13] According to the Texas Demographic Center, 95% of the state's 2010 to 2050 population growth will occur in metropolitan areas, and the non-metropolitan counties will account for only 5.4% of the growth.[14] In the years to come, Texas's population will increasingly center around its cities.

Photo by Eddie Seal for The Texas Tribune

FIGURE 1.6 Hispanics are expected to become the largest population group in Texas as soon as 2022.

FIGURE 1.7

Growth Among Texans of Color Outpaces White Population

While white Texans remain the largest population group in Texas, their growth rate since 2010 has been easily outpaced by other major population groups.

Race	2010 Population Estimate	2017 Population Estimate	Percent Change
Asian	960,543	1,366,658	42% ↑
Hispanic	9,460,921	11,156,514	18% ↑
Black	2,899,884	3,368,473	16% ↑
White	11,428,638	11,886,381	4% ↑

Source: the U.S. Census Bureau

Urbanization: *refers to the population shift from rural areas to urban areas.*

Challenges from Growing Urbanization

The increasingly urban and fast-growing population in Texas will present some changes and challenges regarding transportation, water, healthcare, and energy.

Transportation: As the population grows and becomes more urban, so will the demand for transportation. The road and highway systems will not be able to meet the existing car culture's demands. Given current trends, the Texas Department of Transportation estimates that road use will grow by 15% by 2033, but road capacity will only grow by 6%.

Water: All these urban-dwelling Texans will demand water. The Texas Water Development Board projects that Texas's water supplies—those that are reliable during a drought—will decline by approximately 11% between 2020 and 2070. Texas would need substantial additional water supplies to meet all its demand for water in 2070.[15]

Healthcare: The rapidly growing Texas population will also need health-care. Texas has the nation's highest rate of uninsured people. In 2018, a Georgetown University Center for Children and Families study found that more than one in five uninsured U.S. children live in Texas—about 835,000 as of 2017. The state saw an increase of about 83,000 uninsured children from 2016 to 2017.[16] Texas's rate of uninsured children in 2017 was 10.7%, up slightly from the previous year and still more than double the national average.

Energy: With high temperatures regularly reaching 107° in Dallas, 105° in Austin, and a humid 101° in Houston, 54 million Texans will demand lots of energy. Texans are estimated to meet energy demands through about 2030 with oil, coal, and natural gas. Once those resources are depleted, Texans must turn to alternative energy sources. Although Texas is best-known for its oil and gas industries, the state leads the United States in wind power use. The state's wind energy projects have the capacity to generate power for some five million homes—triple the installed capacity of the number-two state, Iowa. The state's wind energy production is expected to increase and to provide a growing share of the state's electricity.[17]

Political Culture and Ideology in a Diverse State

By now, it should be evident that Texas is a very diverse state and is growing more so every year. All that diversity means the state's political culture is difficult to describe and ever changing. Political culture is set of attitudes, norms, and values that provide the underlying assumptions and rules that govern a society. A societies' political culture promotes specific values, and those values are reflected in the political system's goals, laws, and policies.

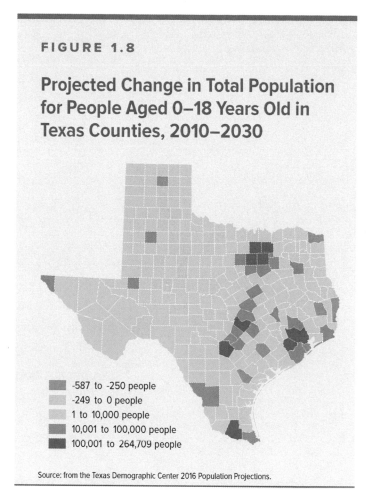

FIGURE 1.8

Projected Change in Total Population for People Aged 0–18 Years Old in Texas Counties, 2010–2030

-587 to -250 people
-249 to 0 people
1 to 10,000 people
10,001 to 100,000 people
100,001 to 264,709 people

Source: from the Texas Demographic Center 2016 Population Projections.

Texan (American) Values

Texans are hardly monolithic, but most, if not all, Texans and Americans agree on six values. Interpretations of these values vary wildly, and different Texans will emphasize some values over others, but most Texans across the ideological spectrum will support liberty, rule of law, self-government, diversity, equal opportunities, and individualism.

Liberty: This political value cherishes freedom from arbitrary powers to restrict people's choices. Americans widely support that freedom, and Texans firmly advocate for each individual's power or right to act, speak, or think without hindrance or restraint. From the Texas legislature's structure to the regulation of school lunches, this value shapes nearly every aspect of Texas politics and policies.

Liberty: a political value that cherishes freedom from an arbitrary exercise of power that restricts a person's choices.

Rule of Law: Texans roundly value and support a legal system with specific rules enforced equally against all people. For Texans, the rule of law includes accountability, (the government and private citizens are accountable under the law), just laws (laws are clear, publicized, stable, and just), and an open government (laws enacted, administered, and enforced are accessible, fair, and efficient). Without the rule of law, a society, person, regime, or group rules arbitrarily.

Rule of law: a system that has specific rules that are enforced equally against all people.

Self-government: Texas and American political cultures roundly support the value of people's sovereignty. To be legitimate, the laws and policies created in Austin and elsewhere must have the people's consent. The social contract in Texas only gives the Texas government the authority accorded it by the Texas citizens. Using a representative democracy, the citizens of Texas elect public officials to make political decisions and enact laws on behalf of the citizens.

Diversity: The diversity of Texas makes it unsurprising that Texans value unique characteristics and respect individual differences across all dimensions of race, ethnicity, gender, sexual orientation, socio-economic status, age, physical abilities, religious beliefs, political beliefs, and ideologies. The value of diversity includes respect for qualities and experiences that differ from one's own. One benefit of diversity is that Texans generally value majority rule and minority rights. With majority rule, society's numerical majority holds the power to make binding decisions for all. Because Texans value diversity, however, they also protect minority rights. By law, minority groups have certain fundamental rights that cannot be taken away.

Equality of opportunity: Texans tend to disdain inherited nobility, wealth, and power and instead believe in human equality. Texan political culture has an egalitarian tradition where all individuals are equal in their moral worth and so must have equality under the law, have equal access to the law and to decision making, and have an equal opportunity in life. Texans generally expect that people may not be discriminated against on account of race, gender, religion, or background and that every Texan should have an equal chance to succeed.

Individualism: The value of individualism dominates nearly every aspect of Texas political culture. Other values are important, but Texas political culture as a whole generally supports individualism. Texans tend to believe that people, not governments, are responsible for their own well-being and personal achievement. Individuals are personally responsible for their own success or lack thereof. Generally, most Texans do not support government programs to help the less fortunate and have not allowed the Texas government to control business enterprises such as railroads and banks. Thus, the Texan political culture supports capitalism (an economic system's enterprises and industries are privately owned and controlled for individual profit) as opposed to socialism (a political and economic system in which enterprises and industries are owned or regulated by the whole community).

These values give order and meaning to Texas's political culture and directly shape the scope and purpose of Texas politics, government, and policy. Various interpretations and the relative importance of these values shape citizens' beliefs about the government's role, and they influence political **ideology** and people's choice of political party.

Liberal and Conservative Ideologies in Texas

A political ideology is a set of consistent political beliefs, and Texans and Americans often hold inconsistent political beliefs. In Texas, political ideologies on a scale from left to right, and Texans who hold fairly consistent views or opinions over a range of policy questions are said to have a political ideology. In the United States, people on the left end of the scale are called **liberals** and typically favor more communal and governmental efforts to improve citizens' lives and society. Liberals tend to favor government participation in the economy and governmental efforts to increase equality, healthcare, public education, and support for the poor and the disadvantaged.

People on the right end of the scale are called **conservatives** and favor less government participation in the economy. Conservatives tend to favor lower taxes and fewer government programs to help poor and disadvantaged people. Liberals may support a government-regulated economy, but conservatives fear governmental regulation will suppress liberty and hurt society. The Texas political culture is largely conservative.

A political ideology concerns more than the economy. Texans on the left–right scale also focus on various values and expectations about the government's scope and purpose regarding social issues. For example, liberals tend to favor less governmental regulation in social issues, but conservatives tend to favor more governmental enforcement of traditional moral values. For example, Texas conservatives will likely support laws that ban same-sex marriages and restrict abortions, and Texas liberals will likely call for less governmental regulation of what they consider private matters, like abortion and marriage.

Liberals: tend to favor government participation in the economy. Liberals tend to favor efforts by the government to increase equality, healthcare, public education, and programs that support the poor and the disadvantaged.

Conservatives: conservative Texans tend to favor lower taxes and fewer government programs to help the poor and disadvantaged.

Political Culture

Political cultures are made up of the widespread attitudes that influence how people view the scope and purpose of government and of policy. Political culture teaches a society's people about politics and how politics ought to be. Political culture is a **social construct** that defines a government's proper scope and purpose and how people should conduct public affairs. Political culture clearly differs among various regions in the United States and around the world. Political scientist Daniel Elazar classified the values found in political cultures. Elazar argued that states and even regions within states held different beliefs and values and that those values established one of three political cultures: moralistic, individualistic, or traditionalistic.[18]

Social construction: a constructed understanding of the world that forms the basis for shared assumptions about reality.

Moralistic subculture: People in a moralistic political culture typically value community and see the common good as the proper scope and purpose of government. In a **moralistic culture** or society, people are taught that proper political positions are those that widely support public interests rather than narrow interests. Government and politics are viewed as being a positive and important for the society's overall health. In a moralistic culture, citizens are socialized to feel an obligation to participate in their democracy. Governments in moralistic cultures are assessed by how well they promote the public good.

Moralistic culture: a political culture typically values community and sees the great common good as the proper scope and purpose of government.

uttyler.edu

uttyler.edu

FIGURE 1.9

How Texas Ranks Among the 50 States: Public Policy and Quality of Life

	TEXAS RANK[19]
Tax Policy	
Taxes paid as percent of income: 7.6%	45th
Income tax collections per capita: $0 (tied)	50th
Property tax collections per capita: $1,635	14th
General sales tax collections per capita: $1,226	6th
Public Education	
State and local spending per student ($9,150)[20]	36th
Pre-K–12 education (ranking measures enrollment in and quality of pre-K, test scores and the public high school graduation rate)	33rd
Higher education (ranking tracks educational attainment, graduation rates, college debt, and tuition costs.)	34th
Healthcare	
Access to healthcare[21]	46th
Per capita spending on mental health[22]	48th
Uninsured adults (percent of adults without health insurance)	1st
Uninsured children (percent of children without health insurance)[23]	1st
Quality of Life	
Percent of adults with a high school diploma	42nd
Percent of children living in poverty 2017[24]	38th
4-Year college graduation rate	33rd
2-Year college graduation rate	45th
Income inequality between rich and poor[25]	8th
Home ownership rate (2018)[26]	41st
Percent living below the federal poverty level (poverty rate: 15.6%)	12th
Teenage birth rate (total births per 1,000 women aged 15–19)	3rd

Note: 1st is the highest and 50th is the lowest.

Individualistic subculture: In the individualistic political culture, on the other hand, citizens are taught to negatively view government as a necessary and practical institution that should further private enterprise. In individualistic societies, governments tend to serve specific interests. This business-like conception of politics limits community support and restricts government action to only areas that encourage private initiative. The **individualistic culture** helps maintain and promote capitalist economies and structures.

Individualistic culture: the idea that individuals should be free of government.

Traditionalistic subculture: Finally, a traditionalistic political culture views government's proper role very differently: politics is a privilege for the elite—not an obligation for everyone. Traditionalistic political culture is found mostly in the southern region of the United States, and the government is limited largely to defending or sustaining traditional values (originally the racial caste system). In this culture, political parties count for less than in the other cultures, and the bureaucracy is underdeveloped and distrusted. Citizens in a **traditionalistic culture** tend to be ambivalent toward the marketplace and have an elitist conception of the common good. People socialized in the traditionalistic political culture tend to accept the inevitability of the existing hierarchical society.

Traditionalistic culture: a political culture views the proper role of government as a privilege for the elite.

The political culture taught to many young Texans is individualistic and traditionalistic. As in an individualistic culture, Texas leaders frequently claim that Texas is a business-friendly state with low taxes. The traditionalistic culture of state politics is exemplified by the long history of one-party dominance in state politics. The Democratic party ruled the state from just after the Civil War until the late 1980s, and the Republican party has dominated Texas politics since then. Historically, Texas has very low voter turnout, reflecting a culture ambivalent toward politics and government. These two cultures are reflected in a history of support for capitalism and private businesses, for negative attitudes about government, and for social and economic conservatism.

Key Terms

Conservative: conservative Texans tend to favor lower taxes and fewer government programs to help the poor and disadvantaged.

Diversity: having or being composed of differing elements.

Ideology: a consistent set of values and ideas that form the basis of political and or economic policy.

Individualistic culture: the idea that individuals should be free of government.

uttyler.edu

Liberals: tend to favor government participation in the economy. Liberals tend to favor efforts by the government to increase equality, healthcare, public education, and programs that support the poor and the disadvantaged.

Liberty: a political value that cherishes freedom from an arbitrary exercise of power that restricts a person's choices.

Moralistic culture: a political culture typically values community and sees the great common good as the proper scope and purpose of government.

Political culture: the set of attitudes, norms, and values that provide the underlying assumptions and rules that govern a society.

Rule of law: a system that has specific rules that are enforced equally against all people.

Self-government: political culture that supports the value that the people are the sovereign.

Social construction: a constructed understanding of the world that forms the basis for shared assumptions about reality.

Traditionalistic culture: a political culture views the proper role of government as a privilege for the elite.

Urbanization: refers to the population shift from rural areas to urban areas.

ENDNOTES

[1] U.S. Census Bureau, 2017 American Community Survey. Retrieved from www.factfinder.census.gov.

[2] Fehrenbach, T. R. Lone Star: A History of Texas and the Texans. EBooks on Demand. Newburyport: Open Road Media, 2014.

[3] Martinez Monica Muñoz. The Injustice Never Leaves You: Anti-Mexican Violence in Texas. Harvard University Press, 2018.

[4] Fehrenbach, T. (2014). Lone Star: A History of Texas and the Texans. Newburyport: Open Road Media.

[5] Handbook of Texas Online, Eugene C. Barker and James W. Pohl, "Texas Revolution." http://www.tshaonline.org/handbook/online/articles/qdt01.

[6] Reséndez, Andrés. The Other Slavery: The Uncovered Story of Indian Enslavement in America. First Mariner Books ed. 2017.

[7] African-American Monument Being Installed at Texas Capitol. Nicole Cobler. The Texas Tribune, September 27, 2016.

[8] Hirschman, Charles, and Samuel Preston, and Vu Manh Loi. 1995. "Vietnamese Casualties During the American War: A New Estimate." Population and Development Review, Vol. 21, No. 4 (Dec): 783-812.

[9] See: The United States Department of Justice. The Language Minority Provisions of the Voting Rights Act at https://www.justice.gov/crt/about-language-minority-voting-rights.

[10]Decades After Clashing With The Klan, A Thriving Vietnamese Community In Texas. John Burnett, National Public Radio, November 25, 2018. https://www.npr.org/2018/11/25/669857481/decades-after-clashing-with-the-klan-a-thriving-vietnamese-community-in-texas.

[11]See: America No Longer A 'Nation Of Immigrants,' USCIS Says. National Public Radio. Richard Gonzales February 22, 2018. https://www.npr.org/sections/thetwo-way/2018/02/22/588097749/america-no-longer-a-nation-of-immigrants-uscis-says.

[12]Texas Sees Significant Decline in Rural Land. Marcos Vanetta and Neena Satija, The Texas Tribune. October 3, 2014.

[13]See: Texas Demographic Center. 2014. Projections of the Population of Texas and Counties in Texas by Age, Sex and Race/Ethnicity for 2010-2050. (http://txsdc.utsa.edu/Data/TPEPP/Projections/06/26/2017).

[14]See: The Texas Demographic Center at the University of Texas at San Antonio.

[15]See: The 2017 State Water Plan by the Texas Water Development Board. http://www.twdb.texas.gov/newsmedia/featured/stories/2016/12/index.asp

[16]Texas has the highest number of uninsured kids in America, report finds. Marissa Evans. The Texas Tribune. November 29, 2018.

[17]How Texas blew to the top in wind power. Ryan Maye Handy. The Houston Chronicle. January 27, 2018.

[18]American Federalism: A View from the States. Daniel J. Elazar. (New York: Thomas Y. Crowell, 1966.

[19]States where Americans pay the least (and most) in taxes. Evan Comen and Thomas C. Frohlich, USA Today. 24/7 Wall Street Published February 28, 2018.

[20]Texas ranks 36th nationally in per-student education spending. Alex Samuels. The Texas Tribune. May 15, 2018. https://www.texastribune.org/2018/05/15/texas-student-teacher-spending-average/

[21]See. US News State Rankings. https://www.usnews.com/news/best-states/texas

[22]National Association of State Mental Health Program Directors Research Institute, Inc. (NRI), http://www.nri-incdata.org/. Table 1: SMHA Mental Health Actual Dollar and Per Capita Expenditures by State (FY2004 - FY2013), accessed May 15, 2015.

[23]Texas has the highest number of uninsured kids in America. Marissa Evans, Texas Tribune, November 29, 2018.

[24]Child Poverty in America 2017: State Analysis. Children's Defense Fund. https://www.childrensdefense.org/wp-content/uploads/2018/09/Child-Poverty-in-America-2017-State-Fact-Sheet.pdf

[25]See: US states with the highest levels of income inequality, March 12, 2018. Emmie Martin. https://www.cnbc.com/2018/03/12/us-states-with-the-highest-levels-of-income-inequality.html

[26]See: States with the Highest (and Lowest) Homeownership Rates June 19, 2018. Lattice Publishing. https://www.latticepublishing.com/blog/states-with-the-highest-homeownership-rates

2

What Is a Constitution?

The U.S. Constitution: Separating
Power and Federalism

The U.S. Constitution Versus
the Texas Constitution

Texas's Extensive Constitution and
its Place in the Federal System

Chapter 2

The Texas Constitution in the Federal System

TEXAS IS A FREE AND INDEPENDENT STATE, subject only to the Constitution of the United States. – Texas Constitution. Art. I, § 1.

What Is a Constitution?

The United States is governed via a **constitution,** which is a written charter that delineates a government's powers and limitations. More simply, a constitution is a political society's fundamental law that lists the rules for all officials who exercise governmental power. Since it was ratified in 1788, the Constitution has governed the United States and had 27 amendments (big and small). Texas, on the other hand, has lived under various constitutions and a plethora of amendments to those constitutions, all reflecting Texas's political situation (e.g., nationhood, statehood) while fulfilling the basic charter of a constitution: defining, distributing, and limiting governmental power. Both constitutions give U.S. citizens various individual and structural protections against their federal and state governments.

To distribute power, the U.S. Constitution creates a governing system called federalism, which divides power between the federal government and state governments. Students often assume Congress possesses a general legislative authority that can govern all facets of American life; as Texas politics

> **Constitution:** *a list of rules for all officials who exercise governmental power. These rules, consequently, are a nation's ultimate law that sets forth the structure and powers of government.*

uttyler.edu

continually shows, however, this is false. Federalism ensures the federal government's primacy in its defined responsibilities while allowing states to regulate the day-to-day lives of its citizens (i.e., local control). Because the Constitution's boundaries are sometimes unclear, conflict can emerge, such as when state politicians argue that the federal government has encroached on states' rights. In 2013, then-Attorney General Greg Abbott characterized his job as: "I go into the office. I sue the federal government. Then I go home."[1]

In addition to defining and distributing power, a constitution safeguards individual rights and liberties from government encroachment and regulation. For example, the U.S. and Texas Constitutions both protect the right of religious freedom. The First Amendment to the U.S. Constitution prohibits the federal government from establishing or coercing citizens into supporting a national religion, and it prohibits the federal government from abridging the free exercise of religious, or nonreligious, practices. Similarly, Article 1, § 6 of the Texas Constitution ensures that Texans have "a natural and indefeasible right to worship" and that no person can be "compelled to attend, erect or support any place of worship." Of course, these dictates are meaningless without a governing structure (e.g., a **separation of powers**) that carefully divides power to ensure that no governmental branch can invade individual liberty.

The U.S. and Texas Constitutions can be boring (after all, they set forth the powers and structures of government), but they create the political system that governs Texans. To understand this system, this chapter will provide an overview of the U.S. Constitution so students can understand the state powers created by the U.S. Constitution. From there, this chapter will examine the Texas Constitution by comparing and contrasting its governing structure to that of the U.S. Constitution. Finally, this chapter will examine political conflicts resolved by the U.S. Supreme Court that highlight the clash of governmental power between the Texas and the federal governments.

The U.S. Constitution: Separating Power and Federalism

Texas, like the other forty-nine states in the Union, is a free and sovereign state. Like every other state, Texas must ensure that its laws and policies are congruent with the U.S. Constitution. Despite the value of the U.S. Constitution, most Americans understand little about it. Worse, most Americans cannot recall basic facts about the document. A survey by the University of Pennsylvania's Annenberg Public Policy Center in 2017 found that only 26% of Americans could name all three branches of government (the legislative, executive, and judiciary branches), and 37% of Americans could not name a right protected by the First Amendment (see the Introduction).[2] This section will dispel the myths of the U.S. Constitution and examine the governing structure it establishes.

The U.S. Constitution is actually the United States' second attempt at a constitutional government. The **Articles of Confederation** (ratified in March 1781 and formally replaced by the U.S. Constitution in 1789) was the first

Separation of powers: the U.S. Constitution's division of the powers of government into three separate and coequal branches of government, vesting the power to create laws with Congress, the power to executive the laws with the President, and the power to resolve legal disputes with the federal judiciary led by the Supreme Court. Article 2 of the Texas Constitution separates governmental power by ensuring that the "powers of the Government of the State of Texas shall be divided into three distinct departments."

Articles of Confederation: the first constitution to govern the original 13 colonies in the Revolutionary War's late years and in the years immediately after the colonies gained independence. The Articles created a confederate system of government, with a weak centralized government. For example, the only institution of government was a unicameral Congress that relied on the states to implement the policies.

written constitution to govern the original 13 colonies during the Revolutionary War's later years and immediately after the colonies gained independence from Great Britain. Indicative of the name, the Articles created a **confederate system of government**—a governing system where independent states delegate specific powers to a relatively weak centralized government. Under the Articles, the states were sovereign (i.e., held the political power) instead of the people. The Articles read more like a treaty among independent sovereign states that ensured the newly created federal government could not abridge states' rights. These states were entrusted to regulate their citizens as they believed best.[3]

In the Articles, the federal government only had powers that were *expressly delegated to it,* and the states retained the remaining political power. Subsequently, the federal government had full responsibility over foreign affairs and relations with Native American tribes, but lacked any meaningful power over domestic affairs (e.g., regulating trade and commerce). A constitution reflects a country's political and social environment, so the colonists hesitated to enumerate significant power to a central government because they had revolted against a king who held all political power in Great Britain (i.e., unitary power).

The Articles established only one institution of government: a unicameral Congress (i.e. there was no separation of powers). In this Congress, every state was entitled to send at least two delegates but no more than seven; regardless of the delegation's size, each state only had one vote. Delegates were sent (and could be recalled) and paid by their respective state legislatures, so delegates were often more interested in polices that helped their states and not the common good of the country. To pass major legislation, nine of the thirteen states had to approve such measures. When Congress did pass laws, it relied on the states to implement the policies because there was no Executive Branch. When states ignored the federal government, Congress had no recourse (e.g., a judicial system) to make the states comply. Further complicating this matter, amending the Articles required the consent of all thirteen states in Congress. This allowed the least populous state (Rhode Island) to block amendments the other twelve states felt necessary, so, unsurprisingly, no amendments were ratified under the Articles. Consequently, and among a host of other economic and domestic issues with this governing structure, a convention in the summer of 1787 was called to consider amendments and revisions to make the Articles workable. The delegates would eventually scrap the Articles altogether and draft what would be become the U.S. Constitution.

If any lesson can be learned from the colonies' experience under the Articles, it is that state delegates at the Constitutional Convention would vigorously protect their sovereignty in whatever government they create. Although the federal government needed vast domestic powers and the ability to execute policies, the trick was granting the federal government those responsibilities while vesting the states with the independence to govern their own affairs. The overarching fear was that granting the federal government power would make it tyrannical toward the people before subsuming the

Confederate system of government: a governing system where separate and independent states delegate very specific powers to a (relatively) weak centralized government. The Articles of Confederation created a confederation where the federal government had full responsibility over foreign affairs and over relations with various Indian tribes, but it lacked meaningful power over domestic affairs (e.g., regulating trade and commerce).

Virginia Plan: *a plan of government, supported by delegates of the larger states that envisioned a powerful bicameral Congress in which a state's population would determine its representation in both houses of Congress. Along with expanded federal powers, Congress would have the ability to veto laws passed by states and, once its membership was determined, the responsibility of selecting a president and judges for the federal judiciary.*

New Jersey Plan: *a plan of government, supported by delegates of smaller states, that would give Congress the powers it lacked, but Congress's structure would remain a unicameral legislature in which states were equal. Further, instead of allowing Congress to veto laws passed by state legislatures, the New Jersey Plan advocated that the federal law would be considered supreme in conflicts between federal and state law. Lastly, Congress would select the president, who would in turn select judges for the federal judiciary.*

Great Compromise: *a compromise between the Virginia Plan and the New Jersey Plan, where the delegates agreed to a bicameral Congress where the population of the lower chamber (the House of Representatives) would reflect states' populations, and the population of the upper chamber (the Senate) would be equal because each state would be guaranteed two Senators. In addition to providing Congress with additional powers, the delegates agreed to the Supremacy Clause, which allows federal law to trump state law in conflicts. Lastly, the delegates agreed to a president selected independently of Congress and to a federal judiciary staffed by judges appointed by the president and confirmed by the Senate.*

state governments, thus creating the centralized (unitary) government they declared independence from. Through a series of compromises, the delegates provided the federal government with more powers, but they checked the exercise of federal power by dividing that power among three branches of government (i.e., separation of powers) and between the federal and state governments (i.e., federalism).

Under the U.S. Constitution, the federal government could establish a uniform currency, regulate foreign and domestic commerce, and tax and spend for defense and for general welfare. The federal government was also provided with implied powers in that Congress can make laws necessary and proper for the federal government to carry out its enumerated responsibilities (e.g., the Articles did not allow Congress to pass any law unless it was expressly delegated the power to do so). With a federal government entrusted with more powers, the question over the new federal government's structure remained.[4]

Two factions emerged at the Convention: states that wanted their populations to determine their representation in Congress and states that wanted to retain equality as structured in the Articles. On the former, the **Virginia Plan** (advocated primarily by James Madison of Virginia and by delegates from larger states) envisioned a powerful bicameral Congress where a state's population would determine its representation in both houses of Congress. Along with expanded federal power, Congress would also be able to veto laws passed by states. After determining its membership, Congress would select a president and judges for the federal judiciary.

Given the amount of congressional power the Virginia Plan envisioned as proportional to population, the smaller states offered the alternative **New Jersey Plan** (advocated primarily by William Patterson of New Jersey). Under this plan, Congress would be given the powers it lacked (which, for many delegates, was the purpose of the Convention) but its structure would remain the same—a unicameral legislature where states were equal. Instead of allowing Congress to veto laws passed by state legislatures, the New Jersey Plan advocated that the federal law would be considered supreme in conflicts between federal and state laws. Lastly, Congress would select the president who, in turn, would select judges for the federal judiciary.

With this background, the Virginia and New Jersey Plan advocates compromised in what would become known as the Great Compromise (which would form the structure of the federal government). In the **Great Compromise,** the delegates agreed to a bicameral Congress where a state's population would determine its representation in the lower chamber (the House of Representatives), and the states would be equal in the upper chamber (the Senate), where they would be guaranteed two Senators. In addition to providing Congress the powers it lacked, the delegates also agreed to the Supremacy Clause, which allows federal law to trump state law in conflicts. Lastly, the delegates agreed to a unitary president who would be selected independently of Congress and to a federal judiciary staffed by judges appointed by the president and confirmed by the Senate.

Separation of Powers with Checks and Balances

Any government has three functions: making laws, enforcing those laws, and peacefully settling legal disputes that arise from those laws. The U.S. Constitution, by way of the Great Compromise, divides federal power into three independent and co-equal branches of government. The power to create laws was entrusted to a bicameral Congress, and the power to execute those laws was given to a unitary president who is elected independently of Congress by the Electoral College. Lastly, the power to judge and settle legal disputes concerning the laws passed by Congress and executed by the President was entrusted to a Supreme Court and to an inferior court system created by Congress. Each branch of government is independent, and they have the ability to check one another. Here are a few examples:

- Congress can pass bills, but the president can veto them.

- Congress can override a presidential veto with a two-thirds vote in both chambers.

- Congress can declare war and raise the armed forces, but the president is the commander in chief of the armed forces.

- The president can appoint Justices to the Supreme Court if the Senate approves these appointments.

- The Supreme Court can declare laws passed by the political branches as unconstitutional.

》 Separating power keeps governmental power balanced because each institution of government is beholden to different electorates at different political times.

Separating power keeps governmental power balanced because each institution of government is beholden to different electorates at different political times. Hence, for any political party to control all branches of political power (e.g., the House, the Senate, and the presidency), the Constitution ensures that its political support must last over six years. House members are subject to reelection by voters in a Congressional district every two years, and a third of the Senate is up for reelection every two years by their statewide constituencies. Every 4 years, a nationwide electorate elects the President. Even when a political party controls the government, their partisan rule tends to be short. For example, the Republican Party had legislative majorities in the House and in the Senate and controlled the Presidency after the 2016 general election, but they lost their majority in the House after the 2018 midterm elections two years later.

For the federal government to properly exercise its powers, the Constitution requires bills to pass a bicameral Congress in which each chamber is elected by different constituencies at different political times. The bills must then be signed by the President, who is elected by a national constituency. The "great lengths" the Founders went to in order to make lawmaking deliberate and difficult included making it difficult for the federal government to pass laws that restrict individual liberty or invade states' rights.[5] Secondly, the lawmaking process ensures that every action taken by the federal government must be traced to a grant of power within the constitutional text. Under the U.S. Constitution, the federal government has defined and limited powers that were either

uttyler.edu

enumerated to it (e.g., the powers to establish a uniform currency, to regulate foreign and domestic commerce, and to tax and spend for the general welfare) or were necessary and proper to carry out its enumerated responsibilities (e.g., implied powers).

Federalism

The remaining power not delegated to the federal government would remain with the states. This division of power, as explained by James Madison in *Federalist Paper No. 45,* would be the basis of the federalist system created by the delegates at the Convention:

> Having shown that no one of the powers transferred to the federal government is unnecessary or improper, the next question to be considered is, whether the whole mass of them will be dangerous to the portion of authority left in the several States....The powers delegated by the proposed Constitution to the federal government are few and defined. Those which are to remain in the state governments are numerous and indefinite....The powers reserved to the several states will extend to all the objects which, in the ordinary course of affairs, concern the lives, liberties, and properties of the people, and the internal order, improvement, and prosperity of the State.[6]

The U.S. Constitution empowers the federal government (i.e., every action must be justified by an enumeration of power), but it is not the source of state power. State power includes all the power not given to the federal government nor restricted to the states by the U.S. Constitution (e.g., the understanding of state power is further protected by the Tenth Amendment to the U.S. Constitution). This power, known as the **police powers of the states,** provides states with the authority to regulate its citizens' health, safety, and morals. In other words, states are given the residual power to perform essential government functions. The states regulate the day-to-day lives of their citizens by, for example, defining when a speeding infraction occurs, running a public-school system, developing a curriculum to teach students, ensuring drivers are licensed by the state and have car insurance, and prohibiting grocery stores from selling beer or wine before noon on Sundays.

As described by Chief Justice Roberts, this expansive power informed the Founders' decision to have the states control police power because the states are the governmental level closest to the people, and states understand the policies that make sense for their citizens (e.g., Texas can pass policies that reflect the conservative nature of its citizens while California can pass policies that reflect the liberal nature of its citizens).[7] States do not use the U.S. Constitution as their authority when enacting policies, but they must consider if any conflicts with a federal prerogative exist or if the U.S. Constitution prohibits them from acting. On the first point, one compromise at the Constitutional Convention involved safeguarding the supremacy of the U.S. Constitution, and all federal law pursuant to it, over state actions. In other words, it rectified the Articles' issue of allowing the states to hamper the federal government's legitimate functions. Under the **Supremacy Clause** in Article 6, the U.S. Constitution and all laws passed in accordance to it by the federal government are the "supreme law of the land." Thus, contrary acts by the states cannot stand if they come into conflict.

Secondly, states must not enact laws or take actions prohibited by the U.S. Constitution. A constitution governs all players within a political system by listing what governments can (and cannot) do, so state governments are constrained as well. Let us examine two clauses of the U.S. Constitution to highlight this notion: Article 1, § 10 and Article 4. Within Article 1, § 10, states (among other regulations) are prohibited from entering into any treaty with a foreign country, nor can any state coin their own currency. States are also prohibited from passing *ex post facto* laws (which retroactively punish illegal behavior that was legal when one engaged in it) or bills of attainder (legislative acts that specifically punish an individual person or groups of persons), and no state can ever bestow a title of nobility to an individual.

Article 4 of the Constitution details how states must interact with each other and with residents from other states. This article stipulates that every state must provide "full faith and credit" to the public acts and judicial proceedings of the other states. Thus, a couple's marriage in Arizona must be honored in Texas. Furthermore, all U.S. citizens are entitled to the "privileges and immunities" of citizenship, so each state is prohibited from discriminating against citizens of other states. For instance, Texas cannot levy penalties on drivers from Oklahoma for speeding on I-20 that are not levied against residents of Texas. Lastly, Article 4 establishes extradition, the process whereby a person must be returned to a state in which they are accused of committing a crime.

When Texas enacts a policy, it must not conflict with a federal power nor be prohibited by the U.S. Constitution in some manner. If it meets both stipulations, Texas (and the forty-nine other states) can enact any policy they desire. Of course, as the federal government's reach has grown over time, the states' power has subsequently decreased.

The U.S. Constitution Versus the Texas Constitution: A Comparison

Federalism guarantees that citizens of Texas receive protection via the U.S. Constitution and the Texas Constitution. Both documents have similarities (e.g., a bicameral legislative body) and vast differences (e.g., a plural executive in Texas vs. a unitary president). The U.S. Constitution is not the only document that protects individual liberties and states' rights, but it does create the structure of the federal government, place constraints on state governments, and serve as the baseline for individual rights and protections secured in the political system.[8] The states, therefore, are allowed to secure additional liberties that do not contradict the U.S. Constitution's minimal protections. For example, the U.S. Constitution does not explicitly bar governmental discrimination on the basis of sex; however, Article 1, § 3 of the Texas Constitution specifically guarantees that "equality under the law shall not denied or abridged because

Supremacy Clause: Article 6 of the U.S. Constitution guarantees the U.S. Constitution, and all laws passed in accordance to it, are the "supreme law of the land." Consequently, states' acts are not allowed to stand if they should come into conflict.

uttyler.edu

of sex, race, color, creed, or national origin." Moreover, Texas has a constitutional structure to secure individual liberty and ensure that its political system cannot become tyrannical. The following sections will compare and contrast the U.S. and Texas Constitutions.

A (Lack of a) Bill of Rights

Article 7 of the U.S. Constitution stipulates that nine of the original 13 colonies needed to ratify the U.S. Constitution before it would take effect. On June 21, 1788, New Hampshire became the ninth state to ratify the Constitution, which officially replaced the Articles of Confederation when the first Congress met on March 4, 1789 (George Washington would assume the Presidency on April 30, 1789). A review of the first seven articles of the U.S. Constitution reveals little mention of individual rights and liberties—the U.S. Constitution's main purpose was to create a durable governing structure. The rights we cherish as Americans (such as the right to free speech, the right against self-incrimination, and the right to bear arms) were added after the ratification of the U.S. Constitution, when the ratification debates identified its major weakness as the omission of a Bill of Rights.

A **Bill of Rights** defines a set of liberties against the government that are so fundamental that no government has the authority to take them away nor infringe upon them for illegitimate reasons. Even when the government can regulate individual behavior, the enumeration of individual rights in a Bill of Rights "trumps (so to speak) that power and limits what the government may constitutionally do."[9] Alexander Hamilton opposed a Bill of Rights in the Constitution and argued in *Federalist Paper No. 84* that the U.S. Constitution itself was a Bill of Rights because Congress (and the federal government) only had powers enumerated to it. Thus, the federal government could never claim the authority to invade fundamental liberties.[10] This argument proved weak, and the Bill of Rights was added to the U.S. Constitution upon ratification.

Importantly, the U.S. Constitution's first ten amendments were intended to only limit the actions of the federal government. The states retained sovereignty over their citizens, as the founders worried the newly created federal government would possess too much power and use it to infringe upon individual liberties. Examine the wording of the First Amendment (specifically the first word):

> Congress shall make no law respecting an establishment of religion, or prohibiting the free exercise thereof; or abridging the freedom of speech, or of the press; or the right of the people peaceably to assemble, and to petition the Government for a redress of grievances.

With no means to incorporate the protections of the Bill of Rights against state governments, the states could protect (or infringe upon) any individual rights. The U.S. Supreme Court could not bind state governments to the same protections the federal government was held to until the Fourteenth amendment was ratified in 1868. The Fourteenth Amendment's Due Process Clause protects people's "life, liberty, and property" from being infringed upon by their state government without a fair judicial hearing, and the Supreme Court would

Bill of Rights: *a set of liberties against the government that are so fundamental that no government has the authority to take them away nor infringe upon them for illegitimate reasons.*

interpret this clause as the basis for making states follow the Bill of Rights. Rejecting the argument that the Fourteenth Amendment automatically incorporated the Bill of Rights, the Supreme Court began in the early 1900s to hold state governments accountable for certain rights in the Bill of Rights that the Court judged to be fundamental. This case-by-case review of fundamental rights is known as **selective incorporation.** Currently, every protection of the Bill of Rights is applicable against the states, except for the Third Amendment, the Fifth Amendment's grand jury indictment requirement, and the Seventh Amendment's right to a civil jury trial.[11]

With these concepts in mind, we can examine the Texas Constitution of 1876, which currently governs the State of Texas. Containing 17 articles, 498 constitutional amendments, and slightly fewer than 90,000 words, it is not brief. Despite its length, the Texas Constitution's first article is a Bill of Rights. If the U.S. Constitution's structure conveys the founders' emphasis on the governing structure they created, the Texas Constitution's structure conveys the importance Texas's founders placed on limiting governmental power, especially to protect individual liberty.

Article 1 of the Texas Constitution: A Bill of Rights

Section 1

Article 1 of the Texas Constitution, entitled "Bill of Rights," begins by establishing the sovereignty of Texas, subject only to the authority of the U.S. Constitution. As discussed, this aptly describes the state's federalist nature because Texas has full sovereignty over issues not enumerated to the federal government nor restricted by the U.S. Constitution. By following the U.S. Constitution, the government of Texas accepts **constitutional supremacy**—Article 6 of the U.S. Constitution commands that the U.S. Constitution and all federal laws pursuant to it are the "supreme law of the land."

For the federal government's responsibilities upon which the states cannot impede, the federal government relies on two main sources of power: **enumerated powers** and **implied powers**. Enumerated, or delegated, powers are specifically written within the text of the U.S. Constitution. Most powers and responsibilities of Congress and, by extension, of the federal government are located in Article 1, § 8. Represented by seventeen broad areas (e.g., Congress can lay and collect taxes, borrow money, and regulate commerce), these are the responsibilities that the Constitutional Convention entrusted Congress to regulate. The last power listed in § 8 allows Congress to pass any legislation that "shall be necessary and proper" to carry out the seventeen issue areas listed in § 8. Referred to as the Necessary and Proper Clause (or the Elastic Clause), the Supreme Court has interpreted this clause as providing Congress with implied powers to pass any legislation necessary and appropriate to implement Congress's enumerated powers.[12] For example, Article 1, § 8 gives Congress the power to raise and maintain an army, but not the power to implement the mandatory enrollment of citizens into the military (i.e., a military draft). Through the Necessary and Proper clause, however,

Selective incorporation: Based on the Fourteenth Amendment's Due Process Clause, the Supreme Court determines, on a case-by-case basis, which rights in the Bill of Rights are fundamental. Those deemed fundamental are enforced against state governments.

Constitutional supremacy: the acceptance that the U.S. Constitution is the "supreme law of the land." Consequently, Texas has full sovereignty over issues not enumerated to the federal government nor restricted by the U.S. Constitution.

Enumerated powers of the federal government: the powers of the federal government that are specifically written within the U.S. Constitution's text. Most of Congress's, and by extension the federal government's, powers and responsibilities are located in Article 1, § 8 of the U.S. Constitution.

Implied powers of the federal government: based on the Necessary and Proper Clause, the Supreme Court interpreted this clause as providing Congress the authorization to pass any legislation that is both necessary and appropriate for Congress to implement its enumerated powers.

Congress can implement a military draft because it is appropriate legislation to carry out its responsibility to raise and maintain an army.

Under the U.S. Constitution, Texas cannot contradict nor undermine the legitimate functions of the federal government. States retain powers not given to federal government, in a relationship reinforced by the U.S. Constitution's **Tenth Amendment**: "The powers not delegated to the United States by the Constitution, nor prohibited by it to the States, are reserved to the States respectively, or to the people."

The U.S. Constitution also prohibits particular state actions. Regarding the constraints listed in Article 1, § 10 and in Article 4, most protections of the Bill of Rights also apply against the states via selective incorporation. Collectively, the Bill of Rights guarantees people the right to conscience (e.g., right to religious freedom), protects expression-based freedoms (e.g., freedom of speech and expression), ensures the right to bear arms for self-defense at home, and contains criminal justice provisions for how government can investigate crimes, conduct trials for the criminally accused, and punish those found guilty at trial.

Examining the remaining amendments to the U.S. Constitution reveals further prohibitions on state power:

- The Fourteenth Amendment (ratified in 1868) ensures that no state can deny due process to its citizens nor deny them the equal protection under the law. Further, this amendment ensures that all people born in the U.S. are citizens of the U.S. and of the state they were born in.

- The Fifteenth Amendment (ratified in 1870) guarantees the right to vote cannot be denied based on race.

- The Seventeenth Amendment (ratified in 1913) ensures popular elections of Senators. Prior to ratifying this amendment, state legislatures could elect their own senators.

- The Nineteenth Amendment (ratified in 1920) guarantees the right to vote cannot be denied on the basis of sex.

- The Twenty-fourth Amendment (ratified in 1964) prohibits states from levying a poll tax to vote.

- The Twenty-sixth Amendment (ratified in 1971) guarantees voting rights to all citizens over the age of eighteen.

Section 2

Article 1, § 2 of the Texas Constitution enshrines the notion that all political power in Texas resides with the people. This ideal, known as **popular sovereignty**, is (mostly) carried out by the Texas Constitution through republican, or **representative government**. The key principle of a representative government is that the people influence the government's actions through frequent and fair elections in which people vote for the officials who govern the state. Neither the Texas nor the U.S. Constitution creates a democracy where the people vote directly on every piece of legislation, nor do they approve every policy taken by government. Instead, guaranteeing people's right to vote for representatives who make those governing decisions fulfills

---

Tenth Amendment: *the understanding of state power is reinforced by the amendment's command that "The powers not delegated to the United States by the Constitution, nor prohibited by it to the states, are reserved to the States respectively, or to the people."*

Popular sovereignty: *the notion that political power rests with the people.*

Representative government: *a governing system, whereby the people influence the government through frequent and fair elections in which they can vote for representatives of their choice.*

America's democratic commitment (i.e., creates accountability at the ballot box).

Because Texas can secure more liberties than what the U.S. Constitution requires, the Texas Constitution allows Texans to vote directly on four issues within the state:

- Article 3, § 24 empowers the Texas Ethics Commission to suggest pay raises for Texas Legislature members. However, these pay raises must be approved by a majority of voters in an election. Currently, Legislature member have an annual salary of $7,200 (plus a per diem when the Legislature is in session).

- Article 4, § 49 allows the Legislature to create state debt after a two-thirds vote in each legislative chamber. However, the debt and the reason for the debt must be approved by a majority of voters in an election.

- Article 17 of the Texas Constitution requires any constitutional amendment proposed by a two-thirds vote in each house of Texas' Legislature to be ratified by a majority of voters in an election.

- Article 8, § 24 of the Texas Constitution stipulates that, if the Legislature levies an income tax, a majority of voters in a statewide referendum must agree on the income tax and on the tax rate. Needless to say, Texas does not have an income tax.

The U.S. Constitution's Preamble contains a similar proclamation about popular sovereignty, but the broader purpose is to ensure that the federal government is empowered by the people, not by the state governments. This arrangement of political power formally abandoned the Articles of Confederation's structure, in which the states enabled the federal government. The U.S. Constitution's Preamble emphasizes the federal government's important role in American life.

Section 3

Article 1, § 3 of the Texas Constitution begins a long list of individual rights citizens of Texas enjoy. Many are redundant because the U.S. Constitution protects them (e.g., most of the protections of the federal Bill of Rights are protected in the Texas Bill of Rights), but the Texas Constitution does provide broader protections in some areas. The additional rights secured by the Texas Constitution include:

- The writ of habeas corpus (the right to know why you are imprisoned) cannot be suspended, by the federal government, unless the U.S. Congress suspends it "in cases of rebellion or invasion the public safety may require it."[13] In Texas, the Legislature can never suspend habeas corpus.

- Texans have a right to access and use the state's public beaches.[14]

- Texans have a right to use a firearm to exercise their right to hunt.[15] In 2008, the Supreme Court interpreted the Second Amendment as only conferring an individual's right to own a handgun for self-defense at home.[16]

uttyler.edu

Article 2 of the Texas Constitution: Separating Governmental Power

One defining feature of the U.S. Constitution is the division of power amongst three separate and co-equal branches of government. However, no specific phrase in the U.S. Constitution calls for this separation of power. Instead, vesting the legislative power to a bicameral Congress in Article 1, the executive power to the President in Article 2, and the judicial power to the Supreme Court (and all other inferior courts) in Article 3 separates and divides governmental power.

Article 2 of the Texas Constitution clarifies that Texas separates governmental power by ensuring that the "powers of the Government of the State of Texas shall be divided into three distinct departments."

Article 3 of the Texas Constitution: The Legislature of the State of Texas

The legislative power—the power to make laws—is entrusted to a bicameral legislature consisting of a 150-member House of Representatives and a thirty-one-member Senate. House and Senate members are elected from single-member legislative districts, divided by population, throughout the state. To ensure that members of the House and Senate represent approximately the same number of constituents, Texas must redistrict the 150 legislative districts for the House and the 31 legislative districts for the Senate every ten years, depending on the results of a federally required census. The **census** mandated by Article 1 of the U.S. Constitution requires the federal government to determine how many people live in each state (and in the whole United States). Based on this count, the federal government tells states how many Congressional seats they have in the federal House of Representatives via a process called reapportionment. Texas reapportions the state's legislative districts to match the population data from the decennial census. Until the results of the 2020 census, a member of the Texas House will represent approximately one hundred sixty-seven thousand Texans, and a member of the Texas Senate will represent approximately eight hundred eleven thousand Texans.[17]

Every two years, the full membership of the House is subject to reelection. Thus, House members serve two-year terms for as long as their constituents reelect them (i.e., members of the House have no term limits). The Texas Constitution requires House members to be at least twenty-one years old, a citizen of the United States, and a resident of Texas for at least two years. Additionally, a House member must have lived in their legislative district for at least a year.

Every two years, about half of the Senate is subject to reelection. Thus, a member of the Senate has a four-year term and serves for as long as they are reelected by their constituents (i.e., Senators have no term limits). The Texas Constitution requires Senate members to be at least twenty-six years old, a citizen of the United States, and a resident of Texas for at least five years. Additionally, a Senator must live in their legislative district for at least a year.

Census: Article 1 of the U.S. Constitution stipulates that the federal government must conduct a census every ten years to determine how many people live in the fifty states and, by extension, the country as a whole.

The Legislature can create and influence public policy by, for example, making laws, defining crimes (e.g., people must be twenty-one to consume and purchase alcohol), paying for specific government programs (e.g., state tuition assistance), and regulating what Texas residents must do (e.g., attend jury duty). In other words, legislative power allows a legislature to "prescribe the rules by which the duties and rights of every citizen are to be regulated."[18] Recognizing this power's reach and effect, the U.S. Constitution provides two checks on legislative power, which are copied by the Texas Constitution. First, **bicameralism** is an internal check on legislative power that requires the House and the Senate to agree on a bill's form and language before it can be sent to the Governor of Texas for her signature. The second **external check on legislature power** is the Governor's ability to veto any bill the Legislature sends to her. The Legislature can override a Governor's veto by a two-thirds vote in both legislative chambers, but the Texas Constitution requires the Legislature to be in session to do so.

Interestingly, the Legislature's **regular session** occurs every two years, meeting on the second Tuesday of January in odd-numbered years (e.g., 2015, 2017, and 2019). When the Legislature meets, its session can only last 140 days.[19] In its regular session, the Legislature can set its own agenda (e.g., pass any bills it can and oversee the executive and judicial branches), and its only constraints during the session are that their business ends when day 140 strikes midnight and that Article 3, § 49 requires Texas to have a balanced budget, which means the Legislature cannot spend more money than it receives from its revenue sources (there are rare exceptions to this rule). At the beginning of every legislative session, the Comptroller of Public Accounts will share the total amount of money the Legislature can appropriate (i.e., spend) until its next legislative session. Article 3, § 49 provides a mechanism for the state to run up its debt, but Texas citizens must approve these expenditures in an election. Thus, Texas has one of the lowest state debts in the country.

If the Legislature cannot complete its legislative priorities during their regular session, they must wait until the next session—unless the Governor calls a **special session** of the Legislature. A special session can only last thirty days, and only the Governor is authorized to call a special session. The governor also sets the legislative agenda for this special session:

> When the Legislature shall be convened in special session, there shall be no legislation upon subjects other than those designated in the proclamation of the Governor calling such session, or presented to them by the Governor; and no such session shall be of longer duration than thirty days.[20]

A legislator's job is important—by carrying out the political goals of their constituents, they make laws and policies that govern the state. However, the Legislature's structure reveals that the 1876 Texas Constitution was wary of governmental power. It made a legislator's job part-time and exceedingly difficult. As a part-time legislature, both House and Senate members are paid only $7,200 a year. For them to receive a raise, the Texas Ethics Commission must suggest a raise that must be approved by a majority of voters in an election.

Bicameralism: *the division of a legislature into two chambers, providing an internal check on legislative power. Bicameralism requires both chambers to agree on a bill's form and language before it can be sent to the executive (e.g., the president or governor of Texas).*

External check on legislative power: *the ability of an executive (e.g., the president or governor of Texas) to veto any bill the legislature sends.*

Regular session of the Texas Legislature: *the Texas Legislature's regular session occurs every two years, meeting on the second Tuesday of January in odd-numbered years. When the Legislature convenes for a regular session it can set its own agenda. A regular session can only last 140 days.*

Special session of the Texas Legislature: *the Governor of Texas is authorized to call a special session of the Texas Legislature and set the legislative agenda for the special session. A special session, therefore, occurs outside of the Legislature's regular session and can only last 30 days.*

uttyler.edu

Therefore, legislators tend to focus on their own careers rather than on the circumstances and issues facing the state. The wariness toward government and toward politicians that prevails in Texas politics shows little desire to make the Legislature a full-time, professional legislative body. For example, then-Governor Rick Perry stated in 2007:

> There are people who always think, "Let's have a full-time legislature." I happen to think that's just asking for trouble. When you have a full-time legislature, they just feel pretty inclined to be doing something. So they are going to dream up new laws, new regulations and new statutes—and generally all of those cost money.[21]

However, low legislative pay, two-year gaps between meetings, and time limits for meetings tend to undermine bicameralism's purpose. The U.S. Congress, a professional and full-time legislative body, has a similar bicameral structure that allows various electorates to elect each Congressional chamber at various times. This division forces a deliberate legislative process and "an arduous one. But that's no bug in the constitutional design: it is the very point of the design."[22] A short, biennial legislative session creates a tremendous workload for confronting issues that arose since the last session, making laws that govern the state, and appropriating money for public policy until the next session. Consequently, bills are rushed through the legislative process without sufficient deliberation, and bills are usually never considered by the Legislature.

For example, the 86th Legislature (which met from January 2019 through May 2019), "legalized hemp and hemp-derived products like CBD oil."[23] However, possession of marijuana is illegal in Texas, and law enforcement has no tools to distinguish marijuana (which is illegal to possess) from hemp (which is now legal to possess). Consequently, top prosecutors from across the state and political spectrum—from Harris to Tarrant counties—have dismissed hundreds of pending marijuana charges since the law was signed by Republican Gov. Greg Abbott and immediately went into effect on June 10. They have also signaled they won't pursue any new charges without testing a substance to indicate if there is more than 0.3% of THC, the now-legal limit to distinguish between hemp and marijuana.[24]

Article 4 of the Texas Constitution: Executive Department

For all the bravado and swagger in the governor of Texas's public persona, Article 4 of the Texas Constitution considers the governor one official out of a **plural executive**. Article 4 stipulates that, in addition to the governor's position as the chief executive officer of the state, the executive branch consists of the lieutenant governor, the secretary of state, the comptroller of public accounts, the commissioner of the general land office, and the attorney general. The only official the governor can select to help run the executive branch is the secretary of state (subject to confirmation by the Texas Senate), who is the chief election officer of Texas. The Texas Constitution creates a weak governor by ensuring that all other executive officials are elected independently of the

Plural executive: *the division of executive power in Texas among executive officials elected independently of the governor in a statewide election (e.g., lieutenant governor, the secretary of state, the comptroller of public accounts, the commissioner of the general land office, and the attorney general). The governor may be the head of the executive branch, but the division of executive power prevents her from controlling all the political output and responsibilities of the Texas executive branch.*

governor in a statewide election, making them politically committed to their constituents—not to the governor. The governor may be the head of the executive branch, but the division of executive power prevents her from controlling all the political output and responsibilities of the Texas executive branch.

The plural executive structure in Texas starkly contrasts with the U.S. Constitution's unitary executive branch, where all executive power is vested in the president. As a unitary executive, the president can select officials to help run the executive branch, from major cabinet officials (e.g., secretary of state and secretary of the treasury) to lesser executive officials (e.g., the FBI director). These executive officials also serve at the pleasure of the president, ensuring that their job security depends on carrying out the president's political agenda. As the sole individual in charge of the executive branch, the president receives full blame (and credit) for all the actions of this governmental branch.

By creating a plural executive, the 1876 Texas Constitution prevents any particular executive official from gaining too much power and, incidentally, prevents any singular official from bearing ultimate responsibility for the executive branch's actions. Some advocated for a plural executive during the U.S. Constitution's ratification, but this idea was rejected primarily because voters would have difficulty holding officials accountable in a plural executive. For example, the governor claims credit for issues he has no formal responsibility over (e.g., Texas's lack of an income tax) but also receives blame for policies he cannot control (e.g., the price of gas, which is regulated by the agriculture commissioner). As Alexander Hamilton explains in *Federalist Paper No. 70,* "But one of the weightiest objections to a plurality in the executive, and which lies as much against the last as the first plan, is, that it tends to conceal faults and destroy responsibility."[25]

Article 4 requires that the governor serve a 4-year term and be a citizen of the United States, at least 30 years old, and a Texas resident for at least 5 years prior to her election. The governor has no term limits, and she can serve for as long as Texas voters reelect her. The longest serving governor in Texas history is Rick Perry, who served from December of 2000 to January of 2015. Perry originally became governor in December of 2000, when then-Governor George W. Bush won the presidency and resigned as governor of Texas. As the lieutenant governor at the time, Rick Perry succeeded Bush and retained his position until he decided not to seek reelection in November of 2014. This story highlights two facts about Texas politics:

- The lieutenant governor of Texas is a member of the executive branch with no formal executive power. As the president of the Senate, his main political power is legislative. His most important executive function is being the successor if the governor cannot complete her duties (e.g., resigns or dies in office).

- When Americans elect the president every 4 years, the election cycle is on-year (e.g., President Trump was elected in November 2016). In 1972, Texas voters passed a constitutional amendment requiring the governor and other executive branch members be elected during off-year election cycles (e.g., Governor Abbott was recently

uttyler.edu

reelected in November of 2018). Also known as midterm elections, these elections occur 2 years after the Presidential election. This change aims to insulate elections for Texas's executive branch from national politics.

As the chief executive, the governor possesses important executive powers to help carry out her responsibilities in support of the state's common good. Arguably, her two most important powers are vetoing legislation and her appointment powers.

Veto Power

The governor has three choices when the Legislature presents her with a bill: do nothing, sign the bill, or veto the bill. If the governor does nothing, a bill automatically becomes law after ten days if the Legislature is in session or after twenty days if they are out of session. If the governor believes the bill is necessary (good) for the state, she signs the bill into law and becomes responsible for executing the law. Once signed, the law will not go into effect for ninety days, unless it was supported by a two-thirds vote in both legislative chambers. If so, the law goes into effect immediately after the governor signs the bill.

During the most recent legislative session in 2019, the 86th Legislature passed 1,429 bills, and Governor Abbott vetoed a little less than 5% of these bills.[26] As an important external check on legislative power, the governor can veto legislation for any reason. Overriding a veto is difficult in Texas, which increases the governor's influence on the legislative process. To override a veto, the Legislature needs a two-thirds vote in both legislative chambers while the Legislature is in session. Major legislation is usually sent to the governor in the waning days of the session, so the governor has immense control over the content of bills the Legislature passes (i.e., the Legislature lacks the opportunity to override a veto).

Line-item veto: the power of the governor to veto particular spending in an appropriations bill without vetoing the entire appropriations bill.

Arguably, the most important bills the Legislature passes are the appropriations bills that authorize the use of state funds for public policies. The governor only possesses the **line-item veto** power for appropriations bills (i.e., this power does not apply to non-appropriations bills). A line-item veto allows the governor to veto particular spending in an appropriations bill without vetoing the entire bill. For example, when funding all the state universities and colleges (e.g., professor salaries and building maintenance), let's assume that legislators from East Texas include $10 million for UT Tyler to create a Division II football program. When the appropriations bill for state universities and colleges reaches the governor's desk, she can veto the $10 million for UT Tyler's football program without vetoing the entire appropriations bill. Interestingly, the president cannot line-item veto Congressional appropriations bills.

Appointment Power

The power of Texas's plural executive is further divided amongst boards and agencies that run state programs (e.g., the Department of Transportation, the Texas Water Development Board, and the Board of Pardons and Paroles). The governor appoints members to these boards and agencies (and the Senate approves them when the Legislature is in session), allowing the governor to influence these boards and agencies by appointing individuals with governing and political philosophies similar to those of the governor. For instance, the Board of Pardons and Paroles determines the conditions for parole (e.g., to grant or to revoke) and which convicted criminals warrant clemency. The governor has little power to contradict these decisions but can appoint members to this board. The types of officials the governor appoints tend to possess political preferences congruent with the governor's.

Lastly, the governor can appoint judges to fill vacancies in the judicial branch. Texas's judges are elected in partisan elections, so the governor's appointment holds the seat until the next scheduled election for that position. Although the judicial branch has independence from the governor, the governor's appointment power allows her to influence the judiciary by appointing judges with judicial (and political) philosophies similar to those of the governor.

In the November 2018 elections, Dallas County voters reelected Democrat Darlene Ewing as judge for Dallas's 254th Family District Court. Sadly, she passed away about a week after she easily won reelection, and Governor Abbott filled this vacancy with Ashley Wysocki, a Republican judge. Judge Wysocki will hold this seat until it is subject to reelection in 2022. In the 2018 November election, Harris County voters ousted Republican Judge Brett Busby from his seat on the 14th Court of Appeals. In February of 2019, however, Governor Abbott appointed Busby to the Texas Supreme Court to fill the vacancy after Justice Phil Johnson retired. Justice Busby will serve out the remainder of Johnson's term, which is subject to reelection in November 2020. Highlighting the governor's appointment power, Justice Busby responded to criticism of his appointment by saying, "The governor was elected statewide to make decisions on appointments. I'm honored that he chose me and I look forward to serving."[27]

>> Texas's judges are elected in partisan elections, so the governor's appointment holds the seat until the next scheduled election for that position.

Article 5 of the Texas Constitution: Judicial Department

The structure of the Judicial Branch, created by the Texas Constitution, uniquely vests judicial power into two supreme courts: the Texas Supreme Court and the Court of Criminal Appeals. The final appellate court for all civil and juvenile matters rests with the nine justices on the Texas Supreme Court, while the final appellate court for all criminal matters rests with the nine justices on the Court of Criminal Appeals. Texas and Oklahoma are the only two states in the country to have a dual supreme court system. Article 5 of the Texas Constitution also creates the courts of appeals, district courts, county courts, commissioners courts, and courts of justices of the peace; it also allows the Legislature to create additional courts.

The U.S. Constitution vests judicial power into one Supreme Court and all other inferior courts that Congress creates. To ensure that federal judges are free from political pressure, federal judges nominated by the president and confirmed by the Senate are guaranteed life tenure with salary protection (i.e., their salary cannot be reduced while they hold office).

uttyler.edu

State and federal judges are entrusted to resolve legal disputes surrounding the laws passed by the Legislature. For example, a person caught speeding on Loop 323 has violated a law created by the Legislature that regulates the lawful speed for travel on the Loop. The Legislature possesses no judicial power, however, so the judiciary is responsible for resolving the dispute by considering the facts to determine the proper punishment.

Secondly, judicial power allows the judiciary to review governmental actions and determine their compatibility with a constitution. Federal judges review the actions of state or federal governments to determine their compatibility with the U.S. Constitution, and Texas state judges review actions of state and local governments to determine their compatibility with the Texas Constitution. With separated governmental power, **judicial review** allows the judiciary to enforce the limits on governmental power enumerated in the Constitution. For instance, Article 8, § 24 of the Texas Constitution stipulates that the Legislature can levy an income tax if a majority of voters in a statewide referendum agree to the income tax and to the tax rate. This limit on legislative power would be meaningless if the Texas judiciary could not strike down an income tax levied by the Legislature that the voters did not approve.

Given this awesome responsibility, the U.S. Constitution provides federal judges with institutional protections from electoral or political pressure. Always wary of governmental power, the 1876 Texas Constitution provides a democratic check on the Texas judiciary's power by subjecting judges to partisan elections. Consequently, trial judges must campaign every four years (e.g., district court judges) and appellate judges must campaign every six years (e.g., Texas Supreme Court justices) to convince voters they deserve another term in office. Any election requires incumbents to defend their record, so judicial elections affect the independence of state judges because the judges must fundraise for an adequate campaign and act in a manner they believe helps their reelection prospects.

Article 6 of the Texas Constitution: Suffrage

Article 1, § 4 of the U.S. Constitution empowers the states to run state and federal elections and to certify valid voters in their state (i.e., states stipulate the qualifications to vote). Of course, later amendments to the U.S. Constitution ensured that no state can disqualify voters on the bases of race (Fifteenth Amendment) or sex (Nineteenth Amendment) and the states must certify voters who are eighteen years old on Election Day (Twenty-sixth Amendment). Article 6 of the Texas Constitution bars the following individuals from voting:

- people under the age of eighteen,

- individuals found mentally incompetent by a court,

- and persons convicted of a felony. However, any felon who has completed their sentence (e.g., served their time in prison or completed their parole or probation) can have their voting rights restored.

Article 6 also reaffirms the Texas Constitution's commitment to a representative government—it does not provide Texans with as many tools for direct

Judicial review: the judiciary's power to review governmental action and determine their compatibility with the constitution (i.e., judicial review allows the judiciary to enforce the limits on governmental power enumerated in a constitution). Consequently, federal judges review the actions of federal or states governments to determine their compatibility with the U.S. Constitution, and Texas state judges review actions of state and local governments to determine their compatibility with the Texas Constitution.

democracy as citizens from other states receive. The State of Arizona became a state during a Populist Movement in the early 1900s that was highly skeptical of representative government, so it allows its citizens to recall elected officials, use the initiative process, and use the referendum process.[28] The **recall process** allows voters to remove a state official before their term of office is complete, and the **initiative process** allows citizens to propose and pass legislation and constitutional amendments on their own, bypassing the Legislature. Both of these direct democracy tools are unavailable to Texas voters.

The **referendum process** allows voters to approve legislation and constitutional amendments proposed by the Legislature. The Texas Constitution does allow its citizens limited use of the statutory referendum by entrusting Texans (in Article 4, § 49) to approve the creation of state debt after a two-thirds vote in each legislative chamber. In addition, Article 8, § 24 stipulates that an income tax proposed by the Legislature, and its rate, must be approved by voters.

Concerning the constitutional referendum, the Texas Constitution gives only Texan citizens the power to approve constitutional amendments. Article 17 of the Texas Constitution stipulates two steps to **amend the Texas Constitution**: proposal and ratification. Any constitutional amendment must be proposed via a two-thirds vote of both legislative chambers (e.g., at least 100 House Members and 21 Senators). Any proposal must be ratified by a majority of voters in either a general election or a special election called by the Legislature to ratify constitutional amendments.[29]

Article 15 of the Texas Constitution: Impeachment

The ultimate check on political power is a legislature's ability to impeach and remove an executive or judicial official from office. Article 15 of the Texas Constitution, which deals with impeachment, does not define impeachable offenses in the Texas government. Hence, the Legislature decides what warrants subjecting a state official to the impeachment process. At the federal level, Congress can subject federal officials to impeachment for "treason, bribery, or other high crimes and misdemeanors."[30]

The **impeachment process** is the same for Congress and for the Texas Legislature. The power of impeachment is solely entrusted to the House of Representatives, which simply means the House determines (by a majority vote) whether sufficient evidence exists to subject an official to an impeachment trial in the Senate. The Senate possesses the actual power to remove an official from office, if two-thirds of the Senate agree to do so at the conclusion of the trial. The only governor in Texas history to be impeached and removed from office was James Ferguson in 1917. Two presidents have been impeached in U.S. history, but neither President Andrew Johnson nor President Bill Clinton were removed from office by the Senate.

Given impeachment's importance in holding state executive and judicial officials accountable, this is the only issue for which the Legislature can call itself into a special session.

Recall process: *the power of voters to remove a state official before their term of office is complete. This tool of direct democracy is available in many states, but not Texas.*

Initiative process: *the power of citizens to propose and pass legislation and constitutional amendments on their own, bypassing the Legislature. This tool of direct democracy is available in many states, but not Texas.*

Referendum process: *the power of voters to approve legislation and constitutional amendments proposed by the Legislature. In Texas, voters have limited use of the statutory referendum (e.g., approving the creation of state debt). However, all constitutional amendments proposed by the Legislature must be ratified by a majority of voters in either a general election or a special elation called by the Legislature to ratify constitutional amendments.*

Amending the Texas Constitution: *Article 17 of the Texas Constitution stipulates two steps to amend the Texas Constitution: proposal and ratification. Any constitutional amendment must be proposed via a two-thirds vote of both legislative chambers (e.g., at least 100 House members and 21 Senators). Any proposal must be ratified by a majority of voters in either a general election or a special election called by the Legislature to ratify constitutional amendments.*

Impeachment process: *the ultimate check on political power is a legislature's ability to impeach and remove an executive or judicial official from office. The power of impeachment is solely entrusted to the House of Representatives, which simply means the House determines (by a majority vote) whether sufficient evidence exists to subject an official to an impeachment trial in the Senate. The Senate possesses the actual power to remove an official from office, if two-thirds of the Senate agree to do so at the conclusion of the trial.*

uttyler.edu

Conclusions: Texas's Extensive Constitution and its Place in the Federal System

The Texas Constitution's Length

The Texas Constitution is a little less than 90,000 words long, spanning seventeen articles and 498 constitutional amendments for governing Texas. The entire U.S. political system, on the other hand, is regulated by a Constitution with seven articles, twenty-seven amendments, and only about 7,500 words. Despite the unequal lengths, both govern by defining and limiting the government's power. But the question does arise: why is Texas's Constitution so long?

One reason for the length of the Texas Constitution is that Texas gets the residual power to govern citizens' everyday affairs. Naturally, legislators and citizens frequently seek to constrain their state government's power by proposing and ratifying constitutional amendments. For instance, in November of 2015, voters ratified an amendment that enshrined their right to "hunt, fish, and harvest wildlife, including the use of traditional methods... [because] hunting and fishing are preferred methods of managing and controlling wildlife."[31]

Secondly, unlike its federal counterpart, the Texas Constitution does not provide the Legislature with a "Necessary and Proper Clause" that gives Congress implied powers—the power to pass laws appropriate for carrying out an enumerated responsibility. The Legislature must show where the Texas Constitution authorizes it to act on issues large and small. This makes Article 3 of the Texas Constitution excessively long because it must enumerate the Legislature's power over all facets of Texan life. A third and related reason for its length is that the Texas Constitution provides many (unnecessary) details that could be handled by simple legislation. Any changes, minor or major, to legislative power or to programs enumerated in the Texas Constitution require a constitutional amendment. Here is a sample of the Legislature's power to provide roadway projects to serve border colonias:

> To fund financial assistance to counties for roadways to serve border colonias, the legislature by general law may authorize the governor to authorize the Texas Public Finance Authority or its successor to issue general obligation bonds or notes of the state of Texas in an aggregate amount not to exceed $175 million and to enter into related credit agreements. Except as provided by Subsection (c) of this section, the proceeds from the sale of the bonds and notes may be used only to provide financial assistance to counties for projects to provide access roads to connect border colonias with public roads. Projects may include the construction of colonia access roads, the acquisition of materials used in maintaining colonia access roads, and projects related to the construction of colonia access roads, such as projects for the drainage of the roads.[32]

» The Texas Constitution is a little less than 90,000 words long. The entire U.S. political system, on the other hand, is regulated by a Constitution with seven articles, twenty-seven amendments, and only about 7,500 words.

The U.S. Constitution is brief mainly because it outlines the structure of government but provides Congress the flexibility to fill in the details. Take the federal court system established by Article 3 of the U.S. Constitution for example: "The judicial Power of the United States, shall be vested in one supreme Court, and in such inferior Courts as the Congress may from time to time ordain and establish." On the other hand, Article 5 of the Texas Constitution specifically enumerates all the courts of the Texas judicial system and discusses retirement, pay, discipline, and the removal of judges in these courts. It also provides the qualifications to be a judge in each court, defines the jurisdiction and geographical boundaries of each court, and describes the use of petit and grand juries.

Fourth, new social and political situations arise over time, and these require new amendments to confront them. The 1876 Texas Constitution provided the governor with unlimited power to grant pardons, parole, and clemency to individuals convicted of committing state crimes. However, a constitutional amendment was ratified in 1936 that revoked the governor's clemency power and gave it to the Board of Pardons and Paroles. The Legislature and the public felt that previous governors had abused their clemency powers.

Finally, a fifth reason for the Texas Constitution's length relates to Texas's standing in the federal system. Texas can regulate anything not given to the federal government nor restricted by the U.S. Constitution, so Texas believes it has a right to enact policies in certain situations (either through state laws or constitutional amendments). Because all policies enacted by Texas must conform to the U.S. Constitution, they are subject to review by the U.S. Supreme Court. If Texas enacts a constitutional amendment, and the U.S. Supreme Court declares that amendment unconstitutional, the provision is not erased from the Texas Constitution. Rather, the provision remains written but unenforceable. These inoperable provisions found throughout the Texas Constitution, are called **deadwood**. Deadwood also appears when constitutional provisions have been superseded, or replaced, by a later constitutional amendment (i.e., the original provision is inoperable).

For example, Texans ratified a constitutional amendment in 2005 that defined marriage in Texas as "the union of one man and one woman."[33] States officials claimed that the regulation and definition of marriage had always been a state issue (i.e., the U.S. Constitution does not provide the federal government any responsibility over marriage). Under the 10th Amendment, Texas argued that defining marriage as "one man and one woman" was a lawful execution of its police power. In 2015, the U.S. Supreme Court disagreed. The Supreme Court recognized marriage as a state issue, but ruled that states' regulation of marriages must respect the federal constitutional rights of its citizens. In other words, marriage is a state power, but the U.S. Constitution constrains how the states may exercise this responsibility. Namely, the Fourteenth Amendment's Due Process Clause protects the right to marry, regardless if the couple is homosexual or heterosexual. The Supreme Court also held that the Fourteenth Amendment's Equal Protection Clause requires states to treat homosexual couples the same as

Deadwood: *provisions of the Texas Constitution that remain in the constitutional text, but are unenforceable (e.g., the U.S. Supreme Court declares the amendment unconstitutional), or have been replaced by a later constitutional amendment.*

uttyler.edu

they do heterosexual couples.[34] With the Supreme Court's ruling, Texas's marriage provision in Article 1, § 32 was held as unconstitutional and cannot be enforced, but it remains in the constitutional text:

Sec. 32. MARRIAGE.

(a) Marriage in this state shall consist only of the union of one man and one woman.

(b) This state or a political subdivision of this state may not create or recognize any legal status identical or similar to marriage.

Views on Federalism

Regarding the types of disputes that arise in a federal system, the U.S. Constitution notably takes policy choices away from Texas and from the other states in the Union. But, this is a natural consequence of living under a political system whose written constitution supersedes all actors in the political system. For example, a Texas law criminalized desecrating either the Texas flag or the U.S. flag. Greg Johnson was charged with violating this law in 1984 after he was caught burning a U.S. flag to protest the Republican National Convention in Dallas. Johnson took his case to the U.S. Supreme Court and argued that his First Amendment right to free speech and expression, which is incorporated against Texas through the Fourteenth Amendment, protects his right to burn a U.S. flag in a political protest. Many people find burning a U.S. flag unappealing and disrespectful and would want Texas to protect these icons, but the Supreme Court agreed with Johnson's argument, stating that no government can "prohibit the expression of an idea simply because society finds the idea itself offensive or disagreeable."[35]

While the term federalism is not found in the constitutional text, it exists due to the careful division of power between the states and the federal government, as detailed in this chapter. However, in practice, the line between the authorities of the state and federal governments is not always clear. The country has grown, society has changed, and the American people now expect more from the federal government (e.g., minimum wage, health care, and the regulation of child labor). The federal government usually addresses these expectations with laws and regulations that determine whether an issue belongs to the federal government via its enumerated or implied powers or if it belongs to the states' police power. Two views create this inherent tension: dual and cooperative federalism.

Dual federalism contends that the authority of the federal and state governments is clearly divided, as the federal government is supreme over its responsibilities and the states retain sovereignty over their affairs. This arrangement creates an enclave of state power that the federal government cannot invade, nor can the federal government directly dictate what states can or cannot do.[36] For example, the Supreme Court ruled in *Murphy v. NCAA* (2018) that it is unconstitutional for the federal government to prevent states from passing laws that legalize sports betting.[37] Here, the Court rationalized the federal government invaded the sovereignty of the states by telling them what laws they could or could not pass.

Dual federalism: *a view of federalism that contends that the authority of the federal and state governments is clearly divided, as the federal government is supreme over its responsibilities and the states retain sovereignty over their affairs. This arrangement creates an enclave of state power that the federal government cannot invade, nor can the federal government directly dictate what states can or cannot do.*

Cooperative federalism, on the other hand, views the federal government as supreme in the legitimate operations enumerated to it by the U.S. Constitution.[38] Therefore, when the federal government carries out its enumerated or implied powers, the states cannot impede the federal government's appropriate actions. For instance, a federal minimum wage was considered unconstitutional prior to 1941 because it improperly invaded the states' sovereignty to regulate workplace conditions within their borders (i.e., dual federalism). In *United States v. Darby* (1941), however, the Supreme Court took a cooperative federalism view and held that federal minimum wage laws are justified under Congress's enumerated power to regulate interstate commerce and could not be challenged by the states.[39]

One way Congress can incentivize the states' actions is via Congress's ability to spend for the general welfare. When offering the states monies (usually through grants), the federal government can attach conditions to these expenditures to encourage the states to pass and promote certain policies. The reason all fiftt states passed laws that prohibit people under twenty-one from buying and consuming alcohol is not because federal government told them to (which is unconstitutional) but because the federal government incentivized the states to do so by threatening to withhold a small percentage of the highway funds they provide to the states.

> **Cooperative federalism:** *a view of federalism that contends that the federal government is supreme in the legitimate operations enumerated to it by the U.S. Constitution. Therefore, when the federal government carries out its enumerated or implied powers, the states cannot impede the federal government's appropriate actions.*

Key Terms

Amending the Texas Constitution: Article 17 of the Texas Constitution stipulates two steps to amend the Texas Constitution: proposal and ratification. Any constitutional amendment must be proposed via a two-thirds vote of both legislative chambers (e.g., at least 100 House members and 21 Senators). Any proposal must be ratified by a majority of voters in either a general election or a special election called by the Legislature to ratify constitutional amendments.

Articles of Confederation: the first constitution to govern the original 13 colonies in the Revolutionary War's late years and in the years immediately after the colonies gained independence. The Articles created a confederate system of government, with a weak centralized government. For example, the only institution of government was a unicameral Congress that relied on the states to implement the policies.

Bicameralism: the division of a legislature into two chambers, providing an internal check on legislative power. Bicameralism requires both chambers to agree on a bill's form and language before it can be sent to the executive (e.g., the president or governor of Texas).

Bill of Rights: a set of liberties against the government that are so fundamental that no government has the authority to take them away nor infringe upon them for illegitimate reasons.

Census: Article 1 of the U.S. Constitution stipulates that the federal government must conduct a census every ten years to determine how many people live in the fifty states and, by extension, the country as a whole.

Confederate system of government: a governing system where separate and independent states delegate very specific powers to a (relatively) weak centralized government. The Articles of Confederation created a confederation where the federal government had full responsibility over foreign affairs and over relations with various Indian tribes, but it lacked meaningful power over domestic affairs (e.g., regulating trade and commerce).

Constitution: a list of rules for all officials who exercise governmental power. These rules, consequently, are a nation's ultimate law that sets forth the structure and powers of government.

Constitutional supremacy: the acceptance that the U.S. Constitution is the "supreme law of the land." Consequently, Texas has full sovereignty over issues not enumerated to the federal government nor restricted by the U.S. Constitution.

Cooperative federalism: a view of federalism that contends that the federal government is supreme in the legitimate operations enumerated to it by the U.S. Constitution. Therefore, when the federal government carries out its enumerated or implied powers, the states cannot impede the federal government's appropriate actions.

Deadwood: provisions of the Texas Constitution that remain in the constitutional text, but are unenforceable (e.g., the U.S. Supreme Court declares the amendment unconstitutional), or have been replaced by a later constitutional amendment.

Dual federalism: a view of federalism that contends that the authority of the federal and state governments is clearly divided, as the federal government is supreme over its responsibilities and the states retain sovereignty over their affairs. This arrangement creates an enclave of state power that the federal government cannot invade, nor can the federal government directly dictate what states can or cannot do.

Enumerated powers of the federal government: the powers of the federal government that are specifically written within the U.S. Constitution's text. Most of Congress's, and by extension the federal government's, powers and responsibilities are located in Article 1, § 8 of the U.S. Constitution.

External check on legislative power: the ability of an executive (e.g., the president or governor of Texas) to veto any bill the Legislatures sends.

Federalism: the U.S. Constitution's careful division of power between the states and the federal government. Federal power is limited to and defined by those powers the Constitution enumerates to it and those powers that can be reasonably implied. The states retain all powers not enumerated to the federal government nor restricted by the U.S. Constitution.

Great Compromise: a compromise between the Virginia Plan and the New Jersey Plan, where the delegates agreed to a bicameral Congress where the population of the lower chamber (the House of Representatives) would reflect states' populations, and the population of the upper chamber (the Senate) would be equal because each state would be guaranteed two Senators. In addition to providing Congress with additional powers, the delegates agreed to the Supremacy Clause, which allows federal law to trump state law in conflicts. Lastly, the delegates agreed to a president selected independently of Congress and to a federal judiciary staffed by judges appointed by the president and confirmed by the Senate.

Impeachment process: the ultimate check on political power is a legislature's ability to impeach and remove an executive or judicial official from office. The power of impeachment is solely entrusted to the House of Representatives, which simply means the House determines (by a majority vote) whether sufficient evidence exists to subject an official to an impeachment trial in the Senate. The Senate possesses the actual power to remove an official from office, if two-thirds of the Senate agree to do so at the conclusion of the trial.

Implied powers of the federal government: based on the Necessary and Proper Clause, the Supreme Court interpreted this clause as providing Congress the authorization to pass any legislation that is both necessary and appropriate for Congress to implement its enumerated powers.

Initiative process: the power of citizens to propose and pass legislation and constitutional amendments on their own, bypassing the Legislature. This tool of direct democracy is available in many states, but not Texas.

uttyler.edu

Judicial review: the judiciary's power to review governmental action and determine their compatibility with the constitution (i.e., judicial review allows the judiciary to enforce the limits on governmental power enumerated in a constitution). Consequently, federal judges review the actions of federal or states governments to determine their compatibility with the U.S. Constitution, and Texas state judges review actions of state and local governments to determine their compatibility with the Texas Constitution.

Line-item veto: the power of the governor to veto particular spending in an appropriations bill without vetoing the entire appropriations bill.

New Jersey Plan: a plan of government, supported by delegates of smaller states, that would give Congress the powers it lacked, but Congress's structure would remain a unicameral legislature in which states were equal. Further, instead of allowing Congress to veto laws passed by state legislatures, the New Jersey Plan advocated that the federal law would be considered supreme in conflicts between federal and state law. Lastly, Congress would select the president, who would in turn select judges for the federal judiciary.

Plural executive: the division of executive power in Texas among executive officials elected independently of the governor in a statewide election (e.g., lieutenant governor, the secretary of state, the comptroller of public accounts, the commissioner of the general land office, and the attorney general). The governor may be the head of the executive branch, but the division of executive power prevents her from controlling all the political output and responsibilities of the Texas executive branch.

Police powers of the states: the U.S. Constitution guarantees that all the power not given to the federal government nor restricted to the states by the U.S. Constitution, is left to the states. This provides states with the authority to regulate its citizens' health, safety, and morals. In other words, states are given the residual power to perform essential government functions (e.g., regulate the day-to-day lives of their citizens).

Popular sovereignty: the notion that political power rests with the people.

Recall process: the power of voters to remove a state official before their term of office is complete. This tool of direct democracy is available in many states, but not Texas.

Referendum process: the power of voters to approve legislation and constitutional amendments proposed by the Legislature. In Texas, voters have limited use of the statutory referendum (e.g., approving the creation of state debt). However, all constitutional amendments proposed by the Legislature must be ratified by a majority of voters in either a general election or a special elation called by the Legislature to ratify constitutional amendments.

Regular session of the Texas Legislature: the Texas Legislature's regular session occurs every two years, meeting on the second Tuesday of January in odd-numbered years. When the Legislature convenes for a regular session it can set its own agenda. A regular session can only last 140 days.

Representative government: a governing system, whereby the people influence the government through frequent and fair elections in which they can vote for representatives of their choice.

Selective incorporation: based on the Fourteenth Amendment's Due Process Clause, the Supreme Court determines, on a case-by-case basis, which rights in the Bill of Rights are fundamental. Those deemed fundamental are enforced against state governments.

Separation of powers: The U.S. Constitution's division of the powers of government into three separate and coequal branches of government, vesting the power to create laws with Congress, the power to executive the laws with the president, and the power to resolve legal disputes with the federal judiciary led by the Supreme Court. Article 2 of the Texas Constitution separates governmental power by ensuring that the "powers of the government of the state of Texas shall be divided into three distinct departments."

Special session of the Texas Legislature: the governor of Texas is authorized to call a special session of the Texas Legislature and set the legislative agenda for the special session. A special session, therefore, occurs outside of the Legislature's regular session and can only last thirty days.

Supremacy Clause: Article 6 of the U.S. Constitution guarantees the U.S. Constitution, and all laws passed in accordance to it, are the "supreme law of the land." Consequently, states' acts are not allowed to stand if they should come into conflict.

Tenth Amendment: the understanding of state power is reinforced by the amendment's command that "The powers not delegated to the United States by the Constitution, nor prohibited by it to the states, are reserved to the states respectively, or to the people."

Virginia Plan: a plan of government, supported by delegates of the larger states that envisioned a powerful bicameral Congress in which a state's population would determine its representation in both houses of Congress. Along with expanded federal powers, Congress would have the ability to veto laws passed by states and, once its membership was determined, the responsibility of selecting a president and judges for the federal judiciary.

ENDNOTES

[1] WFAA Staff. (2013, October 30). Greg Abbott: 'I go into the office, I sue the federal government.' Retrieved from https://www.wfaa.com/article/news/politics/greg-abbott-i-go-into-the-office-i-sue-the-federal-government/306072905

[2] Somin, Ilya. (2017, September 15). Public Ignorance about the Constitution. The Washington Post. Retrieved from https://www.washingtonpost.com/news/volokh-conspiracy/wp/2017/09/15/public-ignorance-about-the-constitution/?utm_term=.20885d36d80f

[3] Paulsen, Michael S., Steven G. Calabresi, Michael W. McConnell, and Samuel L. Bray. 2010. The Constitution of the United States. pgs. 23–24. Second Edition. Foundation Press.

[4] Under the Articles, the federal government only had a unicameral Congress and no institutions to neither execute its laws nor resolve conflicts that emerged when its laws were ignored.

[5] Gundy v. United States. 588 U.S. (2019). (Justice Gorsuch dissenting opinion)

[6] Madison, James. (1778, January 26). Federalist #45: The Alleged Danger From the Powers of the Union to the State Governments Considered.

[7] National Federation of Independent Business v. Sebelius. 567 U.S. 519 (2012).

[8] The American Legion v. American Humanist Association. 588 U.S. _ (2019). (Justice Kavanaugh concurring opinion)

[9] Paulsen, Michael S., Steven G. Calabresi, Michael W. McConnell, and Samuel L. Bray. 2010. The Constitution of the United States. pg. 827. Second Edition. Foundation Press.

[10] Hamilton, Alexander. (1778). Federalist #84: Certain General and Miscellaneous Objections to the Constitution Considered and Answered.

[11] Paulsen, Michael S., Steven G. Calabresi, Michael W. McConnell, and Samuel L. Bray. 2010. The Constitution of the United States. pg. 830. Second Edition. Foundation Press.

[12] McCulloch v. Maryland. 17 U.S. 316 (1819).

[13] United States Constitution. Article 1, § 9.

[14] Texas Constitution. Article 1, § 33.

[15] Texas Constitution. Article 1, § 34.

[16] District of Columbia v. Heller. 554 U.S. 570 (2008).

[17] Texas House of Representatives. How a Bill Becomes a Law. Retrieved from https://house.texas.gov/about-us/bill/

[18] Hamilton, Alexander. (1778). Federalist #78: The Judiciary Department.

[19] Texas is 1 of 4 states to have a biennial regular session. The other states to have a biennial session are Montana, North Dakota, and Nevada.

[20] Texas Constitution. Article 3. § 40.

[21] Bumsted, Brad. (2007, April 27). Texas Gov. Rick Perry says part-time legislature suffices. Trib Live. Retrieved from https://archive.triblive.com/news/texas-gov-rick-perry-says-part-time-legislature-suffices/

[22] Gundy v. United States. 588 U.S. (2019). (Justice Gorsuch dissenting opinion)

[23] McCullough, Jolie and Alex Samuels. (2019, July 3). This year, Texas passes a law legalizing hemp. It also has prosecutors dropping hundreds of marijuana cases. The Texas Tribune. Retrieved from https://www.texastribune.org/2019/07/03/texas-marijuana-hemp-testing-prosecution/

[24] Ibid.

[25] Hamilton, Alexander. (1788, March 18). Federalist Paper #70: The Executive Department Further Considered.

[26] Young, Stephen. (2019, June 18). Catching Up With Texas Gov. Greg Abbott's Veto Pen. Dallas Observer. Retrieved from https://www.dallasobserver.com/news/dallas-just-cant-stop-losing-to-the-car-wash-on-mlk-11704185

[27]Vertuno, Jim. (2019, March 10). Abbot fills courts with GOP judges voters rejected. Austin American-Statesman. Retrieved from https://www.statesman.com/news/20190310/abbott-fills-courts-with-gop-judges-voters-rejected

[28]McClory, Toni. 2010. Understanding the Arizona Constitution. pgs. 80–103. Second Edition. The University of Arizona Press.

[29]To amend the U.S. Constitution, Article 5 provides two methods for proposing constitutional amendments. First, Congress can propose a constitutional amendment provided that the amendment receives a 2/3rds approval vote in both the House and the Senate. While Article 5 stipulates that amendments can be proposed by a constitutional convention called by 2/3rds of state legislatures, this proposal method has never been used. Next, a proposed amendment needs to be ratified by 3/4ths of state legislatures for it to become part of the U.S. Constitution. Reflecting the republican nature of government created by the U.S. Constitution, the founders left the people (through their representatives in Congress and state legislatures) the decision to examine whether an amendment is necessary to alter the country's fundamental law.

[30]United States Constitution. Article 2, § 4.

[31]Texas Constitution. Article 1, § 34.

[32]Texas Constitution. Article 3, § 49-1.

[33]Texas Constitution. Article 1, § 32.

[34]Obergefell v. Hodges. 576 U.S. _ (2015).

[35]Texas v. Johnson. 491 U.S. 397 (1989).

[36]Epstein, Lee and Thomas G. Walker. 2017. Constitutional Law for a Changing America: Institutional Powers and Constraints. pg. 349. 9th Edition. CQ Press.

[37]Murphy v. National Collegiate Athletic Association. 584 U.S. _ (2018)

[38]Epstein, Lee and Thomas G. Walker. 2017. Constitutional Law for a Changing America: Institutional Powers and Constraints. pg. 349. 9th Edition. CQ Press.

[39]United States v. Darby. 312 U.S. (1941).

3

The star on the ceiling of the capitol building rotunda dome in Austin, Texas.

istock.com/xjben

Chapter 3

Voting and Elections in Texas

THE UNITED STATES AND TEXAS ARE GOVERNED by a representative democracy in which the public is represented by elected officials who make policies on behalf of the people. Thus, elections link the government and the people. Voters are theoretically rational and know about political issues and the candidates' stances on issues. These voters cast rational ballots to elect people who reflect their political and policy preferences. Elected officials will then initiate voters' favored policies, and, if voters are satisfied with the elected official's record, they will reelect the official. As this chapter shows, voter turnout is low in the United States and even lower in Texas. What happened to American and Texan voters, and does this electoral link—a link necessary for democracy—still exist today?

To study the low voter turnout in the United States and in Texas, we must compare them to the rest of the democratic world. First, however, we must understand two terms. The **voting-age population**, or VAP, refers to the whole population of people eighteen or older in the United States or in Texas. The term **registered population**, or REG, refers to eligible adults who are registered to vote.

In the United States, a large discrepancy exists between the two numbers, which reflects poorly on American voters. In 2016, for example, the Census Bureau found that the VAP—the number of Americans eighteen years and

Voting-age population (VAP): *the total number of individuals in the United States who are eighteen and older.*

Registered population (REG): *the total number of United States citizens registered to vote.*

uttyler.edu

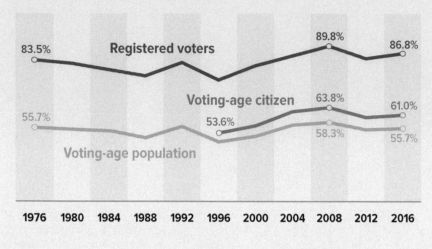

FIGURE 3.1

Turnout in U.S. Presidential Elections[7]

Votes cast as a share of ...

Registered voters
83.5%   89.8%   86.8%

Voting-age citizen
55.7%   63.8%   61.0%
53.6%
58.3%   55.7%

Voting-age population

1976 1980 1984 1988 1992 1996 2000 2004 2008 2012 2016

Source: Pew Research Center; Census Bureau (population estimates), House Clerk's office and Pew Research Center (vote totals)

older—stood at 245.5 million people.[1] Only 157.6 million, or 64.2% of the VAP, were registered to vote, and only 137.5 million, or 56%, actually did vote.[2] It looks like a big majority of Americans do not care about voting, and the voter turnout numbers look comparatively low. Further analysis shows, however, that the VAP number in the United States includes legal and illegal immigrants who are not citizens and therefore cannot vote. They can comprise up to 10% of the VAP, and even more in Texas.

Today, Texas is home to about 4.7 million legal and illegal immigrants. Among states, Texas has the seventh-biggest share of residents born in foreign countries. Only about one-third of these 4.7 million immigrants have become American citizens, and two-thirds are currently permanent residents or undocumented immigrants. This inflates the VAP in Texas because many eighteen-year-olds cannot legally vote. According to the U.S. Census Bureau, Texas had a population of 20,172 million people in 2016. Only 17,378 million, or about 86%, were U.S. citizens.[3] That means a full 14% of the people were legal and illegal immigrants not eligible to vote. Only 58% of all adults in Texas were eligible to vote, and 67.5% of all eligible citizens were registered to vote in 2016.[4] Out of these, 47.7% of the VAP voted. A better, still not great, 55.4% of all registered adults voted.[5]

Thus, for Texas and for the country overall, a more accurate number when analyzing voter turnout would be voting-age citizens. For **voting-age citizens**, voter registration numbers would be closer to 71% in the United States and 67.5% in Texas, which would be comparable with many European countries. Voter turnout for the voting-age citizen population climbs to 61% in the United States and 55.4% in Texas.

Voting-age citizens: *U.S. citizens who are eighteen and older.*

FIGURE 3.2

Votes Cast in Most Recent National Election

Country	Voting-age population	Registered voters	Country	Voting-age population	Registered voters
Belgium (2014)*	87.21%	89.37%	Czech Republic (2018)	63.44%	66.57%
Sweden (2014)	82.61%	85.81%	U.K. (2017)	63.25%	69.31%
Denmark (2015)	80.34%	85.89%	Greece (2015)*	62.14%	56.16%
Australia (2016)*	78.96%	90.98%	Canada (2015)	62.12%	68.28%
South Korea (2017)	77.92%	77.23%	Portugal (2015)	61.75%	55.84%
Netherlands (2017)	77.31%	81.93%	Spain (2016)	61.17%	66.48%
Israel (2015)	76.10%	72.34%	Slovakia (2016)	59.43%	59.82%
New Zealand (2017)	75.65%	79.01%	Ireland (2016)	58.04%	65.09%
Finland (2015)	73.14%	66.85%	Estonia (2015)	56.82%	64.23%
Hungary (2018)	71.65%	69.68%	United States (2016)	55.70%	86.80%
Norway (2017)	70.59%	78.22%	Luxembourg (2013)*	55.12%	91.15%
Germany (2017)	69.11%	76.15%	Slovenia (2014)	54.09%	51.73%
Austria (2017)	68.79%	80.00%	Poland (2015)	53.83%	55.34%
France (2017)	67.93%	74.56%	Chile (2017)	52.20%	49.02%
Mexico (2012)*	65.97%	63.08%	Latvia (2014)	51.69%	58.80%
Italy (2018)	65.28%	73.05%	Switzerland (2015)*	38.63%	48.40%

Source: Pew Research Center calculations based on data from International Institute for Democracy and Electoral Assistance, European Election Database, United States Election Project, Office of the Clerk of the U.S. House of Representatives and various national election authorities[8]

When looking at registered voter turnout, America's numbers are very positive. The United States had 157.6 million people registered to vote in 2016, and 137.5 million—almost 87%—did vote in 2016. This number puts the United States in the top five regarding election turnout in democracies.[6]

Figure 3.1 depicts voter turnout numbers in the United States for the last 40 years (1976–2016) and compares VAP, voting-age citizens, and registered voters.

As **Figure 3.2** shows, the 55.7% turnout for the VAP in 2016 puts the United States at the bottom of turnout in various democracies. When analyzing turnout for registered voters, however, the United States and even Texas fare well, ranking fourth.

What conclusions can be drawn from Figure 1.2? The United States does not have a problem with registered voter turnout; the problem is trying to get voters registered. The big difference between the United States, Texas, and European democracies is that many democracies automatically register eligible adults. In Sweden and in Germany, the government registers citizens to vote when they turn eighteen. All people have to do is show up on Election

FIGURE 3.3

Voter Turnout by State in the 2016 Presidential Elections[9]

STATE	TURNOUT	RANK '16 ('12)	STATE	TURNOUT	RANK '16 ('12)	STATE	TURNOUT	RANK '16 ('12)
Minnesota	74.8%	1 (1)	Delaware	64.6%	18 (17)	Kentucky	59.7%	35 (39)
Maine	72.8%	2 (6)	Montana	64.3%	19 (15)	Alabama	59.3%	36 (32)
New Hampshire	72.5%	3 (3)	Ohio	64.2%	20 (13)	California	58.4%	37 (42)
Colorado	72.1%	4 (4)	Pennsylvania	64.0%	21 (28)	Indiana	57.9%	38 (41)
Wisconsin	70.5%	5 (2)	Nebraska	63.8%	22 (23)	Utah	57.7%	39 (40)
Iowa	69.0%	6 (5)	Illinois	63.4%	23 (30)	Nevada	57.3%	40 (38)
Massachusetts	68.3%	7 (9)	Missouri	62.3%	24 (18)	New York	57.3%	41 (44)
Oregon	68.3%	8 (14)	North Dakota	61.9%	25 (26)	South Carolina	57.3%	42 (37)
Maryland	67.2%	9 (7)	Alaska	61.8%	26 (34)	Mississippi	56.5%	43 (29)
Virginia	67.2%	10 (8)	Dist. of Columbia	61.1%	27 (20)	Arizona	56.2%	44 (45)
Florida	65.7%	11 (16)	Idaho	60.9%	28 (24)	New Mexico	55.2%	45 (43)
Washington	65.7%	12 (10)	Louisiana	60.6%	29 (25)	Oklahoma	53.2%	46 (49)
Michigan	65.7%	13 (12)	Wyoming	60.4%	30 (33)	Arkansas	53.1%	47 (47)
New Jersey	65.5%	14 (19)	Georgia	59.9%	31 (31)	Tennessee	52.0%	48 (46)
Connecticut	65.4%	15 (21)	South Dakota	59.9%	32 (27)	**Texas**	**51.6%**	**49 (48)**
North Carolina	65.2%	16 (11)	Rhode Island	59.7%	33 (35)	West Virginia	50.8%	50 (50)
Vermont	64.8%	17 (22)	Kansas	59.7%	34 (36)	Hawaii	43.0%	51 (51)

Note: 2012 turnout rank in parenthesis

Source: U.S. Elections Project

Day, show identification, and cast a ballot. In the United States, on the other hand, individuals must register to vote, which can be very time-consuming, especially in states like Texas. For this reason, only about 71% of voting-age citizens are registered in the United States. As many as 91% of all citizens are registered in Canada, and 96% of all citizens are registered in Sweden.

Political Participation

Political participation: activities Americans engage in to influence governmental decision-making.

Political participation refers to any activity Texas residents take when they attempt to influence governmental decisions. The most common form of political participation in Texas is voting. However, voting is only one of many forms of political participation that Texans engage in. Other forms include volunteering to help a political campaign, attending campaign rallies, donating money to specific political candidates or political parties, contacting a local- or state-elected official, and putting up a yard sign or bumper sticker to show support for certain political candidates.

FIGURE 3.4

Texas Voter Turnout in Off-Year Elections Since 1994

	1994	1998	2002	2006	2010	2014	2018
United States	36.0	36.4	36.2	37.1	37.8	33.9	49.3
Texas	31.3	26.1	28.8	25.8	26.7	23.9	46.3
Rank *(out of 50 states and D.C.)*	45	47	49	50	50	50	44

Source: Texas Secretary of State at https://www.sos.state.tx.us/

Voting continues to be the number one method of participating in Texas politics, but Texans overall do not compare favorably across the nation regarding actual voter turnout in national, state, and local elections. **Figure 3.3** shows voter turnout in Texas and in the other forty-nine states in the 2012 and 2016 **general elections**. It compares Texas to the rest of the country.

Texas had the third-lowest turnout, 51.6%, for the 2016 presidential election, and the state actually saw lower turnout in 2016 than in the 2012 presidential elections. Only Hawaii and West Virginia had lower voter turnout in 2016.

What about off-year non-presidential elections? Studies show that fewer voters turn out for non-presidential elections, as they tend to be less excited if the presidency is not on the ballot. Do these studies also hold true for Texas? Yes, and voter turnout for off-year elections was even worse for Texas up to 2018, as **Figure 3.4** shows.

As Figure 3.4 shows, Texas had the lowest voter turnout of any state from 2006 until 2018 in **off-year elections**. The Republican and Democratic parties, however, had record turnout numbers during their March 2018 primaries, as **Figure 3.5** shows. The Republican Party increased its turnout by 200,000 voters, and the Democratic Party did even better by increasing its turnout by 440,000.

This record in primary voting would continue into the 2018 mid-term election, as Texas experienced an upswing in voting. A full 46.3% of all registered Texans did vote, a dramatic increase in voting compared to 2014. Therefore, Texas followed a nationwide trend in voter turnout in 2018. With both party bases motivated, the United States saw its best voter turnout in an off-year election cycle since 1914. However, despite a dramatic increase in voting, about 41.07% of all registered voters in Texas stayed home. Accounting for the

FIGURE 3.5

Texas Primary Voting, 2018 and 2014

2018 total primary election voter turnout

Republicans

1,500,000

Democrats

1,000,000

2014 total primary election voter turnout

Republicans

1,300,000

Democrats

560,000

Source: the Texas Secretary of State, the Texas Election Code, and the Texas Democratic and Republican parties

General election: *an election in which candidates from more than two parties compete for political office.*

Off-year elections: *midterm elections, or elections held in non-presidential election years.*

12.61% of unregistered voters, only a minority of Texans, 46.32%, voted in 2018. Analyzing these numbers further reveals that Senator Ted Cruz got reelected with 23.58% of the vote. Clearly, voting is not a priority for the average Texan. However, the 2018 off-year election does provide some hope. The turnout in Texas did increase quite dramatically, and these figures will hopefully improve in the 2020 presidential election.

These statistics beg the question: Why do Texans not exercise their right to vote in higher numbers? Are there legal, historical, cultural, or personal reasons why Texans vote in such low numbers? The next sections will deal with these and other questions.

Voting Requirements

Article I, Section 4 of the U.S. Constitution guarantees the right to vote for local, state, and national representatives. However, the article allows every state to set "time, place and manner" of elections. For this reason, election laws vary in every U.S. state regarding voter registration, the closing of polls, candidate selection, and voter-identification requirements.

As previously mentioned, Texas voters must register to vote before they can cast a ballot on Election Day. How does registration work in Texas and who can register to vote in Texas? According to the Texas Secretary of State's website, people eligible to vote in Texas must be:

- a U.S. citizen;

- a resident of the Texas county in which registration application is made;

- at least eighteen years old on Election Day;

- not finally convicted of a felony (if convicted, voters must have fully discharged the sentence—including any term of incarceration, parole, or supervision—or completed a period of probation ordered by any court, or have been pardoned or otherwise released from the resulting disability to vote); and

- not determined by the final judgment of a court exercising probate jurisdiction as totally mentally incapacitated or partially mentally incapacitated with no right to vote.

After meeting the above requirements, prospective voters must follow Texas's specific procedures to register to vote. First, voters must get a registration card either in person or by mail at least 30 days before the election. The registration card can be requested on the Texas Secretary of State's website or picked up at the Department of Motor Vehicles or at a post office. The completed card must be mailed to the voter registrar's office in the county of residence. Annual registration was declared unconstitutional in 1971, so people stay registered to vote as long as they do not move. After moving within the state, people must start the process all over. Some states make voter registration easier. In North Dakota, for example, people do not need to register to vote—they only show up on Election

58

UNCOVERING TEXAS POLITICS IN THE 21ST CENTURY

Day, present their driver's license or state identification card, and vote. Turnout in North Dakota in the 2016 general election was about 10% higher than in Texas.

After registering to vote in Texas, the voting process is fairly easy. People have several choices of when and how to vote. They can show up with their voter ID on Election Day and cast ballots in person at a local polling place. Many Texans take advantage of the early voting that begins on the 17th day before Election Day and ends 4 days before the election is held. Early voting has been popular with many Texas voters, and 74% of them cast their vote early during the 2016 presidential election. In addition, voters can request an absentee ballot if they are sick, disabled, over the age of 65, or out of town on Election Day. Absentee ballots can be filled out at home and then mailed in.

As an important side note, the Voting Rights Act does require counties with an ethnic minority that comprises 5% or more of the county's voting-age residents, or 10,000 people overall, to print ballots in their native language. For example, many counties in Texas print ballots in English and Spanish. Harris County, which includes Houston, even prints ballots in Chinese and Vietnamese.

In 2011, the Texas legislature passed one of the country's most restrictive voter identification laws. After two court challenges, the law was declared unconstitutional, and the legislature made changes to the law effective in 2016. The amended law was upheld in April of 2018 by the 5th U.S. Circuit Court of Appeals in New Orleans and was used in the 2018 elections in Texas.

According to the law, voters must bring a form of photo identification to the polling station to be able to vote. There are seven approved forms of photo identifications and also other forms of supportive identification, as shown in **Figure 3.6**, that can be brought to the polls to allow a voter to fill out a reasonable impediment declaration, which will allow the voter to still cast a ballot, even if not in possession of one of the seven required photo identifications.

FIGURE 3.6

Identification Requirements for Voters to Cast a Ballot in Texas

The seven approved forms of photo identification are:

Texas Driver License issued by the Texas Department of Public Safety (DPS);

Texas Personal Identification Card issued by DPS;

Texas Election Identification Certificate issued by DPS;

Texas Handgun License issued by DPS;

United States Military Identification Card containing the person's photograph;

United States Citizenship Certificate containing the person's photograph;

United States Passport (book or card)[10]

If a voter does not possess one of the forms of acceptable photo identification the voter may execute a Reasonable Impediment Declaration and present a copy or original of one of the following supporting forms of identification:

A government document that shows the voter's name and an address, including the voter's voter registration certificate;

A current utility bill

A bank statement

A government check

A paycheck

A certified domestic (from a U.S. state or territory) birth certificate or a document confirming birth admissible in a court of law which establishes the voter's identity (which may include a foreign birth document).[11]

Voter Turnout in Texas

As previously discussed, voter turnout in the United States, especially in Texas, is low. In 2016, about 65% of Texans were of voting age (i.e., VAP). However only 58% of the population could legally vote, and only 67.5% of those people

uttyler.edu

were registered to vote.[12] Even worse, only 51.6% of registered voters turned out on Election Day to cast a ballot. Because 2016 was a presidential election year, these numbers were actually quite high for Texas. In the off-year elections of 2014, turnout was even lower. Only 23.9% of all Texans turned out to vote. Many reasons that explain why the United States and Texas have lower voter turnout rates than other democracies are discussed below.

First, studies show that having frequent elections causes low voter turnout. In Texas, average residents can vote several times a year. From primaries to local, state, and national elections, an election always seems imminent. Along with other elections (such school board and city council elections) and votes on constitutional amendments (changes to the Texas constitution), most Texan voters get to vote at least twice a year. Studies show that more elections leads to a lower voter turnout. Voting loses its significance and importance. In France, on the other hand, voters can cast their ballot only once every 5 years for president and for the legislature (the National Assembly). Therefore, voting is special, it matters, and the turnout in France is higher.

To make matters worse, Texas elects public officials to almost every local and state office, which can make ballots lengthy and confusing. Studies show that a longer ballot makes voters less likely to complete it and to vote again in the next election.

The decline of party identification can also explain why people do not vote. The more strongly people identify with a party, the more likely they are to vote. Thus, **partisans** (people who strongly identify with a political party) are more likely to vote than **independents** (voters who do not identify with a political party). Unfortunately for voter turnout, more Americans and Texans today identify as independents than ever before.

The decline of electoral competitiveness resulting from a decline in two-party conflict in the United States and in Texas also causes low voter turnout. Most parts of Texas are dominated by one of the two major parties, and the other party has no chance of winning office. Today, East and West Texas are heavily Republican and it is rare to see a Democrat winning office. At the same time, South Texas and some of the larger urban areas, such as Houston and Dallas, are becoming more Democratic. With both parties dominating certain parts of the state, voter turnout will decline. In solid Republican parts of Texas, Democratic supporters will stay home because their candidates never win. Ironically, Republicans will also stay home because they know their candidates always win. So both Republican and Democratic voters will decide not to vote because the races are not competitive anymore. Why vote if your party's candidate already has won or always loses? We see the same phenomenon at the national level during presidential elections. Turnout is higher in competitive states such as Ohio and Florida compared to non-competitive states such as New Jersey or Alabama.

The level and type of election also influences voter turnout in Texas. The lowest turnouts are usually associated with local elections, primary elections, run-off elections, and off-year elections. Local elections often see single-digit turnouts. For example, in 1999 the race for mayor of Dallas saw a 5% turnout

Partisan: a voter who identifies with a political party.

Independent: a voter who does not identify with a political party.

rate. Presidential elections and competitive races for governor, the Senate, or the House of Representatives usually see higher turnout numbers. Generally, a higher level of office leads to a higher turnout.

Legal Barriers to Voting

The voting history of a specific group of citizens within a state or country can impact voting. For example, long-disenfranchised groups historically experience a lower voter turnout rates when they become enfranchised. Voting is a habit people must develop, and groups with a history of not voting take time to acquire this habit. Many members of formerly disenfranchised groups do not believe they should vote and/or are unfamiliar with the practice of voting. It usually takes a generation or two for newly enfranchised groups to reach the turnout levels of other groups with a history of voting. For example, women were disenfranchised in Texas until 1918 and in the United States until 1920, when they received the right to vote with the Nineteenth Amendment. Women's turnout did not catch up with men's turnout until 1980, or 60 years later, and today women are more likely to vote than men.

The largest decline in overall electoral turnout occurred in 1972, when eighteen- to twenty-year-olds received the right to vote with the Twenty-sixth Amendment to the U.S. Constitution. Overall turnout declined dramatically, and this specific age group still has lower turnout than other age groups, which is one major reason for low voter turnout in Texas and in the United States.

A legacy of legal voting restrictions for certain groups also impacts voter turnout. Historically, Texas has been one of the most restrictive states regarding voting. For example, Texas adopted a poll tax in 1902. A **poll tax** is a fee people must pay before casting a ballot. The poll tax was $1.75 plus an additional $0.25 fee Texas counties levied. This amount represented an average daily wage for Texans in 1902. Many poor Texans could not pay the poll tax and were thus disenfranchised. The poll tax in Texas was finally declared unconstitutional by the United States Supreme Court in 1966 in the case *United States v. Texas*, 384 U.S.155.

Poll tax: a fee that must be paid to vote.

Another mechanism used by the state to disenfranchise certain groups of people was the **white primary**. Implemented in 1906, the White primary disenfranchised African Americans and Latinos in the general election. Because Texas was a one-party state at the time and the Democratic Party controlled all aspects of Texas government, only White citizens could join and vote in the Democratic Party's primary. Whoever won the Democratic Party primary was then assured election during the general election. The White primary was coded into state law and was not declared unconstitutional until 1944.

White primary: primary held by the Democratic Party in Texas that excluded African Americans.

Residency requirements have also disenfranchised certain groups of people from voting. U.S. military members and their families were not allowed to vote in Texas under the 1876 state constitution, because they did not meet residency requirements when stationed in Texas. It took until 1965 for the Supreme Court to overrule this statute in *Carrington v. Rash*.

In addition, young and mobile voters who moved frequently for job requirements were disenfranchised. Most states had no or very brief residency requirements, but Texas imposed a 1-year residency requirement that was not changed until 1972. Today, the residency requirement has been lowered to thirty days.

As mentioned earlier, cumbersome voter registration laws are another major reason for low voter turnout. In the United States, and especially in Texas, voters must put effort into registering to vote before they can actually vote. Studies have shown that registration requirements lower turnout by about 9% nationwide. Texas has imposed fairly stringent voter requirements while other states have made voter registration easier. Some states, like North Dakota, have actually eliminated voter registration requirements.

Determinants of the Vote

As outlined above, Texas has one of the lowest voter turnout rates in the United States. However, a little over half of all Texans voted in the 2016 presidential elections. This section discusses what determines who votes, who does not vote, and which political party Texans favor. Studying the voting behavior of Texans reveals several characteristics that determine the way Texans vote. The following demographic factors influencing voting will be analyzed: ethnic background, education, age, and gender.

When studying the Texas electorate and the reasons for low voter turnout in the state, demographic factors come into play. Currently, 28.3 million people live in the state of Texas, and 18.2 million are eligible to vote because they are eighteen or older.[13] Breaking the Texas population into demographic factors reveals that 11.2 million Texas residents are Latino, which means that 39.4% of the population in Texas is of Hispanic origin.[14] However, only 5.4 million, or 29.8%, of Latinos in Texas are eligible to vote.[15] This low number is not a result of legal disenfranchisement, it is because Latinos make up the youngest ethnic group in Texas, and many are either legal or illegal immigrants who cannot vote.

Texas residents of Hispanic descent also have lower education levels than average Texans. Of this population, 24% do not have a high school degree, and only 7% of the white population does not have a high school degree.[17] Only 13.8% of all Latinos in Texas have a bachelor's or other advanced degree compared to 18.8% of the black population, 33.6% of the white population, and 52% of the rapidly growing Asian population. Studies show that education is a major determinant of the vote, and more educated people are more likely to vote. A low educational level leads to low Latino voter turnout in Texas, which in turn leads to overall low voter turnout for the state. Ethnic background and education are therefore major factors determining voting behavior in Texas.

A third major determinant of the vote in the United States and Texas today is age. Many studies show that voter turnout tends to increase with age. Among the eighteen- to twenty-four-year-old group, voter turnout was a measly 27.3% in the 2016 general election that President Trump won.[18] On the

FIGURE 3.7

Younger Adults Voted Democratic by a Wide Margin in 2018

% who say they voted for the _____ candidate in the election for House of Representatives

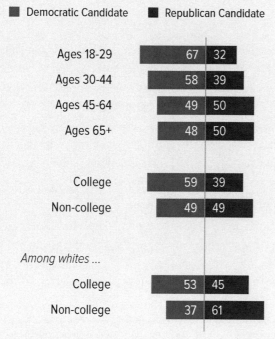

■ Democratic Candidate   ■ Republican Candidate

	Dem	Rep
Ages 18-29	67	32
Ages 30-44	58	39
Ages 45-64	49	50
Ages 65+	48	50
College	59	39
Non-college	49	49

Among whites ...

	Dem	Rep
College	53	45
Non-college	37	61

Source: Pew Research Center; based on exit polls conducted by Edison Research for the National Election Pool, as reported by CNN

FIGURE 3.8

Hispanic Women Voted Extensively for Democrats in 2018

% who say they voted for the _____ candidate in the election for House of Representatives

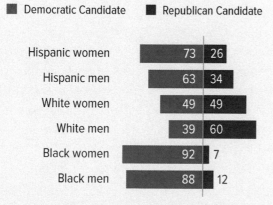

■ Democratic Candidate   ■ Republican Candidate

	Dem	Rep
Hispanic women	73	26
Hispanic men	63	34
White women	49	49
White men	39	60
Black women	92	7
Black men	88	12

Source: Pew Research Center; based on exit polls conducted by Edison Research for the National Election Pool, as reported by CNN

FIGURE 3.9

In 2018 Vote, Sizable Gender, Race and Educational Divides

% who say they voted for the _____ candidate in the election for House of Representatives

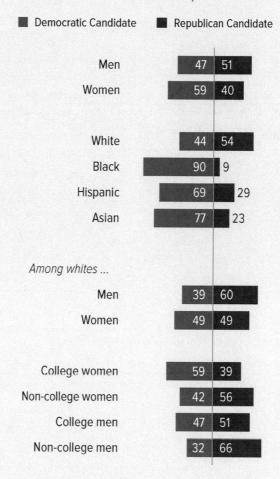

■ Democratic Candidate   ■ Republican Candidate

	Dem	Rep
Men	47	51
Women	59	40
White	44	54
Black	90	9
Hispanic	69	29
Asian	77	23

Among whites ...

	Dem	Rep
Men	39	60
Women	49	49
College women	59	39
Non-college women	42	56
College men	47	51
Non-college men	32	66

Source: Pew Research Center; based on exit polls conducted by Edison Research for the National Election Pool, as reported by CNN

other hand, the sixty-five and older group had a turnout rate over 65%.[19] Why does this voting discrepancy regarding age exist? The explanation is situational; older voters have higher incomes, own homes, and are more likely to be married and have children. Thus, they are more interested in issues that cause them to become politically active and to vote. These issues include property and income taxes and the quality of schools in their neighborhoods. Older voters also are more likely to have a history of voting and involvement in previous campaigns. Finally, they are more likely to identify with a political party and have a more coherent ideology. These factors all contribute to higher voter turnout.

Turnout based on age also correlates with ethnic background. Almost two thirds of all adults over sixty-five in Texas are white, and half are between forty-five to sixty-four years old.[20] These two age groups are the most likely to vote in Texas, giving them disproportionate power in local and state governments. In other words, the most likely voter in Texas today is a sixty-five or older white resident. Whites are more likely to vote, but African Americans have made great strides and are now almost even with white voters when it comes to turnout. Hispanics, on the other hand, still trail badly in all age groups and have the lowest voter turnout of any major ethnic group.

Politically, white voters are more conservative than non-white voters, including African Americans, Asian Americans, and Hispanics. White people are also more likely to support the Republican Party. As older white voters are most likely to vote on Election Day, they are responsible for the Republican Party's domination of the Texas government and for pursuing conservative policies.

Party preference correlates with age and education in Texas and in the United States, as **Figure 3.7** shows below. Younger voters tend to be liberal and prefer the Democratic Party over the Republican Party, and older voters support the Republican Party. Accounting for ethnicity and education reveals that older, white voters with no college education vote particularly heavily Republican and that young voters, especially young minority voters, favor the Democratic Party. Education therefore impacts party preference. Educated people were more likely to vote for the Democratic Party in the 2016 general and in the 2018 off-year election. In 2018, white college-educated women were the most Democratic group among white voters, and white males with no college education were the most Republican group of voters **(Figure 3.9)**. **Figure 3.7** presents data on age, education, and party preference from the 2018 off-year elections.

The final determinant of voting is gender. For several decades, one of the hottest topics in political science has been the gender gap. In 1980, women became more likely to vote than men, and differences in turnout numbers and in political party and candidate preferences have appeared. Interestingly, this holds true for Texas and for the United States as a whole. In the 2016 general election and in the 2018 off-year elections, major differences appeared between men and women regarding political issues and voting. Women were more likely to vote in the 2016 general election, with 63.3% reporting that they voted.[21] Only 59.3% of men reported that they voted.[22] The gender gap also existed in Texas—51.3% of all voters were female, and 48.7% were male.[23]

Interestingly, the turnout gender gap also appears with other ethnic backgrounds. For example, more African-American women (63.7%) reported voting than African-American males (54.2%), and more Hispanic women (50%) voted than Hispanic men (45%).[24] For party preferences, minority female voters tend to mirror white female voters because they are more liberal than minority male voters, as **Figure 3.8** shows.

Women in Texas and nationwide tend to be more liberal on many economic and social issues like abortion and the death penalty, so they tend to support the Democratic Party and its candidates more than men do.

Figure 3.9 shows that in 2018 women nationwide preferred Democratic candidates for the House of Representatives by 19%. Men, on the other hand, preferred the Republican candidates by 4%. Breaking down the numbers further reveals that ethnic backgrounds also impacted gender when it came to voting behavior. White voters preferred the Republican Party by 10 percentage points, while black voters overwhelmingly voted Democratic (90%). Hispanic voters also favored the Democratic Party, 69% to 29%. Finally, white men were the most loyal Republican voters and gave the party 60% of their vote; white women were evenly split between the two parties.

The Latino Vote in the 2018 Elections

In the 2018 off-year elections, the share of Latinos eligible to vote increased dramatically in several states, including in Texas. The share of eligible Latino voters in Texas climbed to 30% of the overall vote, and in Florida it hit a record 20% of the vote. It stood at 23% in Arizona and at 19% in Nevada.[25]

As **Figure 3.10** shows, 64% of all Latinos in Texas voted for Democratic candidate Beto O'Rourke, and 35% voted for Republican incumbent Ted Cruz. In the race for governor, only 53% of Latinos voted for the Democratic candidate, and 42% backed the incumbent Republican Greg Abbott. The Latino vote is not as cohesive as the African-American vote; it is split regionally and ethnically, and various voter turnout rates and political ideologies impact voting preference. For example, Cuban Americans and Venezuelan Americans, many living in Florida, are staunchly conservative, oppose socialist-sounding policies, and favor Republican candidates. Many Mexican Americans in Texas tend to be more conservative and support Republican candidates, but Mexican Americans in California, Nevada, and Arizona tend to be more liberal and staunch supporters of the Democratic Party. Three crucial Senate elections held in 2018 prove this point. As Figure 3.10 shows,

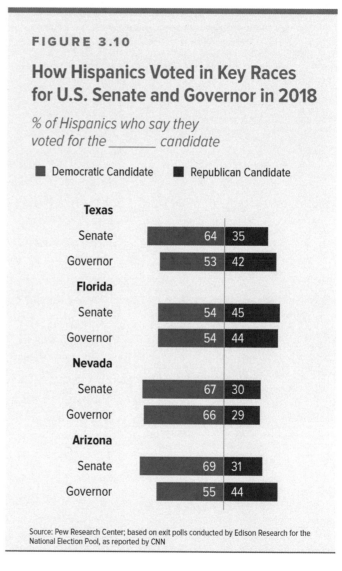

FIGURE 3.10

How Hispanics Voted in Key Races for U.S. Senate and Governor in 2018

% of Hispanics who say they voted for the _____ candidate

■ Democratic Candidate ■ Republican Candidate

	Democratic	Republican
Texas		
Senate	64	35
Governor	53	42
Florida		
Senate	54	45
Governor	54	44
Nevada		
Senate	67	30
Governor	66	29
Arizona		
Senate	69	31
Governor	55	44

Source: Pew Research Center; based on exit polls conducted by Edison Research for the National Election Pool, as reported by CNN

uttyler.edu

FIGURE 3.11

Many More Latinos Voted for Democrats than Republicans in 2018

% who say they voted for the _____ candidate in the election for House of Representatives

■ Democratic Candidate   ■ Republican Candidate

	Democratic	Republican
Hispanic	69	29
White	44	54
Black	90	9
Asian	77	23

Source: Pew Research Center; based on exit polls conducted by Edison Research for the National Election Pool, as reported by CNN

Direct primary: *election held by a political party to determine the party's nominee for political office.*

Closed primary: *a primary in which only registered partisans can participate.*

Open primary: *a primary in which all registered voters can determine which party's primary to vote in on primary election day.*

Raiding a primary: *supporters of one party vote in the other party's primary to select the weakest nominee.*

the Republican candidate for Senate in Florida, Governor Rick Scott, received close to 50% of the Latino vote, and Nevada's incumbent Senator Dean Heller only received 30% of the Latino vote and lost reelection.

Nationwide, however, Latino voters solidly supported the Democratic Party in 2018. As **Figure 3.11** shows, 69% of all Latinos voted for the Democratic Party, and only 29% voted Republican. The most loyal Democratic supporters were African Americans—90% of them voted Democratic. A majority, 54%, of all white voters cast a ballot for the Republican Party.

Types of Elections

Texans can engage in many types of elections. At the national level are general elections for the presidency, the U.S. Senate, and the House of Representatives. Next, state-level elections include those for governor, for state executive positions, for the Texas legislature, and for many local offices. Beginning in 1974, Texas changed the two-year terms for the Governor and for all other elected members of the executive branch to four years. Texas also scheduled executive elections during off-year (non-presidential election years) cycles. Besides local, state, and national elections, Texas also holds occasional special elections. These elections fill local and state level vacancies when a state legislator dies, resigns, or retires; they also occur whenever a constitutional amendment is proposed.

Next, **direct primaries** are a way of selecting party nominees before they run in a general election. The Republican and Democratic parties are the two major parties in Texas, as they are in the other 49 states and at the national level. Both parties must use primaries to select their nominees. As mentioned previously, the U.S. Constitution allows each state to decide how the public chooses its elected office holders. Before the public chooses, however, the two major parties must decide who will be the party's standard bearers in the general election. Some states use state conventions or caucuses to select their party's nominees for office. Texas uses the direct primary to do so. Three types of primaries exist in the United States:

Closed Primary: Most states use closed primaries, in which voters must declare their party affiliation in advance. Only then can they vote in that party's primary. For example, only registered Republicans can vote in the Republican primary. This allows for some party control by ensuring that only registered partisans can vote in a party's primary.

Open Primary: In an open primary, registered voters decide on the primary election day which party's primary to vote in. For example, a Democrat can choose to vote in the Republican primary on a primary election day. However, voters can only vote in one party's primary—not in both. This allows for **raiding a primary**. Republicans, for example, might have only one candidate in a primary, making the result a foregone conclusion. So, the Republican Party might urge Republican supporters to vote in the Democratic primary to select the weakest possible Democratic candidate. This would make it easier for the Republican candidate to win in the general election. One great advantage of open primaries is that they allow for independents, voters not registered with any party, to request a ballot and vote in the primary.

Blanket Primary: Several states use blanket primaries, including California, Louisiana, and Washington State. In a blanket primary, voters receive only one ballot listing all the offices and all the candidates from all the parties. This often includes more than one candidate from the same party. The two candidates with the most votes, even if they are from the same party, will move on to the general election. The United States Supreme Court ruled in 2000 in *Democratic Party et al. v. Jones* that a blanket primary must be truly non-partisan, meaning that all candidates, including those from third parties, are listed on the ballot.

Blanket primary: a primary in which voters do not have to be partisans and ballots contain the names of all candidates from all parties.

Texas has used a variation of the open primary since 1906. On primary election day, any registered voter can choose a party's primary to vote in. The only stipulation is that, after voting in the Republican or Democrat primary, voters are stuck with their choice and cannot vote in the other party's primary or run-off election for a whole year.

Runoff elections: a second vote in which the top two candidates face off against each other if neither received an absolute majority.

Like many Southern states, Texas uses **runoff elections**. In most states, whoever wins the most votes in a primary is declared the winner and moves on to the general election. In Texas, however, a candidate must receive an absolute majority of the votes. If no one receives an absolute majority of votes in a primary, the top two primary candidates will move on to a runoff election, and whoever wins will be the nominee for the general election.

Under Texas law, any party receiving 20% of the gubernatorial vote must hold a primary to select candidates for an election. A party that receives less than 20% can select its candidates in a state convention. Only two parties have a chance to get 20% of the vote and get their candidates elected to office in Texas, so candidates for the Democratic and the Republican parties have to run in primaries to become nominees for the general election.

FIGURE 3.12

Texas Primary Filing Requirements for Democratic and Republican Party Nominees

In order to become a nominee for one of the following offices, candidates must file an application with the state party chair.

Public Office Sought	Filing Fee	Minimum Number of Signatures
President[2]	$5,000	5,000
United States Senator	$5,000	5,000
United States Representative	$3,125	500
Statewide Elected Offices (except US Senator[4,5])	$3,750	5,000
State Senator	$1,250	500
State Representative	$750	500

Source: the Texas Secretary of State, the Texas Election Code, and the Texas Democratic and Republican parties

To be on the Republican or Democratic primary ballot, candidates must either collect the names of registered voters on a petition (the number of names is office-specific) or pay a filing fee to the county or to the state's party chair. The filing fee provides revenue to pay for the primaries, but most of the primary costs are paid for by the Texas Secretary of State's office. **Figure 3.12** shows the costs of getting on parties' primary ballots for Texas offices.

uttyler.edu

The primaries are then administered by the counties or the state depending on the level of office, and drawings are held to determine the order of names placed on the ballot. State and county parties select voting devices and arrange for polling places. By law, primaries in Texas must be held on the first Tuesday of March of even numbered years. If the results require a run-off, it has to be held on the fourth Tuesday in May.

The General Election

The most important election officer in Texas is the Texas Secretary of State. His office is responsible for funding primaries for the two major parties and for funding the general election. He also keeps the state's electoral records for all federal, state, or local elections and is responsible for preparing the general election's ballots and for canvassing votes on Election Day.

In 1892, Texas adopted the **Australian ballot**, which has four essential features. First, it is printed at public expense and lists all the candidates for office on one ballot. Second, the ballot is distributed to every eligible voter at the polls, and then voters cast their ballots in secret. Currently, two versions of the Australian ballot are used in the United States. First is the **Massachusetts ballot**. On it, candidates are listed randomly under each office. This ballot does not allow for straight party voting and encourages **ticket splitting**, where voters vote for some Republican candidates and for some Democratic candidates. The second type of ballot is the **Indiana ballot**. It contains a party column, in which all candidates of the same party are listed in parallel columns under the same party label.

The two major parties are assured a place on the ballot, but the rules differ a bit for minor political parties. If a political party receives 5% of the vote in any statewide office or 2% of the vote in the last gubernatorial election, all its candidates are automatically placed on the ballot. Thus, all Republican and Democratic candidates always appear on a Texas ballot. Currently, only the Green Party and the Libertarian Party have earned a place on the Texas ballot next to the two established parties. A political party that does not receive 5% for any statewide office can still get on the ballot by collecting a certain number of signatures from registered voters on a petition. The number of signatures varies with the office and is a percentage of the total votes in the last gubernatorial election. For statewide office, 1% of the last gubernatorial vote is needed. When candidates qualify for the ballot, their placement is determined by the candidate's or their party's showing in the last election. **Incumbents**, or the winning party's candidates, are always listed first for each office on Texas ballots.

Texas law for recounts is very liberal. In other states, such as Florida, people can only request a **recount** if candidates lose by 0.5% or less, but Texas only allows a recount if candidates lose by 10% or less. However, the candidate who requests the recount has to pay for it, unless he/she wins or ties in the recount, so recounts are usually only requested if the electoral results are 1% or less.

Finally, how do average Texan voters cast their ballots? Since the 2000 presidential election disaster that had to be decided by the U.S. Supreme Court

Australian ballot: *introduced to Texas in 1892, the Australian ballot is cast in secret and is counted by the state.*

Massachusetts ballot: *lists all candidates by office, encouraging ticket splitting.*

Ticket splitting: *instead of voting straight party line, where a voter casts all of his or her votes for one party, the voter divides his or her votes between the parties.*

Indiana ballot: *lists all candidates on the ballot by party, encouraging party voting.*

Incumbents: *elected officials who currently hold office.*

Recount: *another count of the votes cast in an election that candidates in Texas can request if they lose by 10% or less—the candidate pays for the cost of the recount.*

because of conflicting counting procedures and outdated ballots in Florida, electronic voting as become normal in Texas. Electronic voting is similar to getting money out of an ATM. Voters just touch an electronic screen to cast their ballot.

Conclusion

This chapter discussed voting and elections in Texas, starting with voter turnout in Texas and in the United States. As studies on the adult voting population show, turnout is low in Texas and in the country overall. However, a closer analysis reveals that voting among adults may be low, but subtracting ineligible adults and focusing on registered voters shows a turnout comparable to many other democracies.

Compared to the other forty-nine states, however, Texas has one of the lowest voter turnout rates. Why would this be the case? First, Texas has a large legal and illegal immigrant population that is ineligible to vote, and it is one of the youngest states in the United States. Texas also has a large Latino population of almost 40% that is younger and less educated than the rest of Texas. Age and education are among the most important determinants of the vote, so Latinos are less politically active. The older and more educate white population, on the other hand, votes in higher numbers and therefore controls the Texas government. This results in more conservative policies for the state.

Decades of research on voting behavior shows that the major determinants of the vote are ethnic background, age, education, income, and a history of voting. The Latino population, which will become Texas's majority by 2022, lacks in all these categories. Latinos are younger, less educated, and poorer than other ethnic groups in Texas. Therefore, they vote in lower numbers, allowing the shrinking white population to dominate state politics. This is why the Democratic Party has not won any statewide office since 1994 and why no Democratic presidential candidate has carried Texas since Jimmy Carter did in 1976. However, the political situation is slowly changing in Texas. The Latino population is getting better educated and more affluent, which will lead to higher voter turnout in the future. Texas's Latino population will very soon resemble Latino voters in other states, such as New Mexico and California, where Latinos have a higher voter turnout that regularly tops 50%. This could possibly change Texas politics, but it is not a given. As discussed earlier, Latinos in Texas are more conservative than their counterparts in California and in New Mexico, and Republican candidates such as George W. Bush have won the Latino vote statewide.

>> Decades of research on voting behavior shows that the major determinants of the vote are ethnic background, age, education, income, and a history of voting. The Latino population, which will become Texas's majority by 2022, lacks in all these categories.

Key Terms

Australian ballot: introduced to Texas in 1892, the Australian ballot is cast in secret and is counted by the state.

Blanket primary: a primary in which voters do not have to be partisans and ballots contain the names of all candidates from all parties.

Closed primary: a primary in which only registered partisans can participate.

Direct primary: election held by a political party to determine the party's nominee for political office.

General election: an election in which candidates from more than two parties compete for political office.

Incumbents: elected officials who currently hold office.

Independent: a voter who does not identify with a political party.

Indiana ballot: lists all candidates on the ballot by party, encouraging party voting.

Massachusetts ballot: lists all candidates by office, encouraging ticket splitting.

Off-year elections: midterm elections, or elections held in non-presidential election years.

Open primary: a primary in which all registered voters can determine which party's primary to vote in on primary election day.

Partisan: a voter who identifies with a political party.

Political participation: activities Americans engage in to influence governmental decision-making.

Poll tax: a fee that must be paid to vote.

Raiding a primary: supporters of one party vote in the other party's primary to select the weakest nominee.

Recount: another count of the votes cast in an election that candidates in Texas can request if they lose by 10% or less—the candidate pays for the cost of the recount.

Registered population (REG): the total number of United States citizens registered to vote.

Runoff elections: a second vote in which the top two candidates face off against each other if neither received an absolute majority.

Ticket splitting: instead of voting straight party line, where a voter casts all of his or her votes for one party, the voter divides his or her votes between the parties.

Voting-age citizens: U.S. citizens who are eighteen and older.

Voting-age population (VAP): the total number of individuals in the United States who are eighteen and older.

White primary: primary held by the Democratic Party in Texas that excluded African Americans.

ENDNOTES

[1] https://www.census.gov/data/tables/time-series/demo/voting-and-registration/p20-580.html

[2] Ibid.

[3] https://www.census.gov/data/tables/time-series/demo/voting-and-registration/p20-580.html

[4] Ibid.

[5] Ibid.

[6] http://www.pewresearch.org/fact tank/2018/05/21/u-s-voter-turnout-trails-most-developed-countries

[7] Ibid.

[8] Ibid.

[9] Ibid.

[10] https://www.sos.state.tx.us/elections/forms/id/acceptable-forms-of-ID.pdf

[11] Ibid.

[12] https://www.census.gov/data/tables/time-series/demo/voting-and-registration/p20-580.html

[13] http://www.pewhispanic.org/interactives/mapping-the-latino-electorate/.

[14] Ibid.

[15] Ibid.

[16] http://www.pewhispanic.org/fact-sheet/latinos-in-the-2016-election-texas/ .

[17] Ibid.

[18] https://www.census.gov/data/tables/time-series/demo/voting-and-registration/p20-580.html

[19] Ibid.

[20] Ibid.

[21] http://www.cawp.rutgers.edu/sites/default/files/resources/genderdiff.pdf

[22] Ibid.

[23] Ibid.

[24] http://www.pewresearch.org/fact-tank/2018/11/09/how-latinos-voted-in-2018-midterms/

[25] Ibid.

4

Political Parties in the
United States and Texas

Characteristics of
Texas Political Parties

Functions of Political Parties

History of Texas Political Parties

The Structure of
Texas Political Parties

Third Parties

The capitol building in Austin, Texas.
istock.com/LMPphotography

Chapter 4

Political Parties

FOR NEARLY A CENTURY political scientists have debated whether political parties are necessary for a democracy to function properly. E.E. Schattschneider claimed in his classic 1942 study "Party Government" that political parties created democracy and that modern democracy is unimaginable without political parties.[1] Samuel Huntington agrees with Schattschneider, claiming that parties are found in every working democracy and that they are necessary for organizing political participation, aggregating interest, and linking social forces to the government.[2] This chapter assumes that Schattschneider's and Huntington's viewpoints are correct and that the United States and Texas need a fully developed and functioning party system.

This chapter has four parts. First, it discusses political parties' characteristics and functions. Then the focus shifts to partisan identification and how it impacts Texas politics. After a brief history of the development of Texas political parties, the concept of realignment is discussed. The fourth section describes the structure of Texas political parties, and the chapter concludes with a brief overview of third parties in the Texas political system.

What is a **political party**? James Madison, who calls parties "factions," gives the classical definition of a political party in Federalist Paper Number 10: "By a faction, I understand a number of citizens, whether amounting to a majority or a minority of the whole, who are united and actuated by some common impulse or passion, or of interest, adverse to the rights of other citizens or to the permanent aggregate interest of the community."[3]

Political party: *a group of citizens, who organize to contest elections, win public office, and impact policy making.*

uttyler.edu

Modern definitions of a political party vary, and most political scientists define a political party as a group that seeks to elect candidates to public office by supplying candidates with a label well-known to the electorate. Anthony Downs provides a more detailed definition of political parties as "a team of men (and women) seeking to control the governing apparatus by gaining office in a duly constituted election."[4] Both definitions agree on two major characteristics that political parties must have. First, political parties want to elect people to public office. Second, they provide a label or cue to their supporters, which facilitates voting for the average citizen.

A political scientist analyzes political parties in Texas, or elsewhere, in three different ways. V.O. Key first suggested this type of analysis in his seminal work "Politics, Parties and Pressure Groups."[5] Key urged political scientists to differentiate between political parties and other groups, such as interest groups, by recognizing that political parties are tripartite structures composed of three components. First, there is the **party in the electorate**, which includes all the individuals who identify with a political party and support the party on Election Day.

Party in the electorate: voters who identify with a political party.

The second component is the **party as an organization**. Here, one studies the party's structure at the national, state, or local level. For example, party officials' national offices, staffs, budgets, and rules of behavior can be analyzed. A party's organizational view also includes an analysis of the party's involvement in recruiting candidates and organizing primaries, conventions, or caucuses to nominate candidates for office.

Party as an organization: the local, state, and national structure of a political party and its paid leaders.

The third component is the **party in government**. This final component of political parties consists of elected party officeholders at all political levels. This includes members of Congress, governors, state legislators, mayors, and city council people. Studies involving this component include, for example, the voting behavior of United States senators.

Party in government: local, state, and national elected or appointed officials who identify or belong to a political party.

Political Parties in the United States and Texas

When studying the United States Constitution, an interesting phenomenon concerning political parties becomes apparent. Unlike other democratic constitutions, such as the German or French constitution, political parties are not mentioned or regulated by the United States Constitution. Believing that parties were a source of corruption and an impediment to people's freedom to judge issues on their own merits, as James Madison argues in Federalist Paper Number 10, the founding fathers perceived parties (or factions, as they were commonly called back then), as a threat to the survival of the newly formed democratic government in the United States.

George Washington perceived political parties as so dangerous that he even mentioned them in his 1796 Farewell Address. In the address, Washington warned the country against political parties, which he called "factions," because they divided the country along partisan lines, undermining the spirit of cooperation so necessary for the new country's survival. This negative attitude toward political parties has persisted in the United States and many Americans still perceive political parties as a necessary evil and a source of corruption.

As political parties were not mentioned or regulated at the national level, the states had to step in. Today, the Texas Constitution, not the United States Constitution, regulates political parties in Texas. As Chapter 3 discussed, the Texas Constitution demands that the two major parties in Texas, the Democratic and the Republican Parties, use primaries to select their candidates for office. The United States Constitution does not.

Characteristics of Texas Political Parties

American political parties, including Texas political parties, are unique. Some claim that the United States has the oldest existing political party in the world, the Democratic Party, but others give that distinction to the British Conservative Party, or the Tories. Despite this disagreement, everybody agrees that American political parties are very different from traditional or European parties.

The first characteristic of the American party system is the enduring **two-party system**. Following **Duverger's Law**, which states that single-member district election rules result in a two-party system, the United States has found itself with a two-party system for most of its history.[6] With a few exceptions (usually in times of crisis, such as before the Civil War), the United States and Texas have always had a two-party system. Why is this the case? One reason is electoral law. The United States uses British electoral law, also referred to as a **single-member district electoral law**. British electoral law is simple: the person who wins the most votes in a district wins the office. At the same time, this type of electoral law discriminates against third or minor parties. Only the two major parties have a shot at winning seats, but a party or candidate who gets 20% of the vote will receive nothing. Most of the democratic world uses **proportional representation**, where political parties receive seats in legislative chambers based on the proportion of the vote they receive. If a political party wins 10% of the vote, it will automatically receive 10% of the seats in the Legislature. This type of electoral law aids smaller or third parties, allowing them to gain representation even if they do not come in first. The result is a multiparty system where more than two parties are represented in the legislative chamber.

Second, American and Texas political parties are characteristically referred to as all-encompassing, which means they are not very ideological or extreme and represent a plethora of political viewpoints. For example, the Democratic Party in Texas historically has been open to liberal and conservative Democrats. Inviting all viewpoints on major political issues allows Texas political parties to absorb any currently popular issue and its various supporters from other parties; this tactic also results in moderate policies. For example, the Democratic Party absorbed progressive issues, such as the creation of a welfare state, from the Socialist Party, resulting in the United States Socialist Party's decline. In Europe, however, each faction within the Democratic Party (conservative, moderate, and liberal) would have its own political party. In the United States, these factions are packed into one party. This means

Two-party system: *a political system in which only two parties have a realistic chance of winning political office.*

Duverger's Law: *the theory that a single-member district electoral system results in a two-party system and proportional representation in a multi-party system.*

Single-member district electoral system: *an electoral system in which the person who wins the most votes in a district is elected to office.*

Proportional representation: *an electoral system in which seats are allocated based on the proportion of the vote a party receives.*

uttyler.edu

party leaders must constantly mediate between the various factions, resulting in moderate policies acceptable to all factions within the party. In other words, the concept of pluralism also works within political parties and reflects the moderate non-ideological nature of the American electorate.

Unlike European parties, American parties are regulated at the state level. Therefore, they are decentralized and, instead of using a national party structure with millions of dues-paying members like many European parties do, American parties differ from state to state. Every state, but not the national government, has the power to regulate state parties, and every state's party must follow a different set of rules. In Texas the state constitution regulates parties and sets guidelines. As previously mentioned, the Texas Constitution determines how nominees are chosen by the state parties for elections, and it sets limits on many party activities, such as holding elections and raising funds.

Another unique characteristic of American and Texas political parties is that they face a public that is negative toward their existence and their functions. Many scholars trace this back to the warnings of our founding fathers, such as Washington and Madison, who considered political parties, or factions, divisive and bad for democracy. Today, the American public distrusts political parties and doubts they are useful and necessary for a democracy and, an ever-growing group of citizens has slowly moved away from supporting parties. As we will see later in this chapter, more Americans are proclaiming that they are independents, unaffiliated with any party and fewer are proclaiming their identification with a party.

Another important characteristic involves Duverger's classification of political parties into mass and cadre parties.[7] Duverger labels decentralized political parties with real power vested at the local level and only informal committee leaders at the national level as cadre parties. **Cadre parties** have no dues-paying mass membership at the national level, and their functions are purely electoral. In other words, their purpose is to win elections at all costs. An electoral party has one overarching objective: to win offices. It sacrifices everything, including its own soul of principled ideological stances on issues, to win. Its policies tend to be moderate, favoring the status quo.

Mass parties, as found in Europe, are very centralized. All power is vested in a small leadership group that runs the party with an iron fist. They have a large dues-paying membership that can include millions of people. Their main purpose is not only to win elections but to stay true to their vision. Winning elections is a major function, but it is not the only major function. Mass parties would rather lose elections than compromise on issues. If elected to power, mass parties tend to be very doctrinaire and uncompromising. Today's British Labour Party is a good example of a mass party.

The next characteristic involves the Constitution itself. By creating a presidential or gubernatorial system based on the separation of powers, the constitution set the foundation for weak parties. The party cannot select the executive, a power found in a parliamentary system, so party discipline is not as imperative in the United States as it is, for example, in Great Britain. This results in weaker political parties.

Cadre party: *a decentralized and part-time political party whose major purpose is to win office.*

Mass party: *a centralized and full-time political party whose major purpose is to represent a certain ideological viewpoint.*

A final and unique characteristic of Texas political parties involves one party's dominance for long stretches of time. In Texas, the Democratic Party was the dominant party for over one century, from the period after Reconstruction until the 1990s, when the Republican Party became dominant. The Republican Party has now dominated Texas politics for over twenty years. During these long periods of one-party rule, the dominant party becomes factionalized over time. Remember, U.S. and Texas political parties are all-encompassing and everybody, regardless of political beliefs, can join. Many do so because joining the dominant party is the only way to get nominated and later win office. For example, early during the Democratic dominance in Texas the Democratic Party was split between progressives and conservatives. After the conservatives prevailed by the early 20th century, divisions between liberals and conservatives began by the 1940s. One can make a good claim that Texas actually had two parties by the end of World War II: a liberal Democratic Party and a conservative Democratic Party. This would last until the 1990s, when the conservative wing of the Democratic Party aligned itself with the Republican Party and ushered in a period of Republican dominance. Therefore, one-party rule does not necessarily mean that a dominant unified party is running Texas. In reality, several factions within the dominant party could be constantly competing for political power. In other words, a small-party system where factions compete for power can exist within a single party.

Functions of Political Parties

As discussed earlier in the chapter, many consider political parties to be essential for a well-functioning democracy. Why is this the case? To answer this question, the next sections of the chapter deals with the functions political parties perform in a democratic political system.

Political parties have become a major determinant of the vote through a process called **party identification**. First discovered in an analysis of the 1952 and 1956 elections, party identification is psychological in nature. The study, conducted by Angus Campbell and his colleagues at the University of Michigan, is entitled *The American Voter* and was published in 1960.[8] They discovered that most voters are psychologically attached to a political party and that this attachment determines how people vote. Therefore, party identification, as a Republican or as a Democrat, determines how you vote. Voters vote Democrat not because they necessarily know about a Democratic candidate's stances on issues, but because they identify with the Democratic Party. Knowledge does not determine the vote for most U.S. citizens and Texans, but party identification does. According to the study, almost 80% of all voters in the United States base their vote on party identification.[9] As a side note, this important study of American voters also discovered **independents**, or Americans who do not identify with a political party at all.

Therefore, one core function of political parties is to facilitate the voting process for the average voter. As Chapter 3 showed, most voters are unfamiliar with most issues and with candidates' positions on these issues. It is therefore tough for them to cast a ballot, and many will not do so. However, identifying

Party identification: people connecting with a political party.

Independent: a voter who does not identify with a political party.

uttyler.edu

>> The political beliefs and values people hold shape how people act within their political system. People acquire political beliefs through the structures that shape a person's political belief system, such as parents, religion, peers, the media, and political parties.

with a political party allows voters to still cast a ballot. In other words, political parties facilitate voting by providing voters with cues and symbols that make voting easier. Political parties allow voters to identify with a political party that represents their political wishes. A Republican voter, even without knowing about a Republican candidate, knows that the candidate will likely have values and beliefs similar to the voter, making voting for the candidate rational.

A second function of political parties is **political socialization**. Political socialization refers to the process of how people acquire their political beliefs and values. The political beliefs and values people hold shape how people act within their political system. People acquire political beliefs through what we call agents of political socialization. These are the structures that shape a person's political belief system. Several agents of political socialization exist, including parents, religion, peers, the media, and political parties. Political parties try to instill political values in the public. By socializing voters, political parties can create lifelong supporters who will support the party during good and bad times. To become an agent of political socialization, however, political parties must have contact with the public, and the public has to perceive them as important and helpful in their lives. In the 19th century, political parties performed this function well. They organized meetings, provided entertainment—such as party picnics and dances—and were in close contact with the average person. In addition, political parties published newspapers and were a major provider of information for average voters. All of this has changed in the United States and in Texas. Today, political parties have ceased to be an agent of political socialization for most U.S. citizens and Texans. Most of their traditional socializing functions have been taken over by the media in the United States. In Europe, on the other hand, parties still perform this core function of maintaining contact with the public via official party functions, like the aforementioned party picnics, travel, or even dances. In addition, European political parties commonly publish newspapers or control other parts of the media.

A basic function of political parties is to recruit and nominate candidates for political office. Traditionally, the party recruits the strongest possible candidate to run for office and then nominates him or her. In turn, the party gains control over the candidate. If candidates deviate from party policy, vote against the party, or in any way oppose their own party, the party can punish candidates for deviating from the party line by denying them re-nomination, which in turn will end a candidate's political career. While U.S. political parties performed this function a century ago, times have changed. With the introduction of the **direct primary** (see Chapter 3), candidates today do not need the party to win nomination for public office. They can recruit and nominate themselves and even run their own campaign if they have the necessary resources. This has decreased party discipline in institutions such as the Texas State Legislature and Congress.

Another traditional function of political parties, one that has been compromised in the United States and Texas, is running candidates' campaigns. Running for office has become increasingly expensive in Texas. In 2018, a run for the state house cost between $400,000 and $550,000.[10] Historically, political parties provided candidates with the funds to run for political office and with specialists and staff to run their campaigns. Due to the direct primary, all of this changed. Today's candidates in Texas must raise their own funds and establish their own campaign organization without party support during primary campaigns (for a discussion of campaign finance reform in Texas please see Chapter 3). This takes the party out of running candidates' campaigns for office, which decreases the control political parties have over their own candidates. After winning the nomination, candidates are unlikely to scrap their winning campaign teams and let the party take over. However, the party is not totally out of the campaigning process in Texas. It can still provide financial help and indirect support by providing campaign specialists, such as pollsters. At the local level, parties are even more important because they register voters and provide volunteers to help candidates' campaigns.

A closely related function is mobilizing voters, especially on Election Day. Political parties help to register voters and get them to vote. As Chapter 3 showed, voting is not a priority for many Texans, so it is important to get as many registered voters as possible to the polls. Political parties therefore contact voters by calling them, stopping by their homes, or even texting and e-mailing them, not just on Election Day, but weeks before an election to make sure voters will go out and vote.

One of a political party's most important functions is providing voters with information they can use to make a rational decision on Election Day. For this reason, political parties formulate ideas and propose policies and programs to voters in their **party platforms**. Every two years, both major parties in Texas, the Republican Party and the Democratic Party, as well as most minor or third parties meet in a state convention to create a party platform, which contains a party's policy proposals. In other words, the party platform introduces policies to the voter. Texas voters are then supposed to read the platform, familiarize themselves with the policy proposals, and then vote for or against the party's candidates. Although political parties create platforms outlining their policy stances and policy proposals, most Texans do not bother to read them. This is a big problem, because the winning political parties implement close to 75% of the policies outlined in their party platforms, and many people are shocked when political parties suddenly begin to implement policies they have never heard of.

Party platform: *a document drawn up every two years at the state convention that outlines a party's policies and principles.*

Political parties are major sources of political information in most democracies, with the exception of the United States. The early years of the republic were quite different. The two major parties, the Federalists and the Democratic–Republicans, published their own newspapers to provide supporters with information, albeit skewed in nature. Today, neither party publishes newspapers nor runs a news channel, as parties do in many European countries. At the same time, U.S. parties do provide voters with limited information, usually during election time. Through television or radio commercials, pamphlets, or even debates, the parties show the public how they stand on the day's most important issues.

One major function of a political party is organizing the policy-making process at all governmental levels. In other words, this function is performed

uttyler.edu

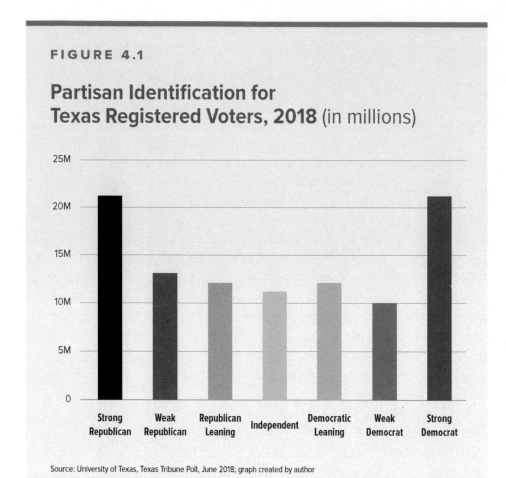

FIGURE 4.1

Partisan Identification for
Texas Registered Voters, 2018 (in millions)

Source: University of Texas, Texas Tribune Poll, June 2018; graph created by author

at the local, state, and even national level. Could you imagine the Texas House of Representatives and its 150 legislators without any kind of machinery in place to run its affairs? You would have to somehow bring together 150 individuals to decide how to run the Legislature, how to write and pass bills, and, finally, how to get enough votes to actually pass legislation. Very likely, nothing would get accomplished. This is where political parties come in. They organize the policy-making process by making sure its members support the party policy line, vote for its bills, and continue to support the parties' policies.

A final function of political parties, one they share with interest groups, is referred to as **interest aggregation**. Most U.S. citizens do not possess much **political power** by themselves. For example, if you travel by yourself to Washington, D.C., to meet with your U.S. Senator and present him with a list of policy demands, he or she would not be likely to meet with you and discuss your proposals. However, if many like-minded people sign a petition to have your policy proposals enacted, the situation changes. Instead of representing only one interest, you now represent possibly millions of people, and your representative will likely meet with you and take your interests into account. This is called interest aggregation, and it is usually accomplished by joining a political party or specific interest group, such as the Sierra Club or the National Rifle Association.

Interest aggregation: *the act of joining with like-minded citizens to acquire political power.*

Political power: *the ability to make people engage in a political act they would not engage in of their own free will.*

As you can see, political parties perform many functions in a democracy. Most of these functions are still performed by parties in the United States and in Texas, and many political scientists therefore believe that democracy without political parties would be impossible.

Party Identification

Most Texans today identify with a political party. People who connect with a political party and base their votes on this party identification are **partisans**. According to a June 2018 University of Texas and Texas Tribune poll, about 89% of all registered voters in Texas have a partisan identification, while only 11% are true independents.[11] Some are strong partisans; 21% of all Texans are strong Republicans or strong Democrats, but some are weak partisans; 13% of all registered voters in Texas are weak Republicans while 10% are weak Democrats.[12] Furthermore, we find leaning independents, registered voters who proclaim to be independent, not identifying with a political party, but after questioning profess to have supported or voted for the same political party over the last few elections. About 24 % of all registered voters in Texas are independent leaners, with 12% each supporting the Democratic or Republican parties.[13]

Overall, 46% of Texans identify in some manner with the Republican Party, and 43% are Democrats. Only 11% of all Texans are considered pure independents (an independent is someone who does not identify with any political party). **Figure 4.1** shows the partisan identification of registered voters in Texas.

In conclusion, party identification still matters in Texas and is still the major predictor of the vote in the state.

Partisan: a voter who identifies with a political party.

History of Texas Political Parties

When studying political parties in Texas, one can observe five distinct party systems, or eras of various party dominance. Uniquely, Texas has a history of one-party dominance, where either the Democratic or the Republican party dominated. After the 2018 off-year elections (see Chapter 3), however, real two-party conflict could be in the future as the Democratic Party gained seats in the Texas Legislature and in the U. S. House of Representatives.

Source: https://commons.wikimedia.org/wiki/File:
Sam_Houston_by_Mathew_Brady.jpg

FIGURE 4.2 Sam Houston, president of the Republic of Texas and governor and United States senator of the state of Texas.

The First Party System (1836–1845)

The first party system actually occurred before Texas joined the United States and is usually called the era of the pre-party system. It lasted from 1836 until 1845, when Texas joined the United States of America. During this time, Texas was an independent republic with a distinct set of political institutions. The era was dominated by Sam Houston **(Figure 4.2)**, who was president of Texas twice (in 1836 and in 1841) and was the driving factor for integrating Texas into the United States. Although many politicians disagreed on issues, such as on whether the Legislature or the president was more powerful, on economic issues like tariffs, and, later, on whether Texas should join the United States of America, no real

uttyler.edu

party structures were created. The leading political figures of the day, disagreed often but were unified by a common foreign threat: Mexico.

However, many political differences similar to those seen in the United States at that time were observed. Populism came to Texas in the form of the Jacksonian Democrats, who were the dominant political party in the United States at this point. Andrew Jackson was president from 1828 to 1836, and his Democratic Party dominated American politics until the outbreak of the Civil War. Populists advocated for common people and were fearful of large businesses, especially banks. A more conservative ideology came from many Southerners who moved to Texas while the state was independent. It included long-held beliefs in social hierarchy, such as slavery, and in religion's importance. Finally, many locals who had been oppressed by the Mexican government and the Catholic Church for many years, advocated for a classical form of liberalism. They favored freedom of religion and believed in a rugged form of individualism with less government interference in the economy and in personal lives. Even though these three dominant ideologies existed and competed vigorously for political power, none became dominant during these early years, and no political parties were formally founded on these divisions. The few divisions that did openly exist were built around support for or opposition to President Sam Houston and his policies.

The Second Party System and Reconstruction (1845–1877)

Texas officially became a part of the United States in 1845. The U.S. party system quickly began to develop in Texas. Sam Houston was elected as a U.S. senator and joined the Democratic Party, mostly because of President Polk's policies regarding Mexico. Similarly to the rest of the country, the issue of slavery would divide Texas. Many Texans believed slavery was necessary for the state's economic survival, and Texas became the seventh state to join the Confederacy in 1861, over Governor Sam Houston's objections. **Figure 4.3** shows the Texas Confederate Flag, with seven stars because Texas was the seventh state to join the Confederacy.

FIGURE 4.3 The Confederate Flag of Texas

After the Civil War's end in 1865, Texas was forced to rejoin the Union and was occupied by Union soldiers for the next twelve years. In other words, Texas experienced the Reconstruction period, where the Republican Party was dominant. The Republican Party was the party of the Civil War's victors, and it took over Texas politics. Texas was put under military rule, and many white Southerners were disenfranchised. With support from the newly enfranchised black electorate, the Republican Party took over. The Republican Party now controlled the governorship and the state legislature and even wrote a new constitution for Texas. Very quickly, the Republican Party became synonymous with military occupation and unpopular policies, such as tax increases and corruption that wasted public monies. After Reconstruction ended with the Compromise of 1877, the Democratic Party quickly regained control of the Legislature and the governorship. Texas would not elect another Republican governor for 101 years, until 1978 when Bill Clements wins office. As a result of Reconstruction, the Democratic Party would control Texas politics for the next century.

The Third Party System (1877–1932)

Despite becoming a one-party state with the Democratic Party controlling Texas well into the 1990s, vigorous party competition existed within the Democratic Party. As usually happens when only one viable party dominates politics, everybody joins it to win office and suddenly the political party is all encompassing and liberal, moderate, and conservative wings compete for control of the party. A good example of this happened in the late nineteenth century when a progressive movement swept through Texas, and the Democratic Party had to deal with many progressive issues, such as the regulation of banks and railroads, the creation of unions, and minority rights. These issues were all supported by the liberal wing of the party and opposed by the conservative wing. Many poor white and black Texans supported the party's liberal wing. When the poll tax came to Texas in 1902, they were disenfranchised (See Chapter 3). Many political scientists argue that one-party rule in Texas was prolonged not by the poll tax but by the direct primary, introduced to Texas in 1906. The various wings of the Democratic Party could suddenly compete against each other in primary elections. Instead of competitive general elections, it was the primaries in Texas that were competitive and that decided elections.

The Fourth Party System (1932–1998)

The Great Depression increased the Democratic Party's dominance in Texas. Dissatisfied with Republican President Hoover's handling of the economic crisis, many core Republican groups left their party and joined the Democratic coalition headed by Franklin Delano Roosevelt. This created the **New Deal Coalition**, which increased Democratic dominance and dominated American politics until the 1960s. The New Deal coalition consisted of groups that switched from the Republican Party, such as Jewish voters and African Americans, and of new voters mobilized by FDR's New Deal programs, such as recent immigrants, who were mostly Southern and Eastern Europeans and Catholic. Overall, the New Deal Coalition consisted of the following groups: unionized voters, Jewish voters, Catholics, African Americans, the Solid Democratic South, the working class, and intellectuals.

After World War II ended and President Roosevelt died, the Democratic Party in Texas began to fracture. On one hand, traditionalists were led by then-Governor Allan Shivers, who was conservative on economic and social issues and opposed integration. On the other hand, the liberal wing of the party continued to support President Roosevelt's New Deal polices and believed in integration. The split became so bad that the Democratic Party of Texas held two state party conventions in 1952 to select their favorite candidate for president. The party's conservative wing supported the Republican Dwight D. Eisenhower, who believed in states' rights, and the liberal wing supported the Democratic Party nominee Adlai Stevenson. Ironically, the conservative wing of the Democratic Party helped the Republican Eisenhower carry Texas in the 1952 presidential elections; this was only the second time a Republican had carried

New Deal Coalition: forged by FDR in the 1930s, the New Deal Coalition consisted of the working class, Catholics, white Southerners, African Americans, Jewish people, and intellectuals. It dominated U.S. politics until the 1960s.

Texas since Reconstruction (Herbert Hoover was the first in 1928). The friction between the party's conservative and liberal wings would increase even more throughout the 1960s and 1970s. By the early 1960s, more conservative Democrats began to vote Republican, and in 1961 a Republican U.S. Senator, John Tower **(Figure 4.4)**, was elected in Texas for the first time in about a century.

More Democrats began to vote Republican at the national level, but the Democratic Party continued to dominate state and local politics. The reason for this was twofold. First, as mentioned earlier, most Texans at this time were Democrats. They had been socialized into the Democratic Party and held strong party identification. Many even proclaimed to be Yellow Dog Democrats, stating that they would rather vote for a yellow dog than for a Republican. Strong partisan identification is tough to change, and it usually takes a specific event or issue to change a person's party identification.

Second, there was the direct primary system. Many Republican voters voted in the Democratic primaries because their own primaries were not competitive or because no viable candidates were running for office, so conservative Democrats usually prevailed. This allowed the party's conservative wing to prevail into the 1990s, and conservative Texas Democrats continued to be elected with Republican support at the local and state levels.

At the national level however, a liberal wing had taken over the Democratic Party after the 1974 off-year elections, and liberal candidates such as Walter Mondale (1984) and Mike Dukakis (1988) became presidential nominees for the party. Most Texans were more conservative than residents of other states **(Figure 4.5)**, so many of them started voting for the more conservative Republican presidential candidate. Throughout the 1970s and 1980s, average Texans would vote Republican for president (with the exception of 1976, when fellow Southerner Jimmy Carter was the Democratic nominee) and Democrat at the local and state levels. This would all change in the 1990s, when the Texas Democratic Party was slowly taken over by its liberal wing. The Democratic Party became more liberal, so more conservative Democrats began to vote in Republican primaries until finally realigning with the Republican Party. Concurrently, many elected Democratic officeholders began to switch political parties. The most famous Texan to switch was former Governor Rick Perry, the longest serving Texas governor (2000-2015). He started his political career as a Democrat in the Texas House of Representatives in 1984. Five years later he switched political parties and subsequently became lieutenant governor and governor of Texas. He is currently (2019) the secretary of energy in the Trump administration.

The last Democrat to win the governorship was Ann Richards in 1990, and the last Democrat to win any statewide office was Dan Morales, who won reelection as attorney general of Texas in 1994.

Write A New Shining Page In Texas History...

A TWO-PARTY TEXAS IS A MUST!

VOTE FOR
JOHN TOWER
REPUBLICAN
SPECIAL ELECTION – MAY 27

Aman Batheja. (2014) Slideshow: John Tower's Historic 1961 Senate Campaign. Retrieved at https://www.texastribune.org/2014/06/06/slideshow-john-towers-historic-1961-senate-campaig/

FIGURE 4.4 John Tower Campaign Poster, 1961[14]

Realignment: *a core group of supporters of a political party switching to the opposition party.*

Realignment

When studying political parties, voters, and elections, **realignment** is one of the most widely used concepts. It was developed by political scientist V.O. Key in a 1955 article and can explain the shifting of party dominance in American and Texas politics.[16] The theory states that all political parties are made of various

FIGURE 4.5

Americans' Political Ideology by State, 2016[15]

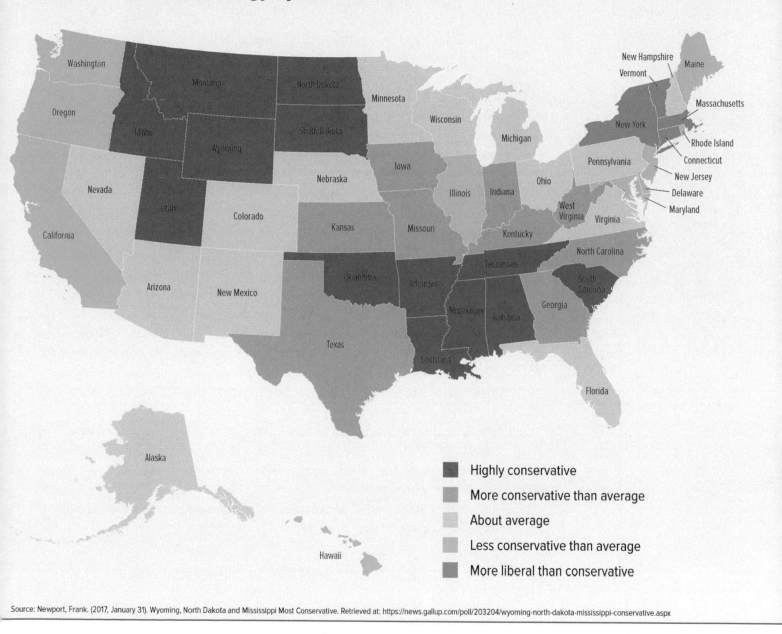

Highly conservative

More conservative than average

About average

Less conservative than average

More liberal than conservative

Source: Newport, Frank. (2017, January 31). Wyoming, North Dakota and Mississippi Most Conservative. Retrieved at: https://news.gallup.com/poll/203204/wyoming-north-dakota-mississippi-conservative.aspx

groups who support a party for different reasons. These groups can be based on ethnicity, on religion, or on various economic characteristics. Therefore, our parties are not homogeneous but very heterogeneous. For example, the New Deal coalition that kept the Democratic Party in power for decades consisted of many groups, such as unionized voters, Jewish voters, Catholics, African Americans, the Solid Democratic South, the working class, and intellectuals. They all supported the Democratic Party for different reasons. After World War II, white Southerners slowly left the Democratic Party. At first, this fractured Democratic politics in Texas, but then many white conservatives moved to the

Republican Party. This is called realignment. Realignment can be defined as follows: One core group of supporters of a political party leaves its old party and aligns itself with a different new party. Realignments are usually caused by issues. A political party gains and loses support when it takes a stance on a specific issue. When the Democratic Party began to embrace civil rights in the 1960s, for example, it gained support from many more African Americans. At the same time, the party lost support from white Southerners who still believed in segregation. White Southerners began to leave the Democratic Party, which led to realignment in the former Solid Democratic South. Only occurring four times in U.S. history, this switch of a political party's core group to a different political party can create a new majority party. This process of creating a new majority party is called a **critical realignment**. Therefore, the switch of the conservative white vote in Texas constitutes a critical realignment at the state level. The Republican Party became the new majority in Texas and has controlled Texas politics since 1998.

Dealignment goes hand in hand with realignment and critical realignment. Dealignment occurs when one core group leaves a political party but fails to realign with a new political party. Instead, the group becomes non-partisan and often splits tickets and varies their votes depending on candidates and on elections. For example, white Southerners moved away from the Democratic Party in 1964, when they voted for Republican Barry Goldwater, because of civil rights issues. Incumbent Democratic President Johnson favored civil rights and voting rights, but Republican Barry Goldwater voted against the Civil Rights Act in the Senate. In 1968, however, white Southerners voted for the American Independent Party headed by Governor George Wallace of Alabama, and in 1972 they voted for Republican Richard Nixon. In 1976, many voted for fellow Southern Democrat Jimmy Carter of Georgia, but then they supported Republican Ronald Reagan in 1980. At that time, they decided to remain with the Republican Party and finally became realigned. Today, white Southerners constitute one of the most heavily Republican voting groups in the United States. Ironically, the solid Democratic South has turned into the solid Republican South.

The Fifth Party System (1998–Present)

Texas was considered a part of the Solid Democratic South before the 1990s. Until 1994, the state had only voted for one Republican governor and for two Republican senators in over one hundred years. As mentioned above, the state would vote Republican at the national level, twice for Eisenhower and twice for Ronald Reagan, but at the local and state level it would remain solidly Democratic. The reasons for this are many. The previously mentioned direct primary allowed for competitive primary elections within the Democratic Party, which took the place of competitive general elections. Party identification for the Democratic Party was strong, and the few years of Republican rule after the Civil War were associated with military occupation and the inept and corrupt rule of Republican Governor E.J. Davis. This attachment would not change for over a century.

Critical realignment: a core group of a political party's supporters switching to the opposition. This switch also creates a new majority party.

Dealignment: a core group of supporters leaving a political party and refusing to join another political party.

FIGURE 4.6

Texas State and National Congressional Delegation, 1973 & 2019

Body	1973 Democrats	1973 Republicans	2019 Democrats	2019 Republicans
Texas House of Representatives	132	17	67	83
Texas Senate	28	3	12	19
U.S. House of Representatives	20	4	13	23
U.S. Senate	1	1	0	2

Source: data collected and rearranged by the author

The realignment process (as discussed above) slowly increased during the 1980s, when Ronald Reagan became president of the United States. His personal appeal and his policies made many white Southerners switch parties permanently, and realignment occurred. At the same time, Texas began to change. Americans from the Midwest and Northeast began to move to Texas, and many were Republicans. The urbanization of Texas also began with large cities such as Dallas and Houston, where a prosperous middle class voted Republican. A platform of cutting taxes, reducing welfare spending, and increasing military spending was tailor-made for them. The president who presented them with this platform would be the Republican Ronald Reagan.

After President Reagan's eight years in power, the split within the Democratic Party became final. With Ronald Reagan as the U.S. president throughout the 1980s, many more conservative Democrats, the so-called Reagan Democrats, began supporting the Republican Party. As conservative Democrats left, the Democratic Party could move to the left, and by the 1990s the liberal wing of the Democratic Party controlled the party. With most Texas voters leaning to the right, the Republican Party soon found itself the majority party in Texas. By 1992, it controlled both United States Senate seats, and in 1994 George W. Bush defeated Democratic Governor Ann Richards to become the second Republican governor since Reconstruction. He was reelected in a landslide in 1998, and the Republican Party won every statewide office that year. In 2002, the Republican Party took control of the Texas Legislature, and finally, in 2004, they took control of the Texas delegation in the U.S. House of Representatives. Even after the 2018 off-year election, no Democrat has won any statewide office in Texas since 1998. **Figure 4.6** shows the transition of Texas from a solid Democratic to a solid Republican state.

Figure 4.6 shows that the Republican Party only controlled 17 seats in the Texas House of Representatives in 1973; it took control of the body in 2002 and today (2019) holds 83 seats. Republicans took over the Texas State Senate in

FIGURE 4.7

Texas Democratic Party Ideological Identification[17]

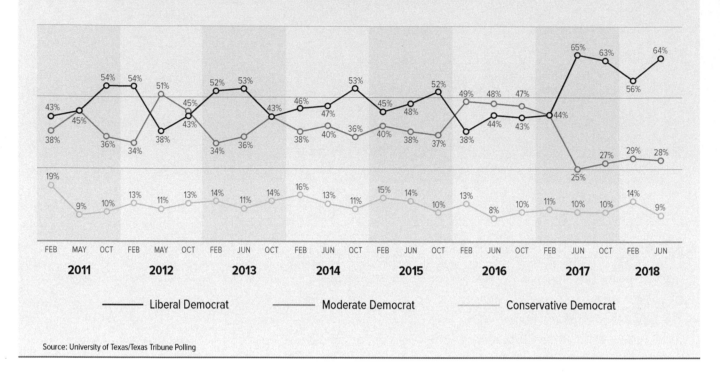

Source: University of Texas/Texas Tribune Polling

Liberal: tends to favor government participation in the economy. Liberals tend to favor efforts by the government to increase equality, healthcare, public education, and programs that support the poor and the disadvantaged.

Conservative: tends to favor lower taxes and fewer government programs to help the poor and disadvantaged.

1996, and in 2019 the party still controls the body with 19 seats. At the national level, the Republican Party controls both United States Senate seats and a majority of the House of Representatives delegation.

Interestingly, the transition from a Democratic state to a Republican state made the Democratic Party in Texas more liberal, as **Figure 4.7** shows. Forty-three percent of all of Texas Democratic Party supporters were liberal in 2011, and by June of 2018 this number increased to 64%. Simultaneously, the number of Texas Democrats professing to be conservative declined from 19% to 9%. If it continues, this trend will lead to even more conservative Democrats leaving their party and will make the Democratic Party even more liberal in Texas.

As a side note, the term **liberal** in this case means that a political party advocates for more government regulation of business, higher taxes on the wealthy, larger social welfare programs, and civil rights. It also means the party opposes more stringent immigration control. A **conservative**, on the other hand, opposes most government regulation of business, high taxes on individuals and businesses, and large social welfare programs that involve government expansion. At the same time, he/she advocates for policies of personal responsibility and immigration control. As previously discussed, however, both parties tend to be more conservative in Texas than their respective counterparts in other states. For example, many Texas Democrats oppose an income tax for the state and increased regulation of business.

The Structure of Texas Political Parties

Using one of V.O. Key's three party distinctions is necessary when studying political parties in Texas. So, let us look at the party as an organization. We will analyze the actual structure of our two major parties, the Democratic and Republican Parties of Texas, at the local and state levels. As discussed earlier, political parties in the United States are decentralized. Real power is held at the local and state level, and political parties differ from state to state. The lowest party level in Texas is the precinct level. Every county in Texas is divided into precincts, and, in a party primary, every precinct elects a precinct chair who then serves for two years. The precinct chair is in charge of recruiting campaign volunteers, coordinating campaign workers, mobilizing voters, and getting them registered to vote. The precinct chair's major function is to serve on a county executive committee. The county executive committee is in charge of planning and conducting local primaries and county conventions.

After the party's primary is over, every primary voter for the party can attend a precinct convention. Here, delegates to the county convention are elected, and every attendee can discuss and pass a set of policy resolutions presented to the county convention. Participation is usually very low; only about 2% of all primary voters show up, and a small dedicated minority can easily dominate the convention and push through its own narrow agenda.

At the county level, the county party chair is in charge. Again, this position is chosen by primary voters for a 2-year term for both parties. The county chair presides over the county executive committee, which is composed of all the precinct chairs within the county. In this capacity, county chairs can determine where to put polling stations within the county. They are also responsible for renting voting machines, printing paper ballots, and constructing the primary ballot. In turn, the whole executive committee is responsible for canvassing votes after the primary and helping the chair prepare the primary ballots and conduct a drawing to determine the order of candidates' names on the ballot.

Another major function of the county chair is recruiting candidates for local or regional offices. County chairs are also in charge of the local party's funds and are considered the party's spokesperson at the local level.

At the county convention, delegates to the state convention are selected. Texas is one of the most populous states and consists of sparsely and heavily populated counties. The most populous counties need more than one convention. In the most populous counties, parties actually hold conventions in each senatorial district.

In Texas, the state party chair is one of the most powerful party officials in the state. She or he recruits candidates for local and state offices and raises funds for candidates and for the party itself. The chair serves a two-year term, certifies all the party's primary winners, and presides over the state executive committee, which determines the site of the next state convention, raises money, disseminates press releases, and works closely with the party at the national level.

Most importantly, the state party chair leads the state party convention. Every even-numbered year, the Democratic and the Republican parties hold

>> Political parties in the United States are decentralized. Real power is held at the local and state level, and political parties differ from state to state.

uttyler.edu

a state convention in Texas. As discussed above, the attendees are selected by the county conventions. The state conventions perform many functions for the two parties, including electing all state party officers and the state executive committee. Crucially, the state party platform is adopted at this level. In the platform, both parties outline their vison and their policies for the state for the next two years. During a presidential election year, the state convention also selects Texas's thirty-eight presidential electors for the party and elects the Texas delegation that attends the national presidential nominating convention.

Third Parties

Throughout its history, many third or minor parties have participated in Texas politics. Most were short-lived and had no visible impact on Texas politics. Some, however, have survived for decades and occasionally impact Texas politics, especially at the local level.

A **third party** is usually formed and supported by a group of voters, who have become dissatisfied with the two major parties, the Republican and Democratic Parties. These voters feel that issues important to them are ignored by the two major parties, so they have no choice but to support a different political party. There are two types of third parties in our political system: single-cause and multi-cause third parties. A single-cause third party exists for and runs candidates based on one major issue. The Prohibition Party of the late 19th century was a single-issue party. Multi-cause parties are similar to our two major parties and run candidates on issues spanning from social and economic policies to foreign policy.

Finally, third parties tend be ideological and not electoral in nature, meaning that winning is not the most important aspect of their political life. Instead, they adhere to their particular political beliefs even if they will lose an election.

Two examples of third parties that exist and do matter in parts of Texas are the Libertarian Party and the Green Party.

The Libertarian Party

The Libertarian Party closely follows the small government ideals set out by Adam Smith in his book *Wealth of Nations.* The party advocates for a very limited governmental role in the economy and in people's lives. Besides providing defense, law and order, and a working infrastructure, the government should not do much more. In other words, the party emphasizes the importance of individual judgement over governmental intrusion. The party currently does not hold any state or federal offices in Texas, but its supporters take away voters from the Republican Party, and it has occasionally impacted the outcome of state-level elections.

The Green Party

The Green Party was founded in the 1970s and advocates for environmental awareness, corporate responsibility, and gender equality. Specifically,

Third party: any political party except the two major parties, the Democrats and the Republicans.

Source: https://en.wikipedia.org/wiki/Libertarian_Party_of_Texas

FIGURE 4.8 Libertarian Party logo

the party supports universal healthcare, universal voter registration in Texas, legalizing medical marijuana, and abolishing the death penalty. The Green Party has not played a major role in Texas politics, but it did impact a presidential election. In the presidential election of 2000, its standard-bearer, Ralph Nader, managed to win close to 3% of the vote nationwide, which proved decisive in Florida, where Ralph Nader won 97,000 votes and arguably took the state and the presidency from Democrat Al Gore, handing it to Republican George W. Bush.

FIGURE 4.9 **Green Party logo**

Conclusion

In a repeat of history, the Republican Party became factionalized after becoming the dominant party in Texas.

Currently, three major groups are competing for power within the Texas Republican Party. First, there are the traditional, or establishment, Republicans. They tend to advocate for low taxes and less spending, but they support most welfare programs and public spending on infrastructure and education. They are also more moderate on social issues.

Second, a new breed of Republican voters was born with the growth of evangelical Christians in the 1980s. They are mainly concerned with social issues, such as abortion and gay rights, and are less concerned with traditional issues, such as foreign policy or tariffs. Interestingly, many evangelicals are fairly moderate on economic issues.

Third, Texas (like many states) saw the rise of the Tea Party after President Obama was elected in 2008. This movement is especially opposed to the Affordable Care Act, more commonly known as Obamacare. Similar to Libertarians, the Tea Party opposes government intervention in the economy and supports low taxes and a smaller welfare state. The Tea Party, often unwilling to compromise on issues, has challenged establishment Republicans in many states, including Texas. In Republican primaries, Tea Party candidates would often upset heavily favored Republican establishment candidates. Tea Party candidates have not fared as well in the general election, however, and many ended up losing to Democratic candidates. Exceptions to the rule are Senator Ted Cruz and Lieutenant Governor Dan Patrick, both from Texas. They both started out as Tea Party challengers to more established Republican candidates, and both won their election and were reelected in 2018.

In conclusion, the Republican Party in Texas today is in a situation similar to the Democratic Party's situation a century ago. It has become factionalized, and these factions are competing vigorously in its primaries. In parts of Texas today, such as in East Texas, the general election does not decide who wins office—the Republican primary does.

Key Terms

Cadre party: a decentralized and part-time political party whose major purpose is to win office.

Conservative: tends to favor lower taxes and fewer government programs to help the poor and disadvantaged.

Critical realignment: a core group of a political party's supporters switching to the opposition. This switch also creates a new majority party.

Dealignment: a core group of supporters leaving a political party and refusing to join another political party.

Direct primary: an election held by a political party to determine the party's nominee for political office.

Duverger's Law: the theory that a single-member district electoral system results in a two-party system and proportional representation in a multi-party system.

Independent: a voter who does not identify with a political party.

Interest aggregation: the act of joining with like-minded citizens to acquire political power.

Liberal: tends to favor government participation in the economy. Liberals tend to favor efforts by the government to increase equality, healthcare, public education, and programs that support the poor and the disadvantaged.

Mass party: a centralized and full-time political party whose major purpose is to represent a certain ideological viewpoint.

Multi-party system: a political system in which more than two parties have a realistic chance of winning political offices.

New Deal Coalition: forged by FDR in the 1930s, the New Deal Coalition consisted of the working class, Catholics, white Southerners, African Americans, Jewish people, and intellectuals. It dominated U.S. politics until the 1960s.

Partisan: a voter who identifies with a political party.

Party as an organization: the local, state, and national structure of a political party and its paid leaders.

Party identification: people connecting with a political party.

Party in government: local, state, and national elected or appointed officials who identify or belong to a political party.

Party in the electorate: voters who identify with a political party.

Party platform: a document drawn up every two years at the state convention that outlines a party's policies and principles.

Political party: a group of citizens, who organize to contest elections, win public office, and impact policy making.

Political power: the ability to make people engage in a political act they would not engage in of their own free will.

Political socialization: the process of how people acquire their political values.

Proportional representation: an electoral system in which seats are allocated based on the proportion of the vote a party receives.

Realignment: a core group of supporters of a political party switching to the opposition party.

Single-member district electoral system: an electoral system in which the person who wins the most votes in a district is elected to office.

Third party: any political party except the two major parties, the Democrats and the Republicans.

Two-party system: a political system in which only two parties have a realistic chance of winning political office.

ENDNOTES

[1]Schattschneider, E.E. (1942). Party Government. New York: Farrar and Rinehart.

[2]Huntington, Samuel. (1980). Political Order in Changing Societies. New Haven, Connecticut: Yale University Press.

[3]Madison, James. (1787, November 22). Federalist No. 10: The Same Subject Continued: The Union as a Safeguard Against Domestic Faction and Insurrection. New York Daily Advertiser.

[4]Downs, Anthony. (1957). An Economic Theory of Democracy. New York: Harper and Row.

[5]Key, V.O. Jr. (1964). Politics, Parties and Pressure Groups. New York: Crowell.

[6]Duverger, Maurice. (1963). Political Parties: Their Organization and Activity in the Modern State (B. North & R. North, Trans.). New York: John Wiley.

[7]Ibid.

[8]Campbell, Angus et al. (1960). The American Voter. New York: John Wiley.

[9]Ibid.

[10]https://www.texastribune.org/2017/11/10/hey-texplainer-how-much-does-it-cost-run-office-texas/

[11]University of Texas, Texas Tribune Poll, June 2018. Retrieved at: https://texaspolitics.utexas.edu/polling

[12]Ibid.

[13]Ibid.

[14]Aman Batheja. (2014) Slideshow: John Tower's Historic 1961 Senate Campaign. Retrieved at https://www.texastribune.org/2014/06/06/slideshow-john-towers-historic-1961-senate-campaig/

[15]Newport, Frank. (2017, January 31). Wyoming, North Dakota and Mississippi Most Conservative. Retrieved at: https://news.gallup.com/poll/203204/wyoming-north-dakota-mississippi-conservative.aspx

[16]Key, V.O. Jr. (1955, August). A Theory of Critical Elections. Journal of Politics, 17(11), 3-18.

[17]Retrieved at: https://texaspolitics.utexas.edu/set/partisan-ideological-identification#democratic-identification

5

Chapter 5

Interest Groups

INTEREST GROUPS HAVE BECOME A MAJOR PLAYER in American and Texas politics. The United States leads the world in the number of interest groups, and in no other democracy have interest groups become as influential. First, we must define interest group. An **interest group** is usually a narrow coalition that seeks to influence public policy. Interest groups attempt to influence all branches of government—the legislative, the executive, and the judiciary—to create policies favorable to their cause. They attempt to influence the passing of policies favorable to their members and to block policies that would harm their cause. Interest groups also actively seek new members and supporters to increase their political muscle, which increases participation in the political process.

Texans who want to impact public policy and share similar goals must combine their resources to acquire political power and influence public policy. Texas has one of the largest economies in the United States, at $1.9 trillion, and both Texas-based interest groups and out-of-state groups compete for a parcel of the biannual $217 billion budget.[1]

With one of the largest markets for textbooks in the United States, for example, many publishers will create new high school textbooks for the Texas market that will then be used in many adjacent states. So, interest groups from Texas and out-of-state groups will compete to determine what materials will go into textbooks. History and political science textbooks in

Interest group: an organization that seeks to influence public policy.

uttyler.edu

Source: https://commons.wikimedia.org/wiki/File:
Alexis_de_tocqueville.jpg

FIGURE 5.1 Alexis de Tocqueville

*Pluralism: a theory that public
policy should be made by
competing interest groups to
ensure that no single interest
group will prevail all the time.*

Source: https://commons.wikimedia.org/wiki/James_Madison#/media/
File:James_Madison.jpg

FIGURE 5.2 James Madison

particular see vicious competition from conservative and liberal groups to determine textbook content.

Europeans join political parties to acquire political power, and Americans join interest groups to influence policy making at the local, state, or national level. As early as 1830, the famous French philosopher Alexis de Tocqueville **(Figure 5.1)** noticed the prevalence of interest group politics in the United States when touring the country and studying its politics. He subsequently labeled the United States "a nation of joiners."[2] His statement is truer today than in 1830, with over 200,000 interest groups active in local, state, and national politics in the United States.

Our founding fathers already knew of people's inclination to join together to acquire political power and push for their often very narrow self-interests. As discussed in Chapter 5, James Madison analyzed factions and labeled them as minorities who get together to push for their own interests, often over the interests of the majority. Both political parties and interest groups can be labeled factions using Madison's definition. Although he foresaw interest groups, or factions, becoming detrimental to the majority, Madison did not believe that the United States should limit or outlaw interest-group politics. He feared that a ban on factions would violate individual freedoms and believed that interest groups should be allowed to flourish and grow. Then, they could compete against each other, limiting their powers in the political process. This theory of **pluralism** will be discussed in more detail in the next section.

Pluralism v. Elite Theory

The right to create and join interest groups was given to us by the First Amendment to the Constitution. The amendment states: "Congress shall make no law respecting an establishment of religion, or prohibiting the free exercise thereof; or abridging the freedom of speech, or of the press; or the right of the people peaceably to assemble, and to petition the government for a redress of grievances." Though our founding fathers were afraid that interest groups could harm the country, they believed that the Constitution provided the right for citizens to come together and create these groups.

Pluralist theory was developed by James Madison **(Figure 5.2)** in Federalist Paper Number 10 and was updated by David B. Truman in his 1951 work *The Governmental Process—Political Interests and Public Opinion.*[3]

Pluralism believes interest groups will arise as societies become more economically and socially complex. People will join together to push for their own interests and for governmental benefits. These interests can be economic, professional, ideological, environmental, or even religious. All of these diverse groups will now compete for public benefits, ensuring that public policy will not benefit only a few people while disadvantaging the majority. As soon as a group feels disadvantaged, it will begin to organize and compete for benefits. Suddenly, many interest groups are competing for political benefits and hopefully balancing each other out overall. Pluralism assumes that everybody will get a little bit from our policymakers, but nobody will get everything they ask for. This balance makes every interest group accept lawmakers' policy decisions without complaining or, more importantly, without taking action against our policymakers.

Elite theory takes a different point of view and believes that not all interest groups are created equal. Some are more powerful than others and eventually acquire a monopoly on political power. Then, they can dominate other interests and push for public policies benefiting only them and their members—not the public overall. Unable to be counterbalanced, they further their very narrow self-interest at the expense of the many. In other words, an elite interest group that the public cannot hold accountable has been created.

Elite theory: a theory that a few powerful interest groups will consistently prevail in public policymaking, often at the expense of the majority.

Interest Groups in Texas

As one of the largest and most economically powerful states, Texas has thousands of interest groups attempting to influence policy making. Some of Texas's largest economic interest groups are the Texas Association of Business, the Texas Farm Bureau, and the Texas branch of the AFL-CIO. Professional interest groups include the Texas Association of Realtors, the Texas State Teachers Association, and the Texas Medical Association. For the environment, we find the Texas League of Conservation Voters. Finally, many powerful ideological interest groups exist, such as Texas Right to Life, Pro-Choice Texas, and the Texas State Rifle Association. The most powerful public interest group in Texas is Public Citizen Texas.

Obviously, Texas has a plethora of interest groups active in politics. So, why do Texas and the United States have so many interest groups active in politics? Here we find five possible answers.

First, the United States and Texas are very heterogeneous, unlike many other democracies. In other words, many divisions exist in Texas and American society. For example, the United States and Texas are ethnically very diverse. Thus, people of the same ethnic group often form interest groups and push for a specific ethnically centered agenda. In Texas, we find interest groups representing Mexican Americans, Asian Americans, and African Americans. The white population is also split among ethnic lines. Most white Texans are of Anglo-Saxon or German descent and are represented by their own interest groups.

Further, many religious divisions exist. The United States and Texas are very religiously diverse, and most religions—including the Catholic faith and many Protestant denominations such as Baptists, Methodists, and Lutherans—are organized into interest groups. Even smaller religions, such as the Mormon Church or Muslims, are organized into interest groups. Each religion now uses interest groups to push for certain faith-based agendas.

Other divisions include ideological splits, such as liberal, conservative, or libertarian, and social or moral divisions. The latter includes pro-choice and pro-life groups. Finally, the divisions can be economic in nature. This topic includes unions or business groups that organize to push for material benefits for their members.

>> What is the difference between a political party and an interest group? Political parties are much broader, and represent large segments of Texans. Interest groups represent a small segment of the population and push for policies that directly benefit their members and supporters.

Second, the United States and Texas constitutions provide many access points for interest groups. In Texas, for example, interest groups can lobby at the local level, which includes cities of all sizes, and at the state level. At the state level, interest groups can impact legislative, executive (a plural executive in Texas), or even judicial policies whenever judges are elected and not appointed. Unlike many European countries, where political power is centralized at the national level, the United States and Texas are decentralized, which provides many access points.

Third, as discussed in Chapter 5, political parties are weak in the United States and in Texas. Interest groups often have more power, measured by the group's size or monetary resources, than political parties, and people flock to interest groups instead of political parties to push for their objectives. In Europe, on the other hand, people join strong political parties rather than the weaker interest groups to push their agenda.

Fourth, governmental structures sometimes push for the creation of interest groups. For example, the national government under President Taft in 1912 urged local structures to create the United States Chamber of Commerce to counterbalance the growing power of labor unions. By 2018, the Chamber of Commerce had become the largest lobbying organization in the United States, spending almost $70 million on lobbying efforts nationwide.

Finally, the government's continuous intervention in the economy has resulted in the creation of interest groups. Studies have shown that the more a government intervenes in an economy, the more impact there is on groups such as unions or businesses. Government regulations change the way businesses conduct daily activities, and businesses will be forced to organize into interest groups to impact the government regulating it. The same goes for private citizens. After the U.S. government legalized abortion in Roe v. Wade in 1973, both pro-life and pro-choice organizations were created to support or combat the decision. Certain segments of the population or economy are impacted whenever the government passes legislation or regulations, and groups form to influence policymaking in their impacted areas.

What is the difference between a political party and an interest group? As discussed in Chapter 4, political parties are much broader, all-compassing organizations. They represent large segments of Texans, in contrast to interest groups' narrower scope. Interest groups represent a small segment of the population and push for policies that directly benefit their members and supporters. In Texas, these groups include the Texas League of Conservation Voters (which represents citizens concerned with the environment) and the Texas State Rifle Association (which represents issues on the right to bear arms, such as gun control). Political parties nominate and run candidates for elected office, but interest groups do not. However, interest groups affect campaigning by publicly supporting candidates who agree with them on certain issues. Interest group can provide campaign funds to candidates or encourage their members to vote for or against candidates.

In the United States, political parties and interest groups are complementary in nature. Although they compete for supporters and donations, political parties and interest groups support each other on passing mutually beneficial legislation. For example, the Texas State Rifle Association has become a close supporter of the Republican Party by turning out its members to vote for Republican candidates and by asking them to financially support the Republican Party. On the other side, interest groups such as the Texas League of Conservation Voters and especially teachers unions strongly support the Democratic Party. Activists from groups closely aligned with political parties will often join political parties and continue their activities in these parties. The reverse can also be true.

Joining Interest Groups

Why do people join interest groups? Three basic explanations exist. First people join to receive material benefits. Workers join unions to receive higher wages, more job protection, and a safe work environment. However, people do not join the Texas League of Conservation Voters or the Texas State Rifle Association for material benefits. These interest groups' followers join for ideological reasons. People join the Texas League of Conservation Voters because they believe in environmental protection. Similarly, people join the Texas State Rifle Association because they believe in the right to bear arms. Many people join pro-life or pro-choice interest groups not to receive material benefits but because they strongly support or oppose abortion.

Finally, solidary incentives have become increasingly prominent. Many people today do not possess a large social support structure. They are separated from their family, are single or divorced, and often feel lonely. Interest groups have tapped into this market. These groups allow people to join a large group of like-minded members to socialize with. Many interest groups hold social activities, such as dinners or game nights, and some have even established permanent places, such as restaurants, where supporters can meet and socialize.

Types of Interest Groups

Are all interest groups the same, or do various types of interest groups exist in our political system? When studying interest groups, we find the following types:

Economic interest groups: Most interest groups in Texas and the United States are economic interest groups. Here we find unions, such as the Texas branch of the AFL-CIO, the American Federation of Labor-Congress of Industrial Organizations, which is a conglomerate of labor unions in Texas and the United States. Businesses, large and small, are represented by the Texas Association of Business or TAB, the leading organization of employers in Texas. TAB makes sure that the business side of issues is heard in the state Legislature.

Professional organizations: One of the most powerful is the American Medical Association or AMA. These organizations represent a small but powerful segment within Texas, and they actively push for legislation

uttyler.edu

benefiting a small group of members, such as medical professionals. Though smaller in size than unions, they are more powerful because of their members' prestige and their monetary resources.

Public interest groups: These groups push for policies benefitting the majority of the people and not just a small minority of members. The most famous one is the Center for Auto Safety. Organized in 1970, it pushed for public policies such as the Lemon Laws, which made auto manufactures and car dealers accountable for selling defective cars to consumers. They were successful not because of monetary reasons but because of support from the American and Texas public.

Governmental structures: These can work as interest groups themselves, and local governmental structures in Texas include cities, such as Houston and Dallas, that hire lobbyists to attend the state legislature and seek benefits such as expanded home rule, tax breaks, or grants.

Ideological interest groups: Usually very ideological in nature, these groups push for very narrow specific policies. A good example is Empower Texans, a conservative interest group headed by Michael Quinn Sullivan. With the rise of the Tea Party movement in the 2010 election, Empower Texans became a political force in Republican politics in Texas. Advocating limited government and personal liberty, Empower Texans supports conservative over moderate candidates in state elections.

Sources of Interest Group Power

What determines the influence that interest groups have in making public policy? Interest groups do not run candidates for office, but they are active in politics via political campaigning and lobbying. They provide public support, mobilize their members to vote, and spent money on behalf of candidates. Interest groups in Texas have six power sources:

Membership size: The more members an interest group has, the more power it has in Texas politics. If an interest group has few financial resources, it can compensate with millions of members who vote on Election Day. For example, the American Association of Retired People does not have large monetary resources to put into a campaign, but it has millions of members who care about issues such as social security or healthcare and are willing to base their vote on them. In 2018, the AARP had 38 million members in the United States, Americans over the age of 50, which is the age group most likely to vote on Election Day.[4]

Monetary resources: The more money interest groups provide to candidates during elections, the more powerful they are. The most affluent interest group in the United States and in Texas is the National Association of Realtors. Founded in 1969, it represents over 1.3 million U.S. realtors. It is widely considered one of the most effective interest groups in the United States and spent almost $14 million on Texas political campaigns in 2018, evenly divided between the two parties' candidates.[5]

Intensity of members' conviction: The more strongly an organization's members feel about a cause, the more likely they are to give money, get involved in politics, and participate in elections. A cohesive group of people held together by a common cause will more likely vote based on certain issues the interest group favors. For example, members of the National Rifle Association, or NRA, feel so strongly about the right to bear arms that they will base their vote on gun-related issues while ignoring other current issues. If the National Rifle Association mobilizes members during elections, they will turn out and vote for candidates favorable to gun-related issues.

Prestige of members: The prestige of interest group members also comes into play. Studies reveal that interest groups that enjoy a lot of prestige, such as the American Medical Association, receive better treatment from policymakers and more public support for policies favorable to their group.

Leadership skills: An exceptional leader can often overcome an interest group's lack of membership or even its lack of monetary resources. A great example is Ralph Nader **(Figure 5.3)** when he founded the Center for Auto Safety, a public interest group in 1970. Public interest groups push for policies that benefit most people while imposing costs on a small minority of economic interests. Under Ralph Nader's leadership, the Center for Auto Safety pushed to implement the so-called Lemon Laws, which made auto manufactures and car dealers accountable for selling defective cars to consumers. So, most citizens benefitted from protection against buying defective cars, while a small minority of manufactures and car dealers bore the costs. Without Ralph Nader's personality and leadership style, these Lemon Laws would have not been passed by every state.

Source: https://commons.wikimedia.org/wiki/File:Naderspeak.JPG

FIGURE 5.3 Ralph Nader

Organizational structure: Interest groups with headquarters in many or all states as well as Washington, D.C., will be more influential than ones located in only one state. In other words, organizational structure determines political power. Locations throughout the country allow interest groups to lobby for their interests in many states and at the national level.

Now that we have discussed sources of power and political influence, let us move on to interest groups' actual functions in Texas and in the United States. In other words, what do interest groups actually do?

Interest Group Functions

This section discusses the functions interest groups fulfill in our democracy. Some are well-known, such as contributing to political campaigns or lobbying lawmakers, but others are unknown to average citizens. Lesser-known functions include providing information for law making and getting average Texans involved in making policies. Two major functions of interest groups in Texas include interest aggregation and electioneering.

Gaining Political Power through Interest Aggregation

Interest aggregation: the act of joining like-minded citizens to acquire political power.

The **interest aggregation** function was included in Chapter 5's discussion on political parties. Remember, an individual usually lacks political power and cannot influence public policy making. If the individual joins other individuals with similar interests, however, they can pool their resources and acquire political power.

What distinguishes political parties from interest groups in regards to interest aggregation? Both types of organizations fulfill the interest aggregation function—having people join for similar reasons and push a similar agenda—but, unlike interest groups, political parties' primary function is to nominate and elect people to office by supplying them with a specific party label. This function allows political parties to directly control the governmental apparatus. On the other hand, interest groups only participate in certain electoral functions, such as providing support, especially monetary support, to candidates during elections.

Influencing by Electioneering

Electioneering: interest groups attempt to influence who gets elected to public office by supporting candidates running for office.

The **electioneering** function is a major way interest groups attempt to influence public policy making. As the term implies, interest groups attempt to influence who gets elected to public office by providing public support for candidates running for office. For example, interest groups can organize rallies for candidates, turn out the vote for them, or provide the electorate with information favorable to candidates. They can walk door-to-door, send out campaign literature, produce voter guides, and even hold rallies and fundraisers for candidates. They can also grade legislators and send these grades to the local media and their members. On the other hand, if an interest group decides to oppose a candidate they can do all of this for the candidate's challenger.

Fundraising through Political Action Committees (PACs)

Political action committees (PACs): interest groups must create these committees to collect and spend money on candidates and on political campaigns.

Please keep in mind that interest groups cannot give money directly to candidates running for office. They first must establish **political action committees (PACs)** to do so.

PACs basically function as the fundraising arms of interest groups. In the 2016 election cycle, Texas PACs spent about $160 million on campaign expenditures.[6] This amount seems very high, but it pales in comparison with the $401 million spent in 2016 by all candidates running for political office in Texas.[7] About half of this amount was spent by business groups, and another 40% was spent by ideological interest groups and groups associated with political parties. Labor PACs, however, only spent about 8% of the $160 million spent by PACs.

Today, interest groups have become a major source of campaign funds for political parties and for candidates running for office. Interest groups, however, must create PACs to raise money to spend on political campaigns. In other words, interest groups cannot directly give money to political campaigns; they

FIGURE 5.4

Top 10 Texas Political Action Committees (PACs) during 2018 Election Cycle

PAC	SPENDING	DESCRIPTION
Texas Association of Realtors PAC-TREPAC	$35,867,910[8]	The realtors in Texas are one of the best-organized and best-funded PACs in Texas. Every realtor in Texas is asked to pay annual dues to the PAC, and this provides the PAC with monetary power unmatched by any other PAC in Texas. Unsurprisingly, realtors have a lot at stake in the financial well-being of their state. When the economy is poor, their business declines. TREPAC is usually non-ideological and supports candidates that are best for the Texas economy, and incumbents who are especially likely to get reelected. In 2018, the PAC supported Democrats and Republicans but favored officeholders. TREPAC's largest donation in 2018 went to one of their own, Cody Harris, who won a coveted seat in the State Senate. He received $140,000 from TREPAC.[9]
ActBlue Texas	$8,239,487[10]	ActBlue Texas is a fairly new Democratic PAC. Some political scientists do not recognize ActBlue Texas as a PAC because most of its money is raised online, but the organization is registered with the state of Texas as a PAC. Not surprisingly, the organization gives only to Democratic candidates and local Democratic Party organizations at the county level. Its major monetary recipient in 2018 was Democratic gubernatorial candidate Lupe Valdez, who received a little over $1 million from the PAC.
Texans for Lawsuit Reform (TLR)	$7,075,912[11]	The third-largest PAC in Texas tends to favor moderate Republican candidates over conservative candidates during primary season. During the general election, however, Texans for Lawsuit Reform favors any Republican candidate over Democratic candidates.
Empower Texans	$5,598,348[12]	While Texans for Lawsuit Reform supports moderate Republicans, Empower Texans supports the most conservative candidates in any race. Their top monetary recipient in 2018 was conservative candidate Mike Canon, who received $349,780 from Empower Texans to challenge moderate Republican Kel Seliger for a State Senate seat.[13] Despite this heavy investment, Empower Texans's candidate ended up losing.
Republican Party of Texas	$4,635,727[14]	The Republican Party of Texas is the fifth-largest PAC in Texas. This organization usually funds political advertising for the party and pays for political consultants if candidates lack the funds to do so.
Associated Republicans of Texas Campaign Fund	$4,168,280[15]	This organization tends to support moderate Republicans running for the state legislature. Its major objective is to maintain the state's Republican majority. It therefore spends most of its money on consulting firms and not necessarily on political candidates.
Republican State Leadership Committee	$3,506,807[16]	This Republican PAC spends its money on down-ballot state offices and not on candidates at the state level.
Texas Justice and Public Safety	$3,379,250[17]	This PAC is funded by billionaire George Soros and advocates for liberal causes, such as criminal justice reform and ending the deportation of illegal aliens. In 2018, it spent most of its money on public relations and on the Texas Democratic Party.
Texas Right to Life (TRTL)	$3,330,085[18]	As the name implies, this PAC supports pro-life candidates in state races. It is mostly funded by Texas billionaires Farris and Jo Ann Wilks.
Annie's List	$2,545,710[19]	This liberal progressive organization favors pro-choice female candidates in Texas.

uttyler.edu

must funnel it through PACs they have created and registered with the state of Texas. Many interest groups in Texas have done so, including unions, corporations, banks, and professional organizations representing business interests (realtors, medical professionals, etc.). See **Figure 5.4** for a list of the top ten political action committees in Texas.

PACs were legalized at the federal level in 1971 especially to allow economic interest groups, such as unions and business organizations, to participate in elections by raising money and financing candidates' campaigns. The Federal Election Campaign Act of 1972 was one of many acts passed by Congress to regulate campaign spending. Disclosing campaign donations and expenditures was required so the federal government could track who donates to political campaigns. This allowed the federal government to ensure that not one source was responsible for funding a whole campaign because the candidate would be beholden to a certain interest group if they were elected. Many of these provisions were later implemented at the state level.

Soft money, or the unlimited raising and spending of monies, was legalized for political parties. Soft money cannot be spent on a specific candidate; it must be spent on political party activities, such as party building and advertising for the party.

Independent Expenditures

Along with money given directly to political candidates, interest groups can independently spend money to support their cause. **Independent expenditures** are monies spent on behalf of candidates without coordination with the candidates or with their campaign. In 2010, independent expenditures were declared constitutional by the Supreme Court in Citizens United v. Federal Election Commission. This declaration resulted in the creation of **Super PACs**, independent organizations that raise and spend unlimited monies solicited from individuals, corporations, and unions. These monies are spent to either help or defeat candidates.

We have recently seen the rise of **dark money** in Texas and American politics. Dark money is raised by nonprofit organizations, or 501(c) 4 and 501(c) 6 organizations. These organizations do not have to report their sources of funding, namely their contributors or the donation amount. In other words, their spending has no limit, and they do not have to disclose where their monies came from. See **Figure 5.5** for rules that apply to raising and spending money for political campaigns.

Use of Litigation

Litigation is another major function of interest groups. In some instances, interest groups must resort to litigation to stop or to advance policies. As previously discussed, individuals might not have the money to file an expensive lawsuit. However, interest groups with many members and deep monetary resources do and are therefore more likely to file expensive lawsuits. In most instances, litigation is an interest group's final attempt to block policies they consider harmful.

Soft money: *unlimited raising and spending of monies; soft money cannot be spent on specific candidates but rather on political party activities, such as party building and advertising.*

Independent expenditures: *monies spent on behalf of candidates by interest groups, without coordination with the candidates or with their campaigns.*

Super PACs: *independent organizations that raise and spend unlimited monies solicited from individuals, corporations, and unions. These monies are spent to either help or defeat candidates, but cannot be directly given to political candidates and/or their campaigns.*

Dark money: *money raised by nonprofit or 501(c) 4 and 501(c) 6, organizations. These organizations do not have to report their sources of funding or the amount of their donations.*

FIGURE 5.5

Fundraising and Spending Rules for Texas Political Campaigns

There are no limits on individual spending for candidates' own campaigns. In other words, candidates can spend as much as they want if they use their own financial resources.

Candidates must appoint a campaign treasurer before they can start spending or raising money. The treasurer reports all campaign contributions and campaign expenditures to the Texas Ethics Commission.

Candidates and political action committees cannot accept cash contributions of more than $100. However, contributions by check are unlimited.

Corporations, unions, professional organizations, and other interest groups cannot directly give money to candidates or to political campaigns. They have to create political action committees and register them with the Texas Secretary of State.

Similar to federal campaign finance laws, candidates must provide statements listing campaign contributions and expenditures to the Texas Ethics Commission.

The Texas Ethics Commission studies campaign contributions and expenditures; if they find violations they can fine a political campaign or even start criminal procedures against it.

Two laws passed in the 1990s further restrict the impact of campaign donations from individuals and interest groups. First, the Texas Legislature passed a law making it illegal to accept campaign contributions while the Legislature is in session. Second, no one can accept campaign contributions inside the Capitol building.

Serving as a Source of Credible Information

A fourth and often forgotten function of interest groups is that they are a major and credible source of information for political officeholders. Keep in mind that most of our elected officials are not specialists in most policy areas, so they rely on information from other people—usually an interest group—to make decisions and pass new laws and regulations. Most work in the state Legislature is done at the committee level, and this is where interest groups can be influential. At the committee level, hearings are held on various topics. During these hearings, interest groups provide information on the policies discussed. For off-shore oil drilling, for example, the oil and natural gas industry will show up and describe the positive impacts of off-shore oil drilling. They present numbers on job creation and tax benefits for the area. Next, an environmental organization, such as the Texas League of Conservation Voters, will show up and present off-shore oil drilling's negative impacts on the environment and eventually on tourism. Our elected officeholders will then consider all the information and base their vote on it. Studies have shown that interest groups present credible information to officeholders because no interest group can afford to lie to a legislature and expect to be invited back or be trusted again. In Texas, presenting false information to policymakers is actually a crime.

Clients paid lobbyists close to $350 million in Texas in 2013.

Approximately 8500 lobbyists worked in Texas in 2015.

The average lobbyist made $109,376 in Texas in 2019.

Lobbying

The last major function of interest groups is **lobbying**. It is such a controversial and important function that it deserves its own section below.

One major function of interest groups in Texas today is lobbying, which is usually defined as contacting members of the legislative, executive, or judicial governmental branches in an attempt to influence policy or administrative decisions. Lobbying in Texas has become big business, with clients paying lobbyists close to $350 million in 2013 alone.[20] According to the **Texas Ethics Commission**, close to 8,500 lobbyists worked in Texas in 2015.[21] Lobbying can be a very profitable profession; in 2019, the average lobbyist in Texas makes $109,376 annually.[22]

Lobbyists tend to be busiest when the Legislature meets every two years. However good lobbyists do not wait until the legislature is in session to contact legislators. They will usually approach lawmakers outside of a session and establish early contacts that will carry into the next legislative session. Some lobbyists are individuals for hire, many of them are former legislators, and some work for large lobbying firms.

Since 2017, former lawmakers must sit out one legislative period before they can become lobbyists. In other words, there is a two-year waiting period after lawmakers leave the legislature before they can become a lobbyist.

An interest group can hire a self-employed lobbyist or a lobbying firm that employs many lobbyists on its behalf. Lobbyists then contact select lawmakers, usually legislators that are already predisposed to their cause. Not all lawmakers matter equally to lobbyists. Freshmen lawmakers especially are of less value then seasoned veterans of the Legislature. Lobbyists will contact lawmakers and offer services, such as providing information, but lobbyists cannot offer lawmakers money or spend an extravagant amount of resources on them—that is illegal in Texas. Texas law actually limits the amount a lobbyist can spend on a legislator to $114 before lobbyists must report the amount to the Texas Ethics Commission. Expenditures on lawmakers can include food, hotel costs, or even tickets to sports events. Many lobbyists get around this limitation by pooling their money. Instead of one oil and natural gas industry lobbyist taking a legislator out to a fancy dinner, five lobbyists will come along and increase the daily limit to $570 instead of $114. That amount will pay for a fancy dinner without being reported to the Texas Ethics Commission. We refer to this practice as **coalition lobbying**.

Lobbyists can also take legislators on fact-finding trips and fully pay for the legislators' costs. All a lobbyist must do is claim that the trip was related to the lawmakers' functions. Therefore, lobbyists can take lawmakers on expensive fact-finding trips to exotic places, pay for all their expenditures, and claim it was a fact-finding trip. Finally, as every lawmaker understands, working with lobbyists from certain organizations means that these organizations will help them financially, usually through political action committees, in subsequent elections.

Three more types of lobbying occur in Texas today:

Grassroots lobbying involves the general public. Interest groups attempt to involve the public in supporting their demands, which facilitates their attempt to influence policymaking. If interested and convinced, the public will push legislators to enact policies that the interest groups favor. In other words, interest groups attempt to influence legislators using public opinion by having the public contact lawmakers, write letters or e-mails, or demonstrate for or against certain policies.

Grasstop lobbying is similar to grassroots lobbying, but the interest groups try to mobilize certain prominent people rather than all or a large portion of the whole citizenry. In other words, well-known community members will contact the legislators, rather than a bunch of average citizens.

Astroturf lobbying involves interest groups spending monies to create the appearance of public support for their agenda. This appearance can involve misinformation to make the public upset about certain policies followed by demands for action from our lawmakers. Interest groups can also create bad polls or fake phone calls to convince legislators to support certain policies.

Coalition lobbying: two or more interest groups pool their financial and contact resources and work together to attain a specific public-policy goal.

Grassroots lobbying: interest groups encourage the public to support their demands, which facilitates their attempt to influence policymaking.

Grasstop lobbying: interest groups attempt to get a few select but very prominent people in the community to contact lawmakers in support of their policies.

Astroturf lobbying: this variation of lobbying involves interest groups spending monies to create the appearance of public support for their agenda.

The 1991 Reforms

The infamous Lonnie "Bo" Pilgrim affair led to campaign and lobbying reforms in Texas in the early 1990s. In 1989, the governor of Texas, Bill Clements, called for a special legislative session to discuss legislation that would force workers to seek mediation with their employers before they could sue and demand a jury trial. This would have saved Texan businesses millions of dollars. When the Legislature deadlocked on the issue, Bo Pilgrim, one of the biggest Republican contributors and owner of Pilgrim's Pride Corporation (which at this time was the largest poultry processing firm in the United States), went to the state Senate and handed out $10,000 checks to nine legislators. Only one would cash the check. No immediate action could be taken as no laws existed to punish Pilgrim or the legislator because the contributions had been public and reported. The speaker of the Texas House, Gib Lewis, was also caught accepting lobbyist money from a law firm, including the payment of his tax bills. It was time for a change. These two events started a series of reforms in the next legislative session. Several bills passed that mandated reporting all gifts and contributions and that limited the amount lobbyists could spend on lobbying. New laws obligated lawmakers to reveal their business holdings and dealings to ensure lawmakers did not personally benefit from the policies they put into place. Most importantly, the Texas Ethics Commission was established.

Source: https://commons.wikimedia.org/wiki/
File:HoustonStateOfficeBuilding.JPG

FIGURE 5.6 Sam Houston State Office Building

The Texas Ethics Commission

The Texas Ethics Commission—headquartered in the Sam Houston State Office Building in Austin, Texas **(Figure 5.6)**—was created in 1991 and has become the most powerful agency dealing with interest groups' lobbying and campaign activity. The commission has eight members appointed by the governor, the lieutenant governor, and the speaker of the House. No more than four can be

FIGURE 5.7

Purpose and Rules of the Texas Ethics Commission

It collects and maintains all campaign fundraising and expenditure records.

It collects and maintains all records of political lobbying activities.

It collects and maintains all the financial records of elected state officials.

All lobbyists who receive a salary of more than $1,000 and spend more than $500 (including gifts such as meals, sports tickets, etc.) in a three-month period on lobbying must register as a lobbyist with the state.

All registered lobbyists must file reports on their compensation; they do not have to list actual amounts but must instead put their salaries into salary range categories.

Lobbyists cannot contribute money thirty days before the start of the Legislature or twenty days after the session ends.

Lobbyists who spend more than $114 on behalf of an elected officeholder must report this expenditure.

Any gift over $50 must be reported and no more than $500 can be spent on gifts annually per office holder.

Only non-cash items of less than $50 can be accepted.

No honoraria or other compensation for speaking events can be accepted.

Elected officials cannot solicit money or employment.

---

of the same party. The Texas Ethics Commission has powers such as collecting and maintaining campaign fundraising records and financial records of elected state officials, and enforces a number of financial rules rules for lobbyists and officials **(Figure 5.7)**. Depending on the violation, the commission can impose fines as high as $10,000, and some violations have resulted in a misdemeanor or in a second-degree felony. Six of the eight members of the Texas Ethic Commission have to agree to impose a fine.

Finally, the Texas Ethics Committee can recommend salaries for legislators, but they must be approved by the voters.

Texas also requires a **full disclosure** for public officials with a financial interest in businesses. Public officials are required to annually report their personal, financial, and business dealings. The idea behind disclosure laws is sound. Policymakers vote on bills that could affect their business holdings, and the state and the public have a right to know how they vote to ensure our office holders do not vote for policies for their personal benefit.

A Theory Explaining Policymaking

One of the best ways to study interest group politics is presented in the book *American Government* by James Q. Wilson **(Figure 5.8)**.[23]

In his work, Wilson tries to predict when interest groups will become active in politics and what other political players might get involved in making policies. Wilson claims that whenever policy is made, the following groups might become active: the media, interest groups, the executive (president or governor), the Legislature, and even the judiciary and the bureaucracy. The final player is the public itself, as expressed via public opinion.

Depending on the issue, all of the above or only two or three players will participate, which determines what type of policies will be implemented. To predict which players will become involved in policymaking, one must study a specific policy's costs and benefits. In other words, we analyze who has to pay for a policy and who actually benefits from the policy. Cost-benefit studies can be further broken down into distributed and concentrated aspects. Distributed refers to everybody paying for or benefitting from a policy. Concentrated refers to only a few paying for or benefitting from a specific policy. After combining all of the above into a policy model, four possible types of politics involving various actors emerge:

https://commons.wikimedia.org/wiki/File:James_q_wilson.jpg

FIGURE 5.8 James Q. Wilson

Majoritarian politics: Everybody pays and everybody gains in majoritarian politics, so benefits and costs are distributed through our society. Therefore, all of the above-mentioned actors, including interest groups, are involved in policymaking. A good example of majoritarian politics at the national level is social security. The public, especially the elderly, become concerned when social security rises to the forefront, so they participate in politics. The media brings the issue to the public's attention, and then interest groups, such as the American Association of Retired People (one of the most powerful interest groups in the United States and in Texas), become active. Congress and the president then actively react to the issue. The judiciary gets involved if lawsuits result, and the bureaucracy must implement any new or changed policies.

Interest-group politics: As the term implies, interest groups are the major players in this type of politics where benefits and costs are concentrated. In other words, only a few people pay and only a few people benefit. The involved players include interest groups, the Legislature, the executive, and the bureaucracy. The public and the media usually stay out of interest-group politics because the issue is unimportant to average Texans, so the media feels no need to cover it. Thus, interest groups can operate behind the scenes. The best example of interest-group politics involves two interest groups fighting over one issue. For example, the oil and the ethanol industries both have well-organized interest groups and lobby heavily at the national and state level. The ethanol industry has long attempted to include more ethanol in gasoline, which would increase their production and sales. The fossil fuel industry, on the other hand, would like to increase their sales by including less ethanol in gasoline. So, both interest groups battle in front

uttyler.edu

of state legislatures and in front of Congress to push for their narrow interests. One wins and the other loses, but most Texans do not care about this and will not be impacted by the end result. Therefore, interest-group politics are battles fought behind the scenes without public involvement.

Client politics: Client politics involve distributed costs and concentrated benefits. In other words, a few benefit, and all have to pay for it. This type of politics involves interest groups pushing for added benefits, and the Legislature and the executive passing legislation that benefits interest groups. Not surprisingly, the bureaucracy must implement any policy changes. A good example would be Texas's dairy industry. Dairy products in the United States and in Texas are subsidized by the federal government. The federal government pays dairy farmers more than their goods are worth, which results in an overproduction of dairy products in the United States. The cost of these subsidies is passed on to U.S. consumers. The cost is so small, about a quarter for a gallon of milk, that the public will not complain, and the media will not cover it. So, everyone pays a little more for dairy products than they should, but the costs are so small that no one complains. The dairy industry, however, benefits handsomely from this policy.

Entrepreneurial politics: The last type of group politics is entrepreneurial politics. One person, the entrepreneur, focuses on a specific issue that he or she brings to the public's attention via the media. The public then gets concerned and demands action. Here, the legislative and executive respond to the public's demands. These types of policies usually involve all the political players, and the public benefits while one specific group bears the costs. Therefore, entrepreneurial politics include distributed benefits and concentrated costs. Interest groups become involved because they must bear the cost of the public's policy demands. Seat-belt laws provide a great example of this type of politics. After the public discovered via the media how many lives seat belts could save, it demanded action. Congress and the president acted, laws were passed, and seat belts became mandatory. The auto industry (interest group) fought the new laws tooth and nail because they had to bear the costs of installing seat belts in automobiles. In the end they lost and seat belts had to be put into every car beginning in 1968.

Why employ Wilson's typology of politics? His model's great benefit is allowing students of public policy to predict which political actors will be involved in policymaking by conducting a cost-benefit analysis of a specific policy. This knowledge allows us to explain and, more importantly, predict how policy is made, who is involved in making it, and who benefits and pays for a specific policy.

Conclusion

Since the creation of the republic, political scientists have debated whether interest groups contribute to democracy or hurt democracy. Pluralists accept that interest groups compete for political benefits and ultimately balance each other out, but elite theorists take the opposite view. According to them, certain groups are so much more powerful and have more resources than other interest groups that they are more likely to prevail on most major issues that concern them. In turn, powerful interest groups could benefit more than smaller ones, which are often public-interest groups. This imbalance will hurt democracy by underrepresenting the majority. The solution seems to be using the public politics model outlined above. Using this model, we can determine when interest groups are the most active and which groups are most likely to prevail in public policymaking. This model can then answer whether pluralism or elite theory is the best fit for explaining a specific policy.

Key Terms

Astroturf lobbying: this variation of lobbying involves interest groups spending monies to create the appearance of public support for their agenda.

Coalition lobbying: two or more interest groups pool their financial and contact resources and work together to attain a specific public-policy goal.

Dark money: money raised by nonprofit or 501(c) 4 and 501(c) 6, organizations. These organizations do not have to report their sources of funding or the amount of their donations.

Electioneering: interest groups attempt to influence who gets elected to public office by supporting candidates running for office.

Elite theory: a theory that a few powerful interest groups will consistently prevail in public policymaking, often at the expense of the majority.

Grassroots lobbying: interest groups encourage the public to support their demands, which facilitates their attempt to influence policymaking.

Grasstop lobbying: interest groups attempt to get a few select but very prominent people in the community to contact lawmakers in support of their policies.

Independent expenditures: monies spent on behalf of candidates by interest groups, without coordination with the candidates or with their campaigns.

Interest aggregation: the act of joining like-minded citizens to acquire political power.

Interest group: an organization that seeks to influence public policy.

Lobbying: usually defined as contacting members of the legislative, executive, or judicial branches of government in an attempt to influence policy or administrative decisions.

Pluralism: a theory that public policy should be made by competing interest groups to ensure that no single interest group will prevail all the time.

Political action committees (PACs): interest groups must create these committees to collect and spend money on candidates and on political campaigns.

Soft money: unlimited raising and spending of monies; soft money cannot be spent on specific candidates but rather on political party activities, such as party building and advertising.

Super PACs: independent organizations that raise and spend unlimited monies solicited from individuals, corporations, and unions. These monies are spent to either help or defeat candidates, but cannot be directly given to political candidates and/or their campaigns.

Texas Ethics Commission: The Texas Ethics Commission, an eight-member commission, was established on November 5, 1991, by the state's voters via constitutional amendment.

ENDNOTES

[1] https://comptroller.texas.gov/about/media-center/infographics/2017/budget-certification/

[2] De Tocqueville, Alexis. (2002). Democracy in America. Chicago, Illinois: University of Chicago Press.

[3] Truman, David. B. (1951). The Governmental Process-Political Interests and Public Opinion. New York, NY: Alfred A. Knopf.

[4] Aarp.com

[5] https://www.opensecrets.org/pacs/lookup2.php?strID=C00030718

[6] https://www.transparencytexas.org/pacs-have-political-tribes-too/

[7] Ibid.

[8] A Closer Look: Top 10 PACs of the 2018 Election Season. (December 11, 2018). Retrieved from https://www.transparencytexas.org/a-closer-look-top-10-pacs-of-the-2018 election-season/

[9] Ibid.

[10] Ibid.

[11] Ibid.

[12] Ibid.

[13] Ibid.

[14] Ibid.

[15] Ibid.

[16]Ibid.

[17]Ibid.

[18]Ibid.

[19]Ibid.

[20]http://info.tpj.org/reports/pdf/
Oldest2013WithCover.pdf

[21]Texas Ethics Commission Annual Reports

[22]https://www.salary.com/research/salary/
benchmark/lobbyist-salary/tx

[23]Wilson, James Q. (2017). American Government:
Institutions and Policies, Brief Version Boston:
MA, Cengage.

6

The House of Representatives chamber
at the capitol building in Austin, Texas.

Chapter 6

The Texas Legislature

FRENCH-CUBAN AMERICAN ESSAYIST, ANAÏS NIN, WROTE, "we don't see things as they are, we see them as we are."[1] Nin observed that people tend to understand and see things from their own individual points of view. She illustrated this human tendency toward distinctive perceptions in a passage in which two characters named Lillian and Jay react very differently to the Seine River in Paris, France. Lillian and Jay "see" the Seine very differently. Lillian sees the river as "silky grey, sinuous and glittering," and Jay sees the very same river as "opaque with fermented mud, and a shoal of wine bottle corks and weeds caught in the stagnant edges."[2] Each individual holds her or his own perspective. So, it is in politics and policymaking. We tend to see issues and concerns not as they are, but as we are. Only seeing the river as opaque mud with stagnate edges and failing to include Lillian's perspective of a beautiful silky grey river would be to miss something critical. For that reason, many humans have decided that it is necessary to include many people and many perspectives in governing and policymaking. Legislatures and parliaments are an attempt to include many voices in governing societies. A *legislature* is a lawmaking body. One hundred and eighty-one people serve in the Texas Legislature. As you read this chapter about the Texas legislature, ask yourself: "Whose point of view is being represented and who might we need to include?"

Photo by Robert Sterken

FIGURE 6.1 Capitol building in Austin, Texas

Does the election of more people of color and or women mean that people of color or women will be better represented? Should the gender, racial, and/or socioeconomic background of legislators reflect the population they represent? Some argue that elected representatives tend to represent the interests of their gender, race, and socioeconomic group. Political scientists call this descriptive representation. From a descriptive point of view, representatives tend to see and interact with politics and policy through their own unique perspective and tend to act in the interest of people like them. Perhaps a representative's gender, background, and perspective have little to do with their decision making. In substantive repsentation a legislator makes decisions based on political party agenda and personal views. A legislator's gender or background matter little and the representative may effectively represent the interests of those unlike him. In other words, men could effectively represent the views of women. However, political scientists have discovered that the number of women in a legislature has a significant and positive impact in terms of policy ramifications.[3] As the numbers of women serving in legislatures across the United States have slowly increased, so has the body of evidence that these increases have policy ramifications. Since Nevada seated the nation's first majority-female state legislature in January 2019, the once male dominated lawmaking body has been shaken up by the perspectives of female lawmakers. Bills prioritizing women's health and safety have soared to the top of the agenda and policy debates long dominated by men, including prison reform and gun safety, are yielding to female voices. In the 2019 session, more than 17 bills were introduced to address issues like sex trafficking, sexual misconduct, equal pay, and child marriage.[4]

Who should we include in governing and decision making in Texas? What perspectives should be included? Who should hold power and how should we be governed? These fundamental questions are at the center of this chapter and are among the most fundamental questions facing all societies. Should the citizens of Texas hold the ultimate power to decide who gets what, when, and how in their society? Should the citizens of Texas get to decide the actions (inactions), scope, and purpose of their government? If so, then how will the people of Texas govern themselves and who will be included in that governing?

We Americans (and Texans) have decided that the best way to include many voices and perspectives, and to govern ourselves is through a representative or participatory democracy. The first words of the United States Constitution — *"We, the People"* — clearly point to the intended source of power in the United States. The people are to be sovereign and hold the power over their own lives. In a participatory democracy the citizens hold the power to make policy decisions and must participate in governing their society. Participatory democracy is not a direct democracy. In a direct democracy, citizens are directly responsible for making policy decisions. In a participatory democracy, citizens influence policy decisions by voicing their opinions and, most importantly, by voting for political leaders who are then responsible for implementing those opinions and policy choices. A participatory democracy only works if citizens participate and if representatives follow the choices of the citizens. In a participatory democracy it is important, even critical, that those who are elected actually represent

FIGURE 6.2 The Texas Senate chamber

the people. Representation of all (or even most) of the people of a state as large and diverse as Texas requires a complex set of rules that foster inclusive participation in governing. The Texas Constitution established the Texas Legislature and its governing rules in order to create a structure that would allow citizens to participate and influence policy decisions for all.

The Legislature in Texas

After achieving statehood in 1845, Texans elected eighty-six men, twenty senators and sixty-six representatives, to meet in the first regular session of the Texas Legislature from February 16 to May 13, 1846. Texans elected eighty-six men to make the rules for their society. The Texas Legislature (called the "Lege" by insiders) is a **bicameral legislature**, meaning that it is made up of two chambers or houses, such as a house of representatives and a senate. A chamber is the place in which the senate or house of representatives meet and is also a generic way to refer to the senate or house of representatives. The two chambers of the Texas Lege are called the Texas House of Representatives and the Texas Senate **(Figure 6.2)**. The Senate is the upper chamber and the House is the lower chamber of the Texas Legislature. The Texas Legislature meets in regular sessions beginning in January of every odd-numbered year for not more than 140 days. A session is the meeting or the convening of the Texas Legislature.

The central function of the Texas Legislature (and any legislature) is to make laws and represent the will of the people. It is important to note that the law enacted by the Texas Lege is a social construction (society created) that reflects the makeup of the existing power structure in Texas. The existing power structure in Texas society is reflected in the Texas Legislature and uses that institution to codify its values and norms to shape and control society.

Bicameral legislature: *is a legislature that is comprised of two chambers or houses, such as a house of representatives and a senate.*

FIGURE 6.3 **Capitol building in Austin, Texas**

Laws passed (or not) by the Lege serve to control (or not) the Texas society. The laws passed by the Lege are the rules of Texas and dictate everything from the number of courses a Texas college student must take and can drop (six), to the age you must be to buy and drink beer, to the taxes you pay, to the vaccinations you must have to enter a Texas college, to the annual inspections and the safety features on your car, and even to the foods you eat. It is hard to overestimate the direct and immediate impact that the Texas Legislature has on the everyday life of the people of Texas.

The Texas Lege not only creates law but holds the power (granted by the Texas Constitution) to make sure that those laws are being followed. The Lege holds the oversight power to review, monitor, and evaluate Texas state agencies, programs, activities, and law implementation. In short, the Lege has the power to make sure that the laws it passes are being followed. To exercise this oversight function, the Texas House and Senate regularly hold committee hearings to investigate the work and actions of the executive agencies. A **hearing** is an official gathering of a group of legislators to discuss and debate legislative business.

Hearing: a hearing is an official gathering of a group of legislators to discuss and debate legislative business.

Structure of the Texas Legislature

The Texas House of Representatives is made up of 150 members who are elected by Texas voters from single districts for two-year terms. A district is the specific geographic region represented by a member of the legislature. Texas House of Representatives meet to debate and make laws in the west wing of the Texas Capitol **(Figure 6.3)**. The House of Representatives is known as the lower chamber of the Texas Legislature. The Texas Constitution requires that a House member must be at least twenty-one years of age,

a citizen of Texas for two years prior to election, and a resident of the district from which elected one year prior to election.

The Senate is made up of thirty-one senators who are elected by Texas voters from single districts to meet in the east wing of the Texas Capitol (Figure 6.3) to debate and make law. In order to be eligible for office, a senator must be at least twenty-six years of age, a citizen of Texas five years prior to election, and a resident of the district from which elected one year prior to election. Each senator serves a four-year term.

How a Bill Becomes a Law in Texas

The Texas legislative process is governed by the Texas Constitution and by the rules of procedure of the Texas Senate and Texas House of Representatives that are adopted at the beginning of a regular session by each respective chamber. Rules are the operating procedures for each chamber. In order to introduce a new law or policy, a lawmaker must introduce a bill. A **bill** is proposed legislation to be considered by a legislature. Legislation is a proposed or enacted law or group of laws. A bill may be drafted by a legislator personally, by an interested outside party, or, as is very often the case, by the professional staff within the legislature. See **Figure 6.4** and **Figure 6.5** for details of the legislative process.

Bill: is proposed legislation to be considered by a legislature.

Types of Bills in the Texas Legislature

There are three types of law or bills debated by the Texas Lege: local bills, special bills, and general bills. Local bills are bills that are limited to a specific geographical area of the state (e.g., local government units such as cities, counties, school districts, precincts, etc.). For example, in 2017, Texas Governor Greg Abbott signed House Bill 7 into law. HB7 allows property owners to offset municipal fees for removing trees on their land by planting new trees in their place. Special bills are laws directed toward a select, special individual or entity. For example, a law intended to apply to people who are blind but not to other people who have other disabilities. Finally, general bills are all other bills that apply generally across the great state of Texas.

The Texas Legislature is a very important center of power in the lives of almost everything in Texas. Here are a few bills introduced in the Lege in 2019:

House Bill 49, by Rep. Lyle Larson, R-San Antonio, would get rid of daylight-saving time in Texas. Texas lawmakers have tried to do this several times in past sessions but failed as HB 49 was left pending in committee at the end of the 86th legislative session.

House Bill 63, by Rep. Joe Moody, D-El Paso, would make it a civil offense — not a crime — to be caught with less than one ounce of marijuana. Mr. Moody's bill was one of several filed in 2019 that were intended to loosen marijuana laws in Texas. HB 63 received final approval in the House in a 103-42 vote but the companion bill (SB 156 in the Senate did not make it out of committee.

uttyler.edu

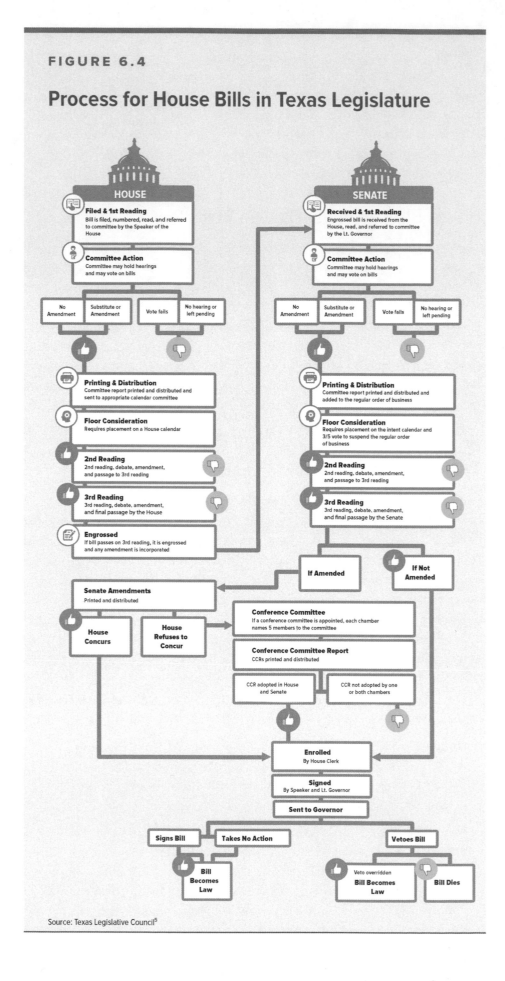

FIGURE 6.4

Process for House Bills in Texas Legislature

Source: Texas Legislative Council[5]

FIGURE 6.5

Process for Senate Bills in Texas Legislature

SENATE

Filed & 1st Reading
Bill is filed, numbered, read, and referred to committee by the Lt. Governor

Committee Action
Committee may hold hearings and may vote on bills

No Amendment	Substitute or Amendment	Vote fails	No hearing or left pending

Printing & Distribution
Committee report printed and distributed and added to the regular order of business

Floor Consideration
Requires placement on the intent calendar and 3/5 vote to suspend the regular order of business

2nd Reading
2nd reading, debate, amendment, and passage to 3rd reading

3rd Reading
3rd reading, debate, amendment, and final passage by the Senate

Engrossed
If bill passes on 3rd reading, it is engrossed and any amendment is incorporated

HOUSE

Received & 1st Reading
Engrossed bill is received from the Senate, read, and referred to committee by the Speaker of the House

Committee Action
Committee may hold hearings and may vote on bills

No Amendment	Substitute or Amendment	Vote fails	No hearing or left pending

Printing & Distribution
Committee report printed and distributed and sent to appropriate calendar committee

Floor Consideration
Requires placement on a House calendar

2nd Reading
2nd reading, debate, amendment, and passage to 3rd reading

3rd Reading
3rd reading, debate, amendment, and final passage by the House

If Amended

If Not Amended

House Amendments
Printed and distributed

Senate Concurs

Senate Refuses to Concur

Conference Committee
If a conference committee is appointed, each chamber names 5 members to the committee

Conference Committee Report
CCRs printed and distributed

CCR adopted in Senate and House

CCR not adopted by one or both chambers

Enrolled
By Secretary of the Senate

Signed
By Lt. Governor and Speaker

Sent to Governor

Signs Bill

Takes No Action

Vetoes Bill

Bill Becomes Law

Veto overridden
Bill Becomes Law

Bill Dies

Source: Texas Legislative Council[5]

FIGURE 6.6

Standing Committees in the Texas Senate Include:

Administration Agriculture

Business & Commerce

Criminal Justice

Education

Finance

Health & Human Services

Higher Education

Intergovernmental Relations

Natural Resources & Economic Development

Nominations

Property Tax

State Affairs

Transportation

Veteran Affairs & Border Security

Water & Rural Affairs

House Bill 84, also by Rep. Joe Moody, would repeal the section of the Texas penal code that lists "homosexual conduct" as a crime. The U.S. Supreme Court has already ruled that the section is unenforceable, but it remains on the Texas law books. Once a bill is filed it is referred to a standing committee for in-depth review and consideration. HB 84 died in committee.

The Committee System in the Texas Legislature

The actual work of the Texas legislature takes place in the committee and subcommittee rooms in the Capitol. A **committee** is a group of legislators appointed by the presiding officer (the officer who presides over a deliberative assembly) of the house or the senate to which proposed legislation is referred. Without committees and subcommittees, the work of the legislature would be impossible as more than eight thousand bills are introduced in the Texas Legislature each legislative session. In the months leading up to each legislative session, representatives and senators file hundreds of bills. While filing early gets a bill a low number, the lowest numbers are reserved for the House speaker and lieutenant governor (The **lieutenant governor** is the presiding officer of the Texas Senate and the speaker of the House is the presiding officer of the Texas House of Representatives), who assign those numbers to their top-priority legislation. In the Senate, the first bill in 2018 came from Senator Judith Zaffirini, D-Laredo. For many years, Senator Zaffirini has had her staff line up outside the clerk's office hours before prefiling starts in order to file the first bill of the coming session. In November 2018, Senator Zaffirini's staff filed the first piece for the 86th legislative session with Senate Bill 31, which was a bipartisan effort—eight senators signed on as authors, with Zaffirini at the top—to create a guardianship, abuse, fraud and exploitation deterrence program within the state Office of Court Administration. The first bill filed in the lower chamber was House Bill 21, authored by state Rep. Terry Canales, D-Edinburg. HB 21 sought to exempt college textbooks from sales taxes during one week in August and one week in January. According to John McGeady and Sarah Keyton of the Texas Legislative Budget Board, as introduced, HB21 would have had a negative impact of $67,690,000 through the biennium ending August 31, 2021.

Once the legislative session begins, bills are assigned to a **standing committee**. Standing committees **(Figures 6.6 and 6.7)** are permanent part of the working structure of the Texas Legislature and exist/stand session after session. Standing committees deal with all of the ongoing (year-in-year-out) issues that the Legislature faces. Standing committees are both the first and last places to which most bills go, as most bills never make it out of the committee to which they were assigned. The bills that are not voted out by a committee are considered "dead" for the session.[6]

Senator Zaffirini's SB31 and Representative Canales's HB 21 were both sent to standing committees for review, discussions, and hearings. SB31 was assigned to the State Affairs standing committee in the Senate and HB21 was assigned to the Ways & Means standing committee in the House. Each

FIGURE 6.7

Standing Committees in the Texas House Include:

Agriculture & Livestock	Insurance
Appropriations	International Relations & Economic Development
Business & Industry	Judiciary & Civil Jurisprudence
Calendars	Juvenile Justice & Family Issues
Corrections	Land & Resource Management
County Affairs	Licensing & Administrative Procedures
Criminal Jurisprudence	Local & Consent Calendars
Culture, Recreation & Tourism	Natural Resources
Defense & Veterans' Affairs	Pensions, Investments & Financial Services
Elections	Public Education
Energy Resources	Public Health
Environmental Regulation	Redistricting
General Investigating	Resolutions Calendars
Higher Education	State Affairs
Homeland Security & Public Safety	Transportation
House Administration	Urban Affairs Ways & Means
Human Services	

standing committee in both the House and the Senate have professional staff who support the members with research and bill-drafting and redrafting.

Senator Zaffirini's bill was voted on favorably by the State Affairs Committee Bill, passed the Senate and the House, and became law on September 1, 2019. Representative Canales's college textbook bill died in committee. The members of each standing committee read, research, amend, and vote (make a formal expression of a preference for a proposed resolution of an issue) on the proposed legislation.

If a bill is voted out of a House standing committee it is then referred to the **Calendars Committee** which schedules it for floor debate. Floor is the term used for the meeting place of either chamber for the conduct of legislative debate and business. Many bills are never set for floor debate and do not go beyond the Calendars Committee, giving the chair of the Calendars Committee significant power over legislation. A chair is a legislator appointed to preside over a specific legislative committee. The speaker of the house appoints chairs of House committees and the lieutenant governor appoints chairs of Senate committees. When a bill is finally approved by both houses, it is enrolled in final form, signed by the presiding officers of both houses, and sent to the governor.

Calendars Committee:
a committee which schedules a bill for floor debate.

uttyler.edu

In the Senate the intent calendar is a long list of bills that could come up for floor debate. A bill cannot pass the Senate unless it has been placed on the calendar. During the first 130 days of the session, Senate rules require a bill to stay on the calendar for two days before it can be debated, and senators must give daily notice to keep bills that don't get brought up for debate to stay on the calendar.

In the Senate (and in the House) a committee must vote to advance a bill for full debate. The bill is then placed on the "regular order of business," an ordered log of all the measures passed out of committee. The Senate has routinely placed what is called a blocker bill at the very beginning of its daily calendar. The blocker bill is introduced and passed through committee as quickly as possible, putting it at the top of the Senate's calendar, where it sits for the rest of the session. No other bill can be passed unless at least two-thirds (nineteen) of the senators agree to "suspend the regular order of business" and skip over the blocker bill. Because of the blocker bill, a piece of legislation can be placed on the intent calendar but not be debated because it does not have the nineteen senators needed to skip the blocker bill. The blocker bill fosters bipartisanship in the Senate by effectively empowering the minority party. In 2003, one Republican, Bill Ratliff (R-Mount Pleasant), joined with the Democrats to use the blocker bill to prevent Lieutenant Governor David Dewhurst from bringing a controversial redistricting bill to the Senate floor.

Texas Legislative Leadership

From the time the Texas Legislature first convened, in February 1846, the leadership and the members of that body have played a critical role in shaping the culture and norms of the Lone Star State. The two houses of the Texas Legislature are led by the lieutenant governor and the speaker of the House. These presiding officers are very influential and even critical to the governing of Texas. Every presiding officer of the Texas Legislature, starting with the first lieutenant governor, Albert Clinton Horton, and the first speaker of the House, William Edmond Crump, in 1846, has been a man. The leaders of the Texas Legislature have not only been all men, but except for Rodney G. Ellis, who was acting lieutenant governor from December 21 to December 28, 2000, they have all been white.

Forty-three men have served as lieutenant governor of Texas, twenty-seven of those men were lawyers, seven were businessmen, three were farmers/ranchers, three were in the newspaper publishing business, one was a medical doctor, one was in the military, and one, Bill Ratliff (Figure 6.8, 6.9), was an engineer.[7] Seventy white men have served as speaker of the Texas House of Representatives, thirty-seven of those men were lawyers, eleven were in business/banking/real estate, nine were in farming/ranching, six were in journalism/newspapers, three had lifelong careers in government, and one, James A. "Jimmy" Turman, was in higher education.[8]

Photo by Texas Senate used with permission of the Texas Senate Media Services

FIGURE 6.8 Lieutenant Governor Bill Ratliff

Photo by Texas Senate used with permission of the Texas Senate Media Services

FIGURE 6.9 On December 28, 2000, with his wife Sally holding Sam Houston's Bible, Bill Ratliff was sworn in as the fortieth Texas lieutenant governor by Chief Justice Tom Phillips.

The Lieutenant Governor

The lieutenant governor is the presiding officer of the Texas Senate and is one of the most powerful leaders in Texas government. The lieutenant governor is normally elected by a statewide popular vote to serve a four-year term of office. The lieutenant governor serves as president of the Senate but is not actually a member of that body. The Texas Constitution assigns to the lieutenant governor a dual executive and legislative role. The lieutenant governor must meet the same qualifications as the Texas governor and serves a term concurrent with the governor. In the event of the governor's death, resignation, refusal to serve, or removal from office, the lieutenant governor assumes the power and authority of that office.

The 2000 United States presidential election marked a milestone in Texas legislative history, for when the state's governor, George W. Bush, was elected president he set in motion an unprecedented chain of events in Texas politics.[9] The 39th lieutenant governor, Rick Perry assumed the newly vacated governorship, leaving Senate president pro tempore Rodney Ellis to fill the position of lieutenant governor until a new lieutenant governor could be elected by the Senate. On December 28, 2000, the thirty-one-member Senate held a secret-ballot vote, electing Bill Ratliff, state senator from East Texas, as the fortieth lieutenant governor and president of the Texas senate. Ratliff's election constituted the first time in Texas history that Senate members had elected one of their own to serve as lieutenant governor.

The Speaker of the Texas House

While the Texas lieutenant governor is selected in a statewide election, the speaker of the Texas House is chosen for the office by his (or her—no women have been chosen yet) peers in the House. The Texas Constitution states that the speaker of the Texas House is to be formally elected by the house of representatives from among its members every two years at the beginning of each regular session. The House speaker is a member of the Texas House of Representatives and, like any other representative, is a full voting member of the legislative branch. Unlike the lieutenant governor who is elected by Texas voters across the entire state, the speaker is elected to the Texas House from only one legislative district.

One of the most important powers of the presiding officers of the Texas Legislature is the handling of the introduced legislation. The presiding officers have enormous power over which bills make it to the floor for a vote and which ones die in committee. When a bill is introduced (or received from the opposite chamber) for consideration, it is referred by the speaker or lieutenant governor to a specific standing committee.

The lieutenant governor and speaker of the House hold significant power and control over law and policy, the operation of Texas government, and the larger Texas society. As presiding officers, they appoint committee chairs, assign and regulate the flow of legislation, and oversee the floor debate of legislation, and both hold enormous influence over not only which bills are

Source: Screengrab by author from Texas Legislature live video April 22, 2019

FIGURE 6.10 Dennis Bonnen, speaker of the Texas House of Representatives, 86th Legislature.

considered but also influence over one of the most important functions of the Legislature: taxing and spending. The presiding officers have the opportunity to influence many issues that personally effect the lives of all Texans. This might be a good time to rethink the question from the top of this chapter: "Whose point of view is being represented and who might we need to include?" You might even visit 📰 6.1 to find out who represents you.

Membership in the Texas Senate and House

The central function of the Texas Legislature (and any legislature) is to make laws and represent the will of the people. It is important to note that the law enacted by the Texas Legislature is a social construction (society created) that reflects the makeup of the existing power structure in Texas.

The Texas Constitution created a part-time citizen legislature and establishes the salary of legislators at $7,200 a year. A **citizen legislature** is a legislative body made up of representatives who have other full-time occupations and are not full-time legislators. The low pay and the part-time structure of the Texas Legislature was intended to foster the spirit of the 'citizen legislator' and promote a limited government.

Apportionment and Voters

Apportionment is the distribution of representation in a legislative body, especially the allocation of representatives based on population. **Reapportionment** is the redistribution of representation in a legislative body according to changes in the census figures. The 150 members of the Texas House of Representatives, like the thirty-one members of the Texas Senate, are elected from the districts that are approximately equal in population size, as required by the U.S. Supreme Court decision in **Reynolds v. Sims**. In this case, the United States Supreme Court held that, "an individual's right to vote for state legislators is unconstitutionally impaired when its weight is in a substantial fashion diluted when compared with votes of citizens living in other parts of the State."[10] With the *Reynolds v. Sims* decision, the United States Supreme Court mandated reapportionment, or the requirement that each legislator should represent approximately the same number of people.

This mandate became known as the **"one person, one vote" rule** and requires states to redraw district lines after each US census in order to maintain equal representation. Thus, every ten years, Texas and all other states in the United States redraw the boundaries of their congressional and state legislative districts after the census.

Redistricting

Every ten years when the federal government completes a census, the Texas Legislature uses that census data to redraw (called **redistricting**) the geographic boundaries for the districts of the Texas House, Texas Senate, and other elected positions. The US census in 2020 will again reshape Texas voter

📰 **6.1**

UTTyler.edu/TexPolBook

Enter your home address to find out who represents you in the state of Texas.

Citizen legislature: is a legislative body made up of representatives who have other full-time occupations and are not full-time legislators.

Apportionment: refers to the distribution of representation in a legislative body, especially the population-based allocation of representatives.

Reapportionment: reapportionment is the redistribution of representation in a legislative body according to changes in census figures.

Reynolds v. Sims: in this case, the United States Supreme Court held that "an individual's right to vote for state legislators is unconstitutionally impaired when its weight is in a substantial fashion diluted when compared with votes of citizens living in other parts of the State."

One person, one vote rule: the one person, one vote rule, requires states to redraw district lines after each U.S. census to maintain equal representation.

Redistricting: when the federal government completes a census every 10 years, the Texas Legislature uses that data to redraw (or redistrict) the geographic boundaries for the districts of the Texas House, Texas Senate, and other elected positions.

districts in 2021. There is a heated and protracted battle in the Texas Legislature every time the state's districts are redrawn.

The redistricting of Texas legislative districts may seem like boring inside-baseball level analysis, but it is anything but. The once-every-ten-year redistricting battle in the Texas Legislature is a monumental struggle for power in the Lege in which those who control the Legislature redraw the districts in order to best maintain control and power for the next decade. Whom Texas will send to Washington and Austin is very often decided by how the districts are redrawn. In short, the legislators redraw districts to select their voters. The way districts are drawn around specific voters will very likely shape the political, ideological, and even the ethnic makeup of the legislative body. It is important to note that the Texas Lege draws the districts for the US House of Representatives. The re-drawing of the districts in Texas has an important and critical impact on the ideological and political makeup of thirty-six seats of the total 435 representatives in the United States House of Representative. In the 2020 redistricting battle, members of the Texas House and Senate will in a very large part be shaping public policy in Austin and Washington for at least the next decade.

Drawing a district to give a certain political party or candidate an advantage is called gerrymandering. Very early in the American democracy, legislators realized the power in selecting those who vote by drawing district lines. In 1812, Governor Elbridge Gerry of Massachusetts wished to secure a Republican party majority and redrew a district in such a strange shape that a political cartoonist just added eyes and the features of a salamander and called it a **"Gerrymander."** In 2019, the shapes of many of the current Texas congressional districts are even stranger than that of the original gerrymander (for example see **Figure 6.11**).

Gerrymandering concentrates political power in the hands of specific voters and has a powerful effect on politics, policy, and our democracy. The influence of gerrymandering in the Texas and American political process has placed the core value of rule-by-the-people at stake.

Gerrymander: drawing a district to give a certain political party or candidate an advantage is called gerrymandering.

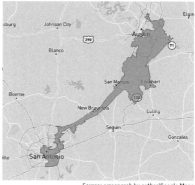

Source: screengrab by author/Google Maps

FIGURE 6.11 U.S House District 35

Selecting Texas Legislators

Selecting legislators with extreme partisan gerrymandering has led to a nationwide outpouring of bipartisan action. With another round of redistricting on the horizon, in 2021, many states are considering redistricting reforms—taking that power from their state legislators. One important way to reshape the power of gerrymandering is to create an independent, **nonpartisan redistricting commission** in each state. Citizens in Arizona in 2000 and in California in 2008 and 2010 demanded and created an independent commission to draw legislative district boundaries in a way that more accurately reflects the voters of specific communities and reduces the power of legislators choosing their voters. Since 2010, voters in Colorado, Michigan, Missouri, New York, Ohio, and Utah have also adopted changes to improve the redistricting process. In 2019, the citizens in Oklahoma are working toward creating an independent commission and in Texas there are six bills that seek to curb the effects of

Nonpartisan: describes an effort or entity free from party affiliation or designation.

Redistricting commission: an independent commission created to draw legislative district boundaries that more accurately reflect the voters of specific communities and reduce legislators' power to choose their voters.

gerrymandering. In 2019, Senator Royce West, D-Dallas, and Representative Donna Howard, D-Austin, have introduced HJR25, seeking a constitutional amendment to create a seven-member political appointee commission and the establishment of new redistricting criteria for congressional and state legislative districts that include a ban on partisan gerrymandering.

Geographic Districts in Texas

The redrawing of geographic districts for partisan advantage is undermining the very core of the intention of representational democracy. Extreme partisan gerrymandering undermines the core value that the people shall govern in several ways. First, the voters in gerrymandered districts do not make much difference, as the district has been created to dilute one party and elect another. Second, with no chance of winning in most districts, the party out of power is not able to recruit good candidates. Third, candidates from the party out of power cannot raise money or even interest its own voters in going to the polls. Fourth, the only elections that actually matter in a district that is gerrymandered are primaries, which makes the general election irrelevant. These four factors also lead to further political polarization.

In March of 2019, the United States Supreme Court once again addressed the question of partisan gerrymandering. Two cases before the Court were from Maryland, where Democrats drew new district lines to eliminate one of the state's two GOP seats in the U.S. House of Representatives, and from North Carolina, where it was Republicans who drew maps to strengthen their political power. In June 2019, the Supreme Court ruled that federal courts are powerless to hear challenges to extreme partisan gerrymandering. Chief Justice Roberts wrote for the majority, stating that the courts are not entitled to second-guess lawmakers' judgments. Speaking for the Court, the chief justice wrote, "We conclude that partisan gerrymandering claims present political questions beyond the reach of the federal courts."[11]

Demographics of the Texas Legislature

Again, as you read this section, ask yourself: "Whose point-of-view is being represented and who might we need to include?"

Does the sex, socio-economic background, ethnicity, or religion of the people who represent Texas in the Lege really matter? Does it make any difference if there are very few women or very few people of color? Does the Texas Lege need to be as diverse as the population of the state? Should the demographic characteristics of the members of the Texas Legislature reflect those of the Texas population? As noted in chapter one, Texas is a very diverse state, but a quick glance at the 2019 Texas House and Senate reveals that current representatives do not reflect the demographics of the general Texas population.

Members of the 86th Texas Legislature are significantly older than the people they represent. In the House, the median age is fifty while in the Senate it's 58. Again, the minimum age to serve in the Legislature is twenty-one. So, if we just look at the population of Texans who are twenty-one and older, we see that Texans ages twenty to thirty-four make up about 30% of the population, but only 3% of the 86th Texas Legislature. Texans ages thirty-five to forty-nine make up 28% of the general population but 39% of the 86th Legislature. Texans ages fifty and older make up 41% of the population but hold 57% of the seats in the Texas Capitol.

In 2019, in a state where people of color are in the majority, most Texas lawmakers are white. While about 42% of Texans are white, 64% of the men and women in the 86th Legislature are white. People of color remain significantly underrepresented in the Legislature.

In 2019, 50.4% of Texas citizens are females and 49.6% are males, but women only hold 23.2% of seats in the 86th Legislature. Thirty-four women serve in the Texas House of Representatives and nine women serve in the Texas Senate making up forty-two (23.2%) of the total 181 seats in the 86th Texas Legislature. Nationwide, women make up only 28.7 percent of all state legislators.[12] The first woman, Edith Wilmans, to serve in the Texas House was elected in 1923 and, in 1927, Margie Neal became the first woman elected to the Texas Senate. Since 1923, only 168 women have been elected to the Texas Legislature. Most women serving in the Texas Legislature are Democrats. In the 86th Legislature thirty-three women serve in the House—twenty-seven are Democrats and six are Republicans. Republican lawmakers control 102 seats in the Legislature but only twelve of those seats are filled by Republican women. According to the Texas Tribune, when House members were sworn in January 2019, there were more men named "John" than there were Republican women.[13]

Women in the Texas Legislature

More than a year before the Me-Too movement (or #MeToo movement)[14] against sexual harassment and sexual assault began in 2017, women who work in the Texas Legislature secretly created their own online network to document sexual harassment and assault in the Texas Capitol.[15] The group of women (including staff, reporters, and legislators) created a document titled the "Burn Book of Bad Men" that lists thirty-eight men along with specific accusations that run from pay discrimination, to creepy comments, and sexual assault. The document is evidence that there are far too many men and the "boys club" culture of the Texas Legislature has not changed since the 1980s and 1990s, when then-Lieutenant Governor Bob Bullock famously said that if Senator Judith Zaffirini, D-Laredo, would "cut her skirt off about six inches and put on some high-heel shoes," she could pass whatever legislation she wanted.[16] Of course, not every male in the Legislature or state government is a predator. There were many legislators about whom one would never hear a word of impropriety.[17] It is the women who have bravely said, "Me-Too" and the women and men who support them that have pushed a cultural change in the Texas Legislature and beyond. As the Me-too movement's success highlights, when women (and supporting men) speak and are heard, a consciousness raising cultural shift occurs. The "boys club" culture of any legislature begins to change when more women are elected and in sufficient numbers.[18]

What changes when more women are elected to a legislature? Political scientists have long sought the answer to this crucial question. Do women representatives govern differently? Do women bring a unique perspective to policymaking? A substantial and growing body of political science research has examined the legislative activities of men and women members of legislatures and parliaments around the world and found that the election of women does have a substantial and distinct impact on policymaking.[19] Studies show that women are more likely to understand the concerns of women, based on life experiences, and that they tend to prioritize policies that are important to women. Female legislators tend to view women as a distinctive part of their constituency and to advocate for women's interests.[20] Women legislators are far more likely to introduce legislation that specifically benefits women.[21] Studies of bill sponsorship show that women offer significantly more bills on issues related to women, children, and families. Women in legislature all around the world (far more than men) introduce feminist and women's rights legislation concerning family leave, equal pay, sexual harassment and assault, and reproductive rights. Women also offer more legislation on social welfare issues such as healthcare and education. In short, gender is a strong predictor of public policy that champions feminists' concerns.[22] Women tend to bring different policy priorities to a legislature. While it is clear that the election of women matters, research also indicates another critical factor. There must be enough women serving in a legislature to actually see a cultural shift in that legislature and to have a significant change in number of bills related to "women's interests." Political science scholars have shown that a legislature needs to be made of at least 30 to 40 percent women before the culture and the resulting legislation changes. In 2019, women hold just 23 percent of seats in the Texas Legislature. In short, the number of women serving in a legislature matters in that with enough women comes a presence and normalization of women's issues on the agenda.[23]

Many nations around the world have implemented a gender quota in order to increase women's legislative representation. The global spread of legislative gender quotas originated with the Fourth United Nations World Conference on Women, which was held in Beijing in 1995. Today many legislatures have a specific number of seats designated specifically for wome in order to address the legislative underrepresentation of women.

Occupation and Education of the Texas Legislature

Most Texas legislators—since the 1860s—have been upwardly mobile white males. Most are from long-established very wealthy Texas families. A quarter of Texans ages 25 or older only have high school diploma, but a vast majority of legislators have a college degree (Figure 6.12). Across the United States and in Texas, legislators generally have much higher educational attainment than the population they serve. In the Legislature—where roughly one out of every three lawmakers are lawyers—most have postgraduate degrees. Some professions, such as law, allow a person the time to devote to legislative responsivities every two years. Political science research shows that a legislator's occupation influences their policymaking more than their education does. And what they do for a living ranges greatly by how much they are paid in the legislature, when they are in session and the main industries in their state.

How Members Make Decisions

Texans (Americans) generally support and place a high value on the ideas of self-government and democracy. While Texans expect their government to be responsive and responsible to the people of the state, many are not familiar with how it all works in the halls in Austin. Many Texans view government with feelings of cynicism, distrust, and in negative terms. The government is often seen as contentious and unresponsive. Understanding the structure and functions of the Texas government is critical for not only the citizens but also the survival of democracy.

As noted above, Texans live in a representative democracy. In a representative democracy, citizens are elected to represent their fellow citizens in governing. The people represented by an elected lawmaker are called constituents. A **constituent** is a citizen residing in the district of an elected official. The representative citizen is directly involved in policymaking and takes on the responsibility of acting on behalf of those who elected her to the position. She is directly responsible to the people and represents the people. The people's representative acts directly in the lawmaking processes in studying policy concerns, creating solutions, drafting laws, and pushing them toward adoption. In short, in a representative democracy, the citizen representatives take care of the governing processes for the citizens.

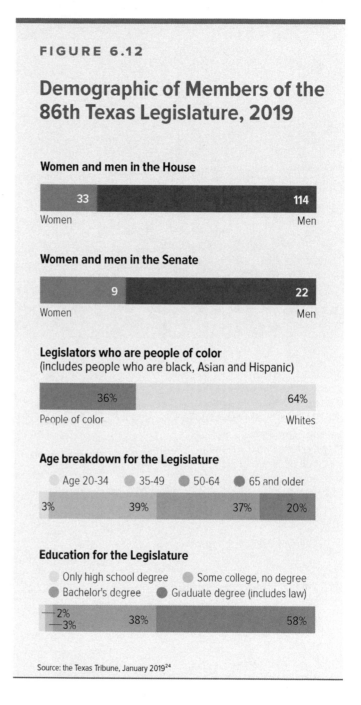

FIGURE 6.12

Demographic of Members of the 86th Texas Legislature, 2019

Women and men in the House

33	114
Women	Men

Women and men in the Senate

9	22
Women	Men

Legislators who are people of color
(includes people who are black, Asian and Hispanic)

36%	64%
People of color	Whites

Age breakdown for the Legislature

Age 20-34 ● 35-49 ● 50-64 ● 65 and older

3%	39%	37%	20%

Education for the Legislature

Only high school degree ● Some college, no degree
● Bachelor's degree ● Graduate degree (includes law)

| 2% | 38% | 58% |
| 3% | | |

Source: the Texas Tribune, January 2019[24]

Members of the Texas Lege must combine and balance the often-competing roles of law and policymaker with the duties of acting as a representative of the people of their district, political party, and sometimes even race, ethnicity, and gender. Political theorists explain that citizen representatives typically tend to take on the responsibility of governing (making policy decisions) in one of four different roles. The representative will act as a delegate, trustee, partisan, or a politico.

Constituent: *the people represented by an elected lawmaker are called constituents and reside in an elected official's district.*

CHAPTER 6 ★ THE TEXAS LEGISLATURE

133

FIGURE 6.12 Governor Greg Abbott signs the beer-to-go bill. Abbott is joined by Austin Beerworks owner Adam Debower (far right), bill sponsors Rep. Chris Paddie (seated left) and Sen. Brian Birdwell (seated right), along with representatives from the TACB and other legislators.

Delegate: citizen representatives serving as delegates see themselves as agents directly responsible for who elected them.

Delegate: Citizen representatives serving in the role of delegate see themselves as directly responsible agents of those who elected them. The representative who is serving as a delegate will speak, act, and vote based on how she believes the people who elected her would want. Delegates attempt to accurately represent the values, desires, and the will of the people they serve. For example, in May 2019, Matt Schaefer (R-Tyler) voted for HB 1554. HB 1554 included a "beer-to-go" provision that was strongly opposed by the Wholesale Beer Distributors of Texas, a large lobby group representing the interests of large beer distributors. Under the intense lobbying of the Wholesale Beer Distributors of Texas, the beer-to-go amendment had died in committee for six consecutive legislative sessions. The beer-to-go provision was supported by the Texas Craft Brewers Guild, which represents the interests of local craft breweries. Representative Schaefer's district, Tyler, Texas, has several small craft breweries. Unlike every other state, before the passage of "beer-to-go" **(Figure 6.13)**, Texas law prohibited customers from purchasing and taking home bottles, cans, and crowlers from craft breweries (operations that produced less than 10,000 barrels of beer annually). Acting as a delegate and directly representing the people of his district, Matt Schaefer voted "yes" to allow beer-to-go from the small craft breweries. State Senator Dawn Buckingham (R-Lakeway) said, "Our constituents elected us to be bold — and with that, I give you beer-to-go, baby."[25] Most Texans would like their representatives to take on the delegate role and act according to the will of the people. However, some representatives chose to act independently of those they represent.

Trustee: A citizen representative who takes on the role of trustee will speak, act, and vote based upon his own judgment. Each decision is decided on its own merits and according to the independent judgement of the representative. The trustee makes the decision based on what he feels is best for the people, not necessarily what might be expressed by the people. Knowing what is best for the people or even the will of the people is often unclear at best. Citizen representatives often represent large numbers of diverse populations. Not all decisions are good for all citizens. Sometimes a policy decision will be good for one subgroup of citizens and harmful to another. Sometimes the citizens will not know or care enough about a given issue to have an opinion. Thus, representatives often find themselves in the role of the politico.

Politico: The politico role is a combination of the delegate and the trustee roles. In the politico role the representative speaks, acts, and votes according to the will of the people — when that will is clear and known. However, without a clear mandate or clearly expressed public opinion, the role of the delegate is nearly impossible. When the people do not hold or express a clear expectation, the representative is then forced to rely on his or her own judgment and becomes a trustee. The citizen representative often finds that she is in the role of the politico as many citizens have neither the information, inclination, or interest in the wide variety of policy decisions she must make. Some citizen representatives find themselves in yet other roles: representing a specific political party or a subset of specific interests.

Politico: the politico role is a combination of the delegate and the trustee roles. In the politico role, the representative speaks, acts, and votes according to the people's will—when that will is clear.

Partisan: The citizen representative who acts as a partisan consistently speaks, acts, and votes along party lines, thus always or nearly always supporting their political party. These men and women make their decisions based on the party leadership and act not in the interest of those who elected them, but rather as loyal party members.

Partisan: citizen representatives who act as partisans consistently speak, act, and vote along party lines, thus always or nearly always supporting their political party.

In 2018, former Texas Lt. Governor Bill Ratliff provided Texas government students at The University of Texas at Tyler with yet another perspective on the way a legislator may make a decision. Governor Ratliff explained what he calls the **"mirror test."** As Ratliff explained to the students, "there were lots of votes in which it was unclear just what the wishes of my constituents might be, so at the end of the day I had to be able to look at myself in the mirror and live with the decisions I made." Using the "mirror test," Lieutenant Governor Ratliff acted as a trustee and voted using his best judgement.

Mirror test: as Governor Ratliff explained, "there were lots of votes in which it is unclear just what the wishes of my constituents might be, so at the end of the day I had to be able to look at myself in the mirror and live with the decisions I made."

Each of these roles tend to produce different answers about the decisions made by citizen representatives. In examining the votes made by citizen representatives, political scientists have grappled with some really challenging questions. Who do the citizen representatives *really* represent? Who *really* governs Texas? To what extent does the Texas Legislature actually represent the will of the people of Texas? Are Texas citizens sovereign, semi-sovereign, or largely powerless? These questions are critical and make up a significant part of the work of political scientists in the study of Texas and American politics. And once again it is important to ask, "Whose point of view is being represented and who might we need to include?"

Constituents and Representation

Do the opinions of Texas voters' matter in the Texas Legislature? Do the citizen representatives actually represent the residents of the Texas? The short answer to that question is mixed: yes, they do, on some issues and, no, they don't, on others. According to a March 2019 University of Texas/Texas Tribune Poll, the Texas Legislature is acting in sync with the people of Texas on some issues, like school finance, property taxes and teacher pay raises.[26] While on other issues—like "red flag" laws, vaccinations and sick leave—voters hold different opinions from those representing them in the Texas Legislature.

In 2019, The University of Texas/Texas Tribune Poll found that voters' thought public school funding and teacher pay were among the most important legislative issues. On the other hand, Texas citizen representatives indicated that problems in public education (low teacher pay, "not enough funding for the public school system as a whole," and "unequal resources among schools and school districts") were the most important issues of the 2019 legislative session.[27] The voters and their representative agreed on these big issues and the actions of the Texas Legislature seem to reflect that agreement. But on other issues there is not the same agreement.

A University of Texas/Texas Tribune poll found that after the mass shootings in 2018, at Santa Fe High School and Sutherland Springs Baptist, Texas voters roundly support "Red Flag" laws.[28] Red flag laws would allow Texas courts to take guns away from people deemed a danger to themselves and/or others. While a full 72 percent of Texas voters support giving judges that power, including 88 percent of Democrats, 60 percent of Republicans, and 65 percent of independents, the Texas Legislature has discussed everything from mental health to armed educators to metal detectors at schools, but not red flag laws. The University of Texas/Texas Tribune poll found very little support among the Texas representatives for the red flag laws.

There is a downside to a representative democracy — the fear that the representatives will not properly represent the citizens they serve. More generally, in Washington and across the states, political science research indicates that when the preferences of economic elites and the positions of organized interest groups are controlled, the preferences of the average American appear to have only a minuscule, near-zero, statistically non-significant impact upon public policy.[29] Professors Gilens and Page found that interest groups do have substantial independent impacts on policy, and a few groups (particularly labor unions) represent average citizens' views reasonably well. But the interest-group system as a whole does not. Political scientists are finding significant evidence that American citizen representatives do not represent the people but instead represent a very small number of wealthy people who shape public policy primarily to benefit themselves financially. This system of government is often called an "oligarchy." An Oligarchy denotes a small, often corrupt, ruling group. Gilens and Page argue that because policymaking is dominated by powerful business organizations and a small number of affluent Americans, then America's claims to be a democratic society are seriously threatened. On way to give the power back to the people would be to reign in the power of gerrymandering. Partisan gerrymandering contributes to a lack of competition. Across the United States, congressional races really aren't much of a race. The number of competitive House seats has been shrinking for years. The non-partisan Cook Political Report indicates that just twenty seats of the 435 seats in the House are competitive toss-ups for 2020.[30] In short, computer-modeling of voters and vote patterns has turned what once was a rather unrefined act of political mischief into a mostly precise art to fix the outcome of elections.

Throughout this chapter we asked, "Whose point of view is being represented and who might we need to include?" We learned the basic structure of the Texas Legislature and the fundamentals of the Texas House and Senate and how a bill is supposed to become a law. We examined the committee structure, rules, and hearings. We examined how the power is obtained and distributed and how older white men have thus become the dominant players in these structures and processes that make up the Texas Legislature. Gerrymandering has played a major role in determining: how the public votes for its representatives; who gets elected; how members represent their districts; the procedural rules governing policymaking, the degree to which the Texas legislature performs functions and most importantly the points-of-view and the type of policies that legislature produces or fails to produce. Since the Texas Legislature is dominated by businessmen, lawyers, and older Texans, beginning in the 1800s and continuing to the present day, this has meant both the passage of legislation that has benefited that specific subset of Texans at the expense of everyone else. These include tax breaks for corporations and the wealthy; limits on tort damage awards, reduced business regulations; the weakening unions and workers' rights; bankruptcy reform; class action reform and failing to adequately increase the minimum wage.

While the Texas Legislature is supposed to represent the will of all Texans, it very often fails to do so. As noted above, the Texas Legislature is not demographically representative of the state of Texas, but skewed by age, race, social class, and gender. Second, given the problems with gerrymandering, the Texas Legislature effectively selects its voters and disenfranchises many voters. Although women (23%) and people of color (36%) have made strides in the makeup of the Texas Legislature, obstacles remain. To move toward a full representative democracy, Texans need to promote greater equality and access when it comes to elections and campaigns, committee assignments, and presiding officer leadership roles, as well as reevaluate how specific interests hinder legislative policy outcomes that could benefit underrepresented groups.

Key Terms

Apportionment: refers to the distribution of representation in a legislative body, especially the population-based allocation of representatives.

Bicameral legislature: is a legislature that is comprised of two chambers or houses, such as a house of representatives and a senate.

Bill: is proposed legislation to be considered by a legislature.

Calendars Committee: a committee which schedules a bill for floor debate.

Citizen legislature: is a legislative body made up of representatives who have other full-time occupations and are not full-time legislators.

Committee: is a group of legislators appointed by the presiding officer (the officer who presides over a deliberative assembly) of the house or the senate; proposed legislation is referred to committees.

Constituent: the people represented by an elected lawmaker are called constituents and reside in an elected official's district.

Delegate: citizen representatives serving as delegates see themselves as agents directly responsible for who elected them.

Gerrymander: drawing a district to give a certain political party or candidate an advantage is called gerrymandering.

Hearing: a hearing is an official gathering of a group of legislators to discuss and debate legislative business.

Lieutenant governor: a statewide elected office who is the Texas Senate's presiding officer.

Mirror test: as Governor Ratliff explained, "there were lots of votes in which it is unclear just what the wishes of my constituents might be, so at the end of the day I had to be able to look at myself in the mirror and live with the decisions I made."

Nonpartisan: describes an effort or entity free from party affiliation or designation.

One person, one vote rule: the one person, one vote rule, requires states to redraw district lines after each U.S. census to maintain equal representation.

Partisan: citizen representatives who act as partisans consistently speak, act, and vote along party lines, thus always or nearly always supporting their political party.

Politico: the politico role is a combination of the delegate and the trustee roles. In the politico role, the representative speaks, acts, and votes according to the people's will—when that will is clear.

Reapportionment: reapportionment is the redistribution of representation in a legislative body according to changes in census figures.

Redistricting: when the federal government completes a census every 10 years, the Texas Legislature uses that data to redraw (or redistrict) the geographic boundaries for the districts of the Texas House, Texas Senate, and other elected positions.

Redistricting commission: an independent commission created to draw legislative district boundaries that more accurately reflect the voters of specific communities and reduce legislators' power to choose their voters.

Reynolds v. Sims: in this case, the United States Supreme Court held that "an individual's right to vote for state legislators is unconstitutionally impaired when its weight is in a substantial fashion diluted when compared with votes of citizens living in other parts of the State."

Standing committee: these committees are a permanent part of the Texas Legislature's structure and stand session after session.

ENDNOTES

[1] Nin, Anaïs. 1961. Seduction of the Minotaur. Swallow Press. The Swallow Press, Chicago, Illinois. page 124.

[2] Ibid.

[3] Numbers and Newness: The Descriptive and Substantive Representation of Women, by Karen Beckwith, Canadian Journal of Political Science / Revue canadienne de science politique, Vol. 40, No. 1 (Mar., 2007), pp. 27-49.

[4] First majority-female legislature pushing for change in Nevada, CBS NEWS June 1, 2019.

Retrieved from https://www.cbsnews.com/news/majority-female-legislature-pushing-for-change-in-nevada-2019-06-01.

[5] Texas Legislative Council. 2019. Retrieved from: https://tlc.texas.gov/publications#p-and-p-section.

[6] Hey, Texplainer: How do I know if my bill died? By Alex Samuels, The Texas Tribune, May 31, 2017. Retrieved from https://www.texastribune.org/2017/05/31/hey-texplainer-how-do-i-know-if-my-bill-died.

[7]See: Presiding Officers of The Texas Legislature 1846–2016. Several presiding officers had multiple occupations, so I selected the occupation in which they spent most of their professional life beyond elected office. Rodney G. Ellis served as acting lieutenant governor from December 21 to December 28, 2000, and has not been assigned a number by the Texas Senate as lieutenant governor, thus there are forty-three men but officially only forty-two lieutenant governors as of 86th Legislature in 2019. Ellis assumed the duties of the office when George W. Bush, was elected president of the United States, and served until the full Senate selected Bill Ratliff as the 40th lieutenant governor. Some historians count Ellis as 40 and Ratliff as 41, but the Texas Senate documents do not.

[8]See: Presiding Officers of The Texas Legislature 1846-2016.

[9]Sterken, Robert Edward. Bill Ratliff: A Profile of Courage and Leadership in American Politics. Lexington Books. 2016.

[10]See: 377 U.S. 533. Reynolds, Judge, Et Al. V. Sims Et Al. No. 23. Supreme Court of United States. Argued November 13, 1963. Decided June 15, 1964.

[11]Rucho et al. vs. Common Cause et al. No. 18–422. Argued March 26, 2019—Decided June 27, 2019.

[12]See: National Conference of State Legislatures Women In State Legislatures. http://www.ncsl.org/legislators-staff/legislators/womens-legislative-network/women-in-state-legislatures-for-2019.aspx.

[13]In Increasingly Diverse Texas, The Legislature Remains Mostly White and Male, by Alexa Ura And Darla Cameron. The Texas Tribune, January 10, 2019. Retrieved from: https://apps.texastribune.org/features/2019/texas-lawmakers-legislature-demographics.

[14]Amentahru Wahlrab, Sarah M. Sass, Robert Edward Sterken Jr. , (2019), The Need to Disrupt Social Control, in Cara E. Rabe-Hemp , Nancy S. Lind (ed.) Political Authority, Social Control and Public Policy (Public Policy and Governance, Volume 31) Emerald Publishing Limited, pp. 245 – 258.

[15]Women Expose The Secret Sexual Predators Inside Texas Politics. By Olivia Messer, The Daily Beast 11.07.17. Retrieved from https://www.thedailybeast.com/women-in-texas-politics-started-their-own-shtty-men-list-a-year-ago.

[16]The Good Old Boys in the Texas Legislature Still Haven't Learned How to Treat Women. By R.G. Ratcliffe. Texas Monthly, November 9, 2017. Retrieved from https://www.texasmonthly.com/burka-blog/good-old-boys-texas-legislature-still-havent-learned-treat-women/.

[17]Sterken, Robert Edward. Bill Ratliff: A Profile of Courage and Leadership in American Politics. Lexington Books. 2016.

[18]Tolleson-Rinehart, Sue, and Jeanie Ricketts Stanley. Claytie and the Lady: Ann Richards, Gender, and Politics in Texas. 1st ed. Austin: University of Texas Press, 1994.

[19]Dolan, J., Deckman, M. M., & Swers, M. L. (2017). Women and Politics: Paths to Power and Political Influence. New York: Roman & Littlefield.

[20]Poggione, Sarah. "Exploring Gender Differences in State Legislators' Policy Preferences." Political Research Quarterly 57, no. 2 (2004): 305-14.

[21]Carroll, Susan J. Impact of Women in Public Office. Bloomington: Indiana University Press, 2001.

[22]Swers, Michele L. Women in the Club: Gender and Policy Making in the Senate. Chicago: University of Chicago Press, 2014.

[23]Devlin, Claire, and Robert Elgie. "The Effect of Increased Women's Representation in Parliament: The Case of Rwanda." Parliamentary Affairs 61, no. 2 (2008): 237-54.

[24]In increasingly diverse Texas, the Legislature remains mostly white and male, by Alexa Ura And Darla Cameron, The Texas Tribune, Jan. 10, 2019. Retrieved from https://apps.texastribune.org/features/2019/texas-lawmakers-legislature-demographics.

[25]Senate moves to let breweries sell beer to go, make it easier to own several liquor stores, by Catherine Marfin, The Texas Tribune, May 22, 2019. Retrived from https://www.texastribune.org/2019/05/22/texas-alcohol-law-could-allow-brewery-beer-go-more-liquor-permits.

[26]Analysis: In step with Texas voters on some things, and out of step on some others. By Ross Ramsey, Texas Tribune. March 8, 2019. Retrieved from https://www.texastribune.org/2019/03/08/in-step-with-texas-voters-sometimes-out-of-step-others.

[27]Ibid.

[28]Ibid.

[29]Gilens, Martin, and Benjamin Page. "Testing Theories of American Politics: Elites, Interest Groups, and Average Citizens." Perspectives on Politics 12, no. 3 (2014): 564-81.

[30]See: The Cook Political Report, 2020 House Ratings, February 2019. Retrieved online https://cookpolitical.com/ratings/house-race-ratings.

7

Rotunda dome at the capitol building in Austin, Texas.

Chapter 7

The Executive Branch in Texas

AS THE STATE'S CHIEF EXECUTIVE OFFICER, the **governor** of Texas serves as the head of state and as the head of the Texas government. The governor of Texas implements state laws and oversees the operation of the Texas executive branch. The Texas executive branch consists of the governor, the lieutenant governor, the comptroller of public accounts, the land commissioner, the attorney general, the agriculture commissioner, the three-member Texas Railroad Commission, the State Board of Education, and the secretary of state.

Texas has had forty-eight governors, and only two have been women. Ann Richards was the first woman to be elected governor of Texas entirely in her own right.[1] However, Richards was the second woman to hold the office. Miriam Amanda Wallace "Ma" Ferguson was the first woman elected governor, but she clarified that she was a puppet candidate for her husband. She said voters would get "two for the price of one," and, in election rally speeches, she always introduced him before giving him the platform to speak.[2]

Ma Ferguson's husband, James Edward Ferguson Jr., was known as "Pa" Ferguson and served as governor of Texas from 1915 to 1917. After his reelection in 1916, Pa Ferguson vetoed the appropriations bill for the University of Texas

Governor: elected official who is the chief executive of the state.

FIGURE 7.1 Governor Greg Abbott (center) signed House Bill 3 during a triumphant ceremony on June 11, 2019, at Parmer Lane Elementary School in Austin.

Photo source: Miguel Gutierrez Jr./The Texas Tribune

uttyler.edu

at Austin in an attempt to close the university. Ferguson had long distrusted the university's faculty and administration and had repeatedly called the faculty "educated fools" and other demeaning names.[3] Governor Ferguson's veto was retaliation against the university because it refused to fire faculty members he found objectionable. Ferguson specifically wanted UT Austin to fire William Harding Mayes, the school of journalism's dean, and historian Eugene C. Barker. Mayes and Barker were vocal critics of Pa Ferguson. The Texas Senate disapproved of Ferguson's actions, impeached him, and prohibited him from holding a state office in Texas again. After her husband's impeachment and conviction, Ma Ferguson successfully ran for governor in his place in 1924.

Texas governors have often clashed with the University of Texas over issues of political interference and institutional autonomy since the university's establishment. Control (or lack thereof) of state colleges and universities—especially of UT Austin—is an excellent example of the Texas governor's formal powers and the limits of those powers. The Texas governor formally holds the power to appoint the Board of Regents that oversees Texas state colleges and universities, but that does not mean the governor can direct policy or interfere in those institutions' operations. In many respects, the office of Texas governor is, by design and by law, a weak executive because of the way the Texas Constitution divides executive powers.

Plural Executive

Plural executive system: *an executive branch in which power is shared among several elected officials who are independent of the governor.*

Texans live under a **plural executive system**; the executive powers are not given to the governor but are spread among several public officials who are independently elected and not controlled by the governor. Thus, the Texas governor is not as powerful as other governors across the United States. Many duties and responsibilities that typically fall under the governor's office in other U.S. states are not under the Texas governor's control.

In 1876, the Texas Constitution's authors severely limited the powers of future Texas governors. When drafting the constitution, the framers of Texas's foundational law considered Governor Edmund J. Davis, who was governor of Texas right after the American Civil War during the reconstruction period. Governor Davis was an ardent supporter of civil rights and freedoms for African Americans. Davis was a Southern Unionist, a general in the U.S. Army during the Civil War, and a vocal supporter of Texas Governor Sam Houston's stand against secession.

In the years right after the Civil War and the end of slavery in Texas, Governor Davis appointed many state leaders who supported civil rights for African Americans, created an African-American militia, and, in 1870, established the Texas State Police. Davis specifically charged the State Police with combatting race-based crimes. The new police force included African-American officers, which caused widespread protest from former slaveowners and segregationists. The State Police were described as "snakes, wolves, and other undesirable things," and were opposed, maligned, and vilified by most Texans. By 1873, Davis's State Police program was replaced by a renewed Texas Rangers force (see Chapter 1 for more on the Texas Rangers).[4] Notably, the State Police employed African Americans, but the Texas Rangers did not until late in the 20th century. Governor Davis's decisions and the powers he used to control the state were on the minds of those writing a new Texas Constitution in 1876, and they wanted to ensure that no future governor could control the state as Davis had from 1870 to 1874. So, they created a plural executive system and spread the Texas governor's powers across nine state officials.

The Plural Executive in Texas

The nine state officials with executive power are the governor, the **lieutenant governor** (see Chapter 6), the Texas attorney general, the general land office commissioner, the comptroller, the commissioner of agriculture, the railroad commissioner, the State Board of Education, and the appointed secretary of state **(Figure 7.2)**. As noted in Chapter 6, the Speaker of the House is also a significant part of the state's executive leadership. This chapter focuses on the governor but let us first acknowledge other officials with significant and important executive powers.

Lieutenant governor: statewide elected official who presides over the Texas Senate.

Texas Attorney General

As noted above, the men who drafted the Texas Constitution in 1876 made the Texas attorney general a statewide elected office independent of the governor. The Texas attorney general is accountable to the people of Texas, not the governor. Since 1836, zero women and 61 men have held the attorney general position in Texas.

The Texas **attorney general** functions as the state's lawyer, bringing lawsuits on behalf of the state, issuing legal opinions, representing the state in litigation, and performing other duties. As the state's chief legal officer, the attorney general protects state interests via judicial proceedings, legal advice, and written opinions. The Texas attorney general represents the state in Texas and U.S. courts.

Attorney general: elected official who serves as the chief lawyer for the state.

The Texas Constitution charges the attorney general with defending state laws and the state's constitution. Notably, that charge has allowed some discretion in how Texas attorneys general can fulfill the office's legal duties. Texas attorneys general have used the office's authority to aggressively pursue some policies and laws and disregard or only moderately pursue others.[5]

Commissioner of the General Land Office

The General Land Office was established in 1836 by the First Congress of the Republic of Texas shortly after Texas won its independence from Mexico. The Texas Constitution states that the **land commissioner** must "superintend, execute, and perform all acts touching or respecting the public lands of Texas." In short, the Texas General Land Office manages Texas's public lands, and its core mission today is to manage those lands and the mineral rights of about 20 million acres. Those acres include beaches, bays, estuaries, and other submerged lands up to 10.3 miles into the Gulf of Mexico; institutional acreage; grazing lands in West Texas; timberlands in East Texas; and commercial sites in

Land commissioner: elected official who is in charge of Texas public lands.

FIGURE 7.2

Executives of the Texas Government, 2019

Elected Executives

Governor	Greg Abbott (Republican)
Lieutenant Governor	Dan Patrick (Republican)
Attorney General	Ken Paxton (Republican)
Commissioner of General Land Office	George P. Bush (Republican)
Commissioner of Agriculture	Sid Miller (Republican)
Comptroller	Glenn Hegar (Republican)
Railroad Commission (three members)	Wayne Christian, Chair Christi Craddick Ryan Sitton
State Board of Education *(There are 15 State Board of Education members elected by Texans to four-year terms. Each member represents about 1.8 million Texans.)*	Donna Bahorich, Houston, Chair Marty Rowley, Amarillo, Vice Chair Georgina C. Pérez, El Paso, Secretary Ruben Cortez, Jr., Brownsville Marisa B. Perez-Diaz, Converse Lawrence A. Allen, Jr., Houston Ken Mercer, San Antonio Matt Robinson, Friendswood Barbara Cargill, Conroe Keven Ellis, Lufkin Tom Maynard, Florence Patricia Hardy, Fort Worth Pam Little, Fairview Aicha Davis, Dallas Sue Melton-Malone, Robinson

Appointed Executive

Secretary of State	vacant

urban areas throughout the state.[6] In 1854, Texas's founders created a public-school fund with a $2 million appropriation to support public education for Texas children. The 1876 Texas Constitution states that certain public lands and all proceeds from those lands go into the Texas Permanent School Fund. In 2019, the $44 billion Texas Permanent School Fund invests and spends money made from state lands. In managing state lands, the General Land Office leases drilling rights for oil and gas production on those properties to produce revenue and royalties that become the state's Permanent School Fund. While the General Land Office manages the property, Article VII § 5 of the Texas Constitution states that the State Board of Education manages the proper use of the Texas Permanent School Fund.

State Board of Education

In the years right after World War II, many Texans focused on public education. During the Great Depression and the war years, little to no funding left most Texas public schools in very poor condition—if they still existed at all. In 1947, Texas House Representative Reuben Senterfitt summed it up: "We have the worst education system that you could possibly have."[7] The task of rebuilding the Texas public school system fell to an East Texas senator, Alexander Mack Aikin Jr., and Texas State Representative Claud Gilmer. For his life-changing work of rebuilding Texas schools, Senator Aikin is known as the "father of modern Texas education."[8]

Passed in 1949, the Gilmer-Aikin laws made school a reality for many Texas children. The Gilmer-Aikin law created the Foundation School Program to fairly apportion state funds to local school districts. The Gilmer-Aikin laws also reorganized Texas public education's administration, created an elected State Board of Education that appointed an education commissioner, and reorganized the Texas Education Agency's administration of the state's public-school policies. Today, the State Board of Education sets policies and standards for all Texas public schools. The primary responsibilities of the State Board of Education include setting curriculum standards, reviewing and adopting instructional materials, establishing graduation requirements, and overseeing the Texas Permanent School Fund. The Texas governor appoints one member to chair the board, but the board itself is made up of members elected from single-member districts.

Comptroller of Public Accounts

The **comptroller** is the chief tax collector, accountant, revenue estimator, treasurer, and purchasing manager for the Texas government. The comptroller writes the checks and keeps the books for the multibillion-dollar business of the state government. The Comptroller is not under control of the governor but is elected by all Texas voters and serves a four-year term. The comptroller is the guardian of the state's fiscal affairs. All state agencies depend on the comptroller's office to pay their bills and to issue paychecks to state employees. Members of Texas Legislature rely on the comptroller's office for economic predictions, annual financial reports, and estimates of future state revenues. Estimating state revenues is one of the comptroller's more important powers.

Comptroller: elected official who directs the collection taxes and other state revenues and estimates revenue for the state budget.

Commissioner of Agriculture

Early Texas leaders largely ignored agriculture management across the state. The early Texas government did not even collect basic crop and livestock statistics until 1908. In 1907, legislators in the 30th Texas Legislature remedied this oversight by creating the Texas Department of Agriculture. The new

uttyler.edu

department would be headed by a statewide elected commissioner of agriculture, responsible for gathering farming and ranching statistics in Texas, publishing agricultural information, and holding farmer conferences to promote advanced farming methods and best practices.

Today, the Department of Agriculture plays a vital role in the lives of all Texans and beyond. The Texas **agriculture commissioner** gathers and shares information, and the office is a regulatory agency. The Texas Department of Agriculture (TDA) and the commissioner directly affect how Texas food producers work. For example, the TDA ensures that pesticides are applied safely, an important responsibility. TDA officials also inspect facilities like grain silos and warehouses for cleanliness and for proper food storage. The Department of Agriculture also certifies which Texas foods are organically produced.

The TDA also oversees weights and measures. When Texans purchase food at Trader Joe's or at Brookshire's grocery, they rely on the Agriculture Commissioner's consumer-protection division, which ensures that scales in stores accurately calculate the weights and prices of foods. The consumer-protection division's regulation of weights and measures also includes fuel sales at gas stations all across the state of Texas. The TDA regularly checks fuel pumps to make sure consumers get exactly the amount of fuel they pay for.

The agriculture commissioner also plays an important role in Texans' diets and food choices. In 2004, for example, Texas Agriculture Commissioner Susan Combs launched the Texas Public School Nutrition Policy, which banned certain unhealthy foods, deep fryers, and soda machines from cafeterias across the state. In 2015, the newly elected agriculture commissioner, Sid Miller **(Figure 7.3)**, used his first official act to grant full amnesty to soft drinks, cupcakes, cakes, pies, and brownies in Texas schools. At a press conference, with cupcake in hand, Commissioner Miller said, "We've been raising big, strapping, healthy young kids here in Texas for 200 years, and we don't need Washington, D.C., telling us how to do it."[9] Whether you are packing cupcakes for school, running a farm or ranch, shopping for dinner, or fueling up the car, the Texas Agriculture Commissioner affects the most ordinary aspects of your daily life.

Agriculture commissioner: elected state official who is responsible for agriculture, food, and rural matters.

Photo: The Texas Tribune by Marjorie Kamys Cotera

FIGURE 7.3 Texas Agriculture Commissioner Sid Miller declares cupcake amnesty at a press conference on Jan. 12, 2015.

Texas Railroad Commission

Despite the name, the Texas Railroad Commission's actions directly affect your life no matter where you live or if you use a train in Texas. The Texas Railroad Commission (RRC) is the state's oldest regulatory agency and one of its most powerful, and it is one of the most interesting state commissions in the United States. Three statewide elected officials, called commissioners, head the RRC regulatory agency. What do the RRC commissioners regulate?

On April 3, 1891, the Texas Legislature established the RRC to regulate rail rates and the operation of railroads, terminals, wharves, and express companies. The Texas Legislature originally created the RRC to combat corruption and monopolies in Texas rail transportation.

Early in Texas history, farmers relied almost solely on railroads to move their goods to markets; so, the men who ran the railroads often took advantage of those who needed to use the rails. As transportation changed from rail to roads, the RRC's focus turned to regulating the Texas oil and gas industry. The RRC's regulatory responsibilities expanded to include regulating oil pipelines in 1917, oil and gas production in 1919, natural gas delivery systems in 1920, bus lines in 1927, and trucking in 1929. It grew from twelve employees in 1916 to sixty-nine in 1930 and 566 in 1939.

The last remaining railroad-related responsibility—rail safety regulation—was transferred to the Texas Department of Transportation in 2005. Today, the RRC has no authority over rail transport in Texas. In 2011, the Texas Legislature considered, but did not pass, a bill (SB 655) to change the Railroad Commission's name to the Oil and Gas Commission. The RRC regulates oil and gas exploration and production and oversees natural gas and pipeline operations across the state.

One legendary RRC commissioner is Ernest Othmer Thompson, who served the RRC and Texans for thirty-two years from 1932 to 1965.[10] Thompson took charge of the RRC and, indeed, the worldwide oil industry by emphasizing Texas's role in regulating global oil production and pricing. At every opportunity, Commissioner Thompson promoted Texas oil and the idea that regulation would enhance, not hamper, the free market. Thompson, nicknamed "Mr. Petroleum," once quipped that "the civil religion of Texas is oil" and that this religion of oil was rooted in the historic vision of Texan independence.[11]

In 2019, the RRC operates in the small Texas community of Altair (west of Houston). For months, Altair's citizens complained that its beautiful waterway called Skull Creek was turning black and reeking of chemicals. The citizens say the source of the problem is obvious: an oil and gas waste-recycling facility near the creek owned by Columbus-based Inland Environmental and Remediation. The RRC ordered the facility to stop storing oil and gas waste in 2017. Although Inland has denied wrongdoing, the Texas attorney general is suing the company and alleging that it illegally discharged industrial waste into the creek and stored that waste without RRC's authorization. As of April 2019, the RRC is considering fining Inland for failing to plug an oil waste disposal well that was sealed last June. The state's lawsuit seeks monetary damages up to $1 million.[12]

Photo source: Miguel Gutierrez Jr. / The Texas Tribune

FIGURE 7.4 **Texas Secretary of State David Whitley, Governor Greg Abbott's appointee, failed to win a two-thirds vote in the full Senate.**

Secretary of State

On December 17, 2018, Texas Governor Greg Abbott appointed David Whitley (Figure 7.4) as the 112th secretary of state of Texas. The **secretary of state** acts as Texas's chief elections officer and protocol officer for state affairs and as a liaison for the governor on Mexican and border affairs. Whitley's appointment filled a vacancy left by outgoing Secretary of State Rolando Pablos but was ill-fated nearly from the beginning.

Unlike the eight other state leaders with executive power, the Texas secretary of state is appointed by the governor. The secretary of state oversees voting and elections across the state, so Mr. Whitley was in charge of increasing the number of registered voters, monitoring and securing elections, collecting election-night ballot returns from the many county judges and clerks, and making those results available to the media and the public. Within these duties, Whitley oversaw a botched review of Texas voter rolls that pulled Texas

Secretary of state: *state official who is responsible for overseeing elections in Texas and is appointed by the governor.*

FIGURE 7.5

Governors of Texas, 1874–present

Richard Coke	1874–1876	Miriam Ferguson	1933–1935
Richard B. Hubbard	1876–1879	James V. Allred	1935–1939
Oran M. Robert	1879–1883	W. Lee O'Daniel	1939–1941
John Ireland	1883–1887	Coke Stevenson	1941–1947
Lawrence S. Ross	1887–1891	Beauford H. Jester	1947–1949
James S. Hogg	1891–1895	Allan Shivers	1949–1957
Charles A. Culberson	1895–1899	Price Daniel	1957–1963
Joseph D. Sayers	1899–1903	John Connally	1963–1969
S.W.T. Lanham	1903–1907	Preston Smith	1969–1973
Thomas M. Campbell	1907–1911	Dolph Brisco	1973–1979
Oscar B. Colquitt	1911–1915	William Clements	1979–1983
James E. Ferguson	1915–1917	Mark White	1983–1987
William P. Hobby	1917–1921	William Clements	1987–1991
Pat M. Neff	1921–1925	Ann Richards	1991–1995
Miriam Ferguson	1925–1927	George W. Bush	1995–2000
Dan Moody	1927–1931	Rick Perry	2000–2015
Ross Sterling	1931–1933	Greg Abbott	2015–present

Source: Texas State Library and Archives Commission

into three federal lawsuits and prompted a congressional investigation over concerns of voting rights violations.

In 2018, Texas was granted $23.3 million as part of U.S. Congress's reauthorization of the Help America Vote Act to improve elections. Congress allowed the state to put the money toward election security enhancements, including replacing voting equipment, upgrading election-related computer systems to address cybersecurity vulnerabilities and funding "other activities that will improve the security of elections for federal office."[13]

Secretary of State Whitley used $121,000 of the funds from the Help America Vote Act to search Texas voter rolls for supposed noncitizen voters. Immediately, civil rights groups sued, claiming that the secretary of state's efforts violated the U.S. Constitution and the Voting Rights Act because they focused on voters of color and immigrants. A federal judge agreed and stopped the review over concerns that "perfectly legal naturalized Americans" were targeted while those born in the country were not.[14]

Whitley's office agreed to stop the review as part of a legal settlement to halt the litigation the state faced. Despite the settlement, Whitley was not confirmed as secretary of state because Democratic senators blocked his confirmation. Whitley resigned as secretary of state and went back to Governor Greg Abbott's office, where he was rehired with a $205,000 annual salary, according to the state comptroller's office.[15] At this writing, Governor Abbott has not yet appointed a replacement for David Whitley.

Qualifications for the Texas Governor

To become Texas governor, a candidate must meet some broad legal qualifications and, possibly, several informal and unwritten qualifications. Although the legal or constitutional qualifications are required by Texas law, the informal qualifications are not required. However, they are a long-established pattern for those elected to the office. For example, nearly all Texas governors have been men (See **Figure 7.5**). This is not a legal requirement, but only two of the forty-eight people elected to the office have been women. Being a man appears to be an informal qualification for the Texas governor. In the years to come, someone who does not meet the historical informal qualifications will probably be elected.

Legal Qualifications

Article 4 of the Texas Constitution requires that the governor of Texas, who is elected every four years by Texas voters, must (a) be at least thirty years old, (b) be a citizen of the United States, and (c) be a resident of Texas for five years immediately before the election. The legal requirements are few, but the informal qualifications are more limiting.

Photo source: Bob Daemmrich: The Texas Tribune

FIGURE 7.6 **Governor Greg Abbott**

Informal Qualifications

Greg Abbott (**Figure 7.6**) exemplifies each informal qualification historically held to win the office. Like Abbott, Texas governors have been white, male (except for two women, as noted above), Christian, middle-aged, politically experienced, and either personally wealthy or with access to wealth. Like Abbott, many Texas governors have been lawyers. Abbott was sixty-two in 2019 and served as the Texas Attorney General from 2002 to 2015.

As noted in Chapter 1, the Texas population is diverse, and women make up more than half of that population. In 2018, former Dallas County Sheriff Lupe Valdez (**Figure 7.7**) won the Democratic gubernatorial nomination in Texas. Valdez ran well ahead of Democratic opponent Andrew White in the primary, and her victory broke historic barriers as she became the first Latina and the first openly gay person to be nominated for governor by a major party in Texas.

The daughter of migrant farmworkers, Valdez grew up in one of the San Antonio's poorest neighborhoods. After high school, she went on to a earn college degree at Southern Nazarene University in Oklahoma and then earned a master's degree in criminal justice from the University of Texas at Arlington. After college, Valdez served in the U.S. Army Reserve and worked for almost thirty years as a U.S. Customs agent. She was ultimately elected as the sheriff of Dallas County. Valdez held only one of the informal qualifications

Photo source: Laura Skelding: The Texas Tribune

FIGURE 7.7 **Democratic gubernatorial nominee Lupe Valdez**

uttyler.edu

(Christian faith) traditionally held by successful candidates for governor. Valdez is not white, male, or middle aged, nor does she have extensive political experience. Further, she did not have substantial personal wealth nor access to wealth. Historically, nonwhite and female candidates have faced several major roadblocks to the governorship: experience, money, and race. At seventy years of age, Valdez faced an uphill battle against incumbent Greg Abbott, who had amassed more than $40 million for his reelection campaign—Valdez had raised only about $220,000.[16] With all of the traditional informal characteristics for the office and a mountain of cash, Greg Abbott easily secured a second term as the 48th governor of Texas.

Removal and Succession of a Texas Governor

Governor James "Pa" Ferguson is the only Texas governor to have been impeached and convicted. As noted above, Pa Ferguson was impeached in 1917 and removed from office. Ferguson had vetoed an entire appropriations bill for the University of Texas in 1916 and was indicted by the Texas House on nine charges, including misapplication of public funds, embezzlement, and the diversion of a special fund.

To impeach means to accuse or to indict. Article 15 of the Texas Constitution governs **impeachment** in Texas and notes that the governor and nonelected officials can be impeached; however, it is silent about the reasons for impeachment and only establishes the impeachment process. For a governor (or any state official) to be impeached, articles of impeachment must be brought forward by the Texas House of Representatives. If the House votes to indict or adopts articles of impeachment, the Texas State Senate must then sit as the court of impeachment.

If two-thirds of the senators present vote to convict, the governor is removed from office. The Texas Constitution states that when the governor's office becomes vacant via impeachment and conviction, death, resignation, or the governor's absence from the state, the lieutenant governor becomes the governor. In December of 2000, Texas Governor George W. Bush was elected president of the United States and resigned as the governor of Texas. Lieutenant Governor Rick Perry was immediately sworn in as governor. The Texas Senate was then forced to elect a new lieutenant governor. As noted in Chapter 6, the Senate elected Senator Bill Ratliff as the lieutenant governor.[17]

Impeachment: *the formal charge by the Texas House of Representatives that leads to a trial in the Texas Senate and possibly removal of a state official.*

The Governor's Compensation

The governor's salary and benefits are set by the Texas Legislature. In 2019, Governor Greg Abbott's annual salary was $153,750. Governor Abbott also receives millions of dollars in nontaxable income as part of a structured settlement resulting from a 1989 personal injury lawsuit following an accident that crushed his spine and left him a paraplegic. The Texas governor

FIGURE 7.8

Top Compensation for Office of the Texas Governor, 2019[19]

Name	Title	Compensation
Thomas D. Williams	Deputy Director III	$265,000
Luis J. Saenz	Deputy Director III	$265,000
Matthew J. Hirsch	Deputy Director III	$265,000
John D. Colyandro	Deputy Director III	$265,000
Jeffrey L. Oldham	Deputy Director II	$220,000
Sarah K. Hicks	Deputy Director II	$205,000
Jordan J. Hale	Deputy Director II	$205,000
David Whitley (see above)	Deputy Director II	$205,000
Walter C. Fisher	Deputy Director II	$198,000
Angela V. Colmenero	General Counsel V	$172,500
Peggy M. Venable	Director V	$164,701

also receives use of the state-owned governor's mansion, state vehicles, and state-owned aircraft.

For comparison, if Greg Abbott (who is a lawyer) were a partner in a top law firm in Dallas or in Houston, he would probably earn an annual salary between $3 million and $10 million, according to disclosed compensation records when top lawyers opted for a government position in the Trump administration in 2018.[18] Governor Abbott's salary is not even among the top 10 for the office of the governor (see **Figure 7.8**). Abbott pays his top staffers six-figure wages that exceed those paid in California, Florida, and other big states.

Formal Powers of Texas Governors

Although several officials lead the Texas government's executive branch, the governor holds important and meaningful political power. In recent years, Texas governors have learned to use legislative powers, media access, inside party politics, and appointment powers to make significant policy for Texans. Rick Perry, the longest-serving governor in state history, became very influential largely because of his long tenure. Perry was the lieutenant governor in 2000 and assumed the office of governor upon George W. Bush's exit, who resigned to take office as president of the United States.[20] With 14 years in office, Perry is the longest-serving governor in the United States. He was reelected in 2002, in 2006, and again in 2010. His fourteen years in office allowed him to dominate Texas politics and policy. He had appointed all of the administrative boards, university boards, and statewide commissions, and even shaped

uttyler.edu

legislator behavior.[21] One of the Texas governor's more important powers is directly appointing the women and men who supervise the state bureaucracy. Many of the most important decisions regarding Texans' daily lives are made by boards and commissions that are appointed by the governor.

Appointment power is the authority of the governor to select the specific people who serve on boards and commissions **(Figure 7.9)**. The Texas Constitution grants the authority to make governmental appointments to the governor of Texas. During a four-year term, a Texas governor will make about fifteen hundred appointments. Most appointments are:

- state officials and members of state boards, commissions, and councils that carry out the laws and direct the policies of state government activities;

- members of task forces that advise the governor or executive agencies on specific issues and policies; or

- state-elected and judicial offices when vacancies occur via the office holder's resignation or death.

The Texas governor appoints members to nearly 500 state boards or commissions that direct the daily operations of state agencies. These state agencies include the Texas Department of Health and Human Services, the Department of Transportation and Safety, the Higher Education Coordinating Board, and the University of Texas. Although the governor can use the appointment power to shape policy and law, the Senate must approve those appointments. The Texas Legislature only meets every two years, however, so an appointee often serves a substantial amount of time before the Senate convenes for approval. As illustrated above with David Whitley, the Senate does not always approve of the governor's appointment. An informal rule, known as **senatorial courtesy**, limits the governor's appointment power and gives some power to individual senators. Informally, the appointee's senator must approve the appointment—without regard to party affiliation—for the Senate to approve. If the appointee's senator does not approve, then the Senate will not approve. An appointee can be removed after approval, but the process is complex. The governor cannot simply fire the appointee, which is an important limitation on the governor's power.

The Texas governor appoints the regents who serve on the governing body for all state colleges and universities in Texas. The regents set the policies and rules for institutions. For example, the regents make decisions about the fees and tuition that students pay. Regents or board members are appointed by the governor and must be confirmed by the Texas Senate. The governor also appoints a student regent to each board for a one-year term. This appointment power gives the governor significant but, as noted above with Governor Pa Ferguson, incomplete power over all state agencies—including colleges and universities.

For nearly a decade, Governor Perry sought to change the operation, focus, and structure of the state's higher education system. Even after appointing boards of regents, Perry struggled to make changes he wanted. The president

FIGURE 7.9

Examples of Texas Governor's Appointment Power[22]

Economic Development
- Aerospace & Aviation Advisory Committee
- Texas Economic Development Corporation
- Economic Incentive Oversight Board
- Jobs and Education for Texans
- Product Development & Small Business Incubator Board
- Real Estate Research Advisory Committee
- Small Business Assistance Advisory Task Force

Higher Education
- Texas A&M University System Board of Regents
- Education Coordinating Board, Texas Higher
- Midwestern State University Board of Regents
- Stephen F. Austin State University Board of Regents
- Texas Southern University Board of Regents
- Texas State University System Board of Regents
- Texas Tech University System Board of Regents
- University of Houston System Board of Regents
- University of North Texas System Board of Regents
- University of Texas System Board of Regents

Public Safety
- Automobile Burglary & Theft Prevention Authority
- Texas Crime Stoppers Council
- Crime Victims' Institute Advisory Council
- Governor's Criminal Justice Advisory Council
- Emergency Communications, Commission on State
- Board of Pardons & Paroles
- Texas School Safety Center Board

State Oversight
- Criminal Justice, Texas Board of
- Education, State Commissioner of
- Environmental Quality, Texas Commission on
- Ethics Commission, Texas
- Health and Human Services, Executive Commissioner of
- Inspector General for Health and Human Services
- Insurance Counsel, Office of Public
- Juvenile Justice Advisory Board
- Library and Archives Commission, Texas State
- Military Preparedness Commission, Texas
- Motor Vehicles Board, Texas Department of
- Parks and Wildlife Commission
- Public Safety Commission
- Sex Offender Management, Governing Board
- Transportation Commission, Texas
- Veterans' Land Board
- Water Development Board, Texas
- Workforce Commission, Texas

of The University of Texas at Austin, Bill Powers, balked at his proposed changes, so Perry waged a years-long and bitter battle with him to reshape UT Austin and higher education across the state. In 2008, Perry endorsed "seven breakthrough solutions" designed to bring market-oriented changes to the state's colleges and universities.[23] Governor Perry proposed dramatically increasing enrollment, emphasizing student ratings in professor evaluations, dividing teaching and research budgets, and using revenue as a measure to decide if a program or course should continue. Powers openly fought Perry's ideas and promoted a different vision for Texas public universities, insisting on valuing and supporting faculty research, limiting online courses, and allowing enrollments to grow at a natural pace.[24]

In June 2013, Governor Perry vetoed a higher education bill, SB 15, that would have limited regents' power and included a provision that regents could not fire a university president without a chancellor's recommendation. Legislators from both parties accused Governor Perry and the University of Texas Board of Regents of micromanaging UT Austin and harassing its president, Bill Powers. But Governor Perry, who appoints university regents, ensured that the regents kept all their power and authority. Governor Perry said, "Limiting oversight authority of a board of regents is a step in the wrong direction."[25]

After defying his Board of Regents, the UT Chancellor, and Governor Perry, Bill Powers faced intense pressure to resign. By the time he retired, however, he was the second-longest-serving president in UT Austin history— and the voices pushing for major changes at UT Austin were quiet. "Bill put every ounce of himself into defending the soul of our university," current UT Austin President Greg Fenves wrote in a letter to the campus community upon Power's death in March 2019.[26] Fenves continued, "He bravely stood up for what was right, and he fought against a view of higher education that would have compromised UT's constitutional charge to be a 'university of the first class,' while setting a dangerous precedent for public research universities across the nation." Although Governor Perry was unsuccessful in changing UT Austin, he had more success with other universities across the state.

Current Texas Governor Greg Abbott has taken a hands-off approach to the state's colleges and universities and has worked very closely with the executive branch's other elected officials and with the Texas Legislature. Governor Abbott vetoed a number of pieces of legislation, but he cooperated with the Legislature when he signed the state's roughly $250 billion 2020-21 budget without issuing a single line-item veto.[27]

Legislative Powers of the Governor

The Texas governor makes policy recommendations that lawmakers in the state's House and Senate chambers may sponsor and introduce as bills. In the months before a new legislative session, the governor begins communicating priorities and expectations for the session. Effective governors use the office's power to call attention to issues and concerns they wish the Legislature to address. Governors often send a message in the form of a formal letter to the legislature's leadership. Then, early in the session, the governor will deliver a

» The Texas governor makes policy recommendations that lawmakers may sponsor and introduce as bills. In the months before a new legislative session, the governor begins communicating priorities and expectations for the session.

State of the State speech to a joint session of the legislature. In this speech, the governor lays out problems and priorities for the legislative session and for the next two years. This agenda-setting power is important for signaling the governor's expectations. If those expectations are not met, the governor has several powerful tools to shape the legislative outcome.

Lobbying: Governors will often send staff or, in important cases, go to the House or Senate floor to persuade members to pass or not pass specific legislation. In 2019, Greg Abbott made it well known that he greatly supported two priority issues of the 86th legislative session: school finance reform and property tax relief.

Veto: The governor has the critical power to sign a piece of legislation or to veto it. A **veto** is the rejection of a decision or proposal made by the Legislature. With a veto, the governor turns down a bill, which usually kills that policy. The Legislature can override a veto with a two-thirds vote of both the House and the Senate. The Texas Legislature has not overridden a governor's veto since 1979 when the House and Senate voted to override Governor Bill Clements's veto of HB2153 regarding the Commissioners Court of Comal County hunting and fishing regulations **(Figure 7.10)**.

Austin, Texas
May 14, 1979

TO THE MEMBERS OF THE HOUSE OF REPRESENTATIVES, SIXTY-SIXTH LEGISLATURE; REGULAR SESSION:

Pursuant to Article IV, Section 14, I herewith return to you House Bill 2153 vetoed, for the following reasons:

This bill continues a trend started in previous legislatures, that if allowed to continue would negate any attempt by the state, through the Parks and Wildlife Department, to regulate the taking of wildlife in this state. If this continues we would have no "uniform" wildlife regulations. If the legislature desires that there be no uniform regulation, and desires each county to regulate wildlife in that county, then the legislature should abolish all of the "uniform" regulations.

If we allowed each county to regulate health regulations applicable to the whole state and establish their own, we would have 254 different "state" health regulations. The same principle holds on various statewide laws -- they should either be applicable to all or applicable to none.

I would hope that future legislatures would repeal Section 61.202 of the Parks and Wildlife Code that sets up veto power by some 20 counties. In that same light, it is obvious I am against adding any more counties to the list, and therefore, I return House Bill 2153 to you unsigned.

Respectfully,

W. P. Clements, Jr.
Governor

FIGURE 7.10 Governor Clements Veto Letter of HB2153, May 14, 1979.

In June 2019, Governor Abbott vetoed more than fifty bills passed during the regular legislative session. Abbott explained that the bills were unnecessary, too costly, or too burdensome.

The Texas governor can also veto individual parts of appropriations bills. Called the **line-item veto**, this is the governor's power to veto specific provisions or items in a spending bill passed by the legislature. This power to cut or include specific budget items can shape the overall budget, act as a political bargaining tool, or punish specific legislators, agencies, or programs favored by the governor. In the final days of the 86th legislative session, a Senate confirmation looked increasingly unlikely for embattled Secretary of State David Whitley, so Governor Abbott lobbied the Senate to confirm his longtime aide. He called several Senate Democrats to his office individually to try to change their votes. The Democrats would not vote to confirm and thus prevented Whitley from keeping his job. Minutes after news broke that Whitley had resigned, Governor Abbott vetoed four seemingly uncontroversial bills authored by several of the Democrats whose opposition had doomed his nominee.[28]

Veto: *the power of the Texas governor to turn down legislation and can only be overridden by a two-thirds vote of both the House and Senate.*

Line-item veto: *power of the governor to veto any specific provision (line) of an appropriations bill passed by the Texas legislature.*

uttyler.edu

FIGURE 7.11 Governor Abbott, House Speaker Dennis Bonnen, and Brig. Gen. Tracy Norris, announce that the Texas National Guard will "provide assistance at temporary holding facilities" in the Rio Grande Valley and in El Paso and help at ports of entry.

Photo: Miguel Gutierrez Jr./The Texas Tribune

The Governor's Judicial Power

As noted in Chapter eight Texas judges are elected. When a vacancy occurs in a Texas district or appellate court due to resignation, retirement, death, or the creation of a new court, however, the governor can appoint a judge to fill the vacancy. Once appointed, judges tend to be reelected. Via this appointment power, the governor shapes the Texas judicial system. For example, District Judge Darlene Ewing, the longtime Democratic Party chairwoman who helped turn Dallas County reliably blue, died in 2018. During a decade as the party's chairwoman, Ewing helped local Democrats dominate for a period. Under her leadership from 2006 to 2012, Democrats won nearly every contested county-wide race they entered in Dallas County. The former chairwoman went on to be elected as the 254th District Court's judge in Dallas County on November 8, 2016, and was reelected in 2018 but passed away on November 16, 2018. Texas Democratic Party Chairman Gilberto Hinojosa praised Ewing: "Darlene was a loyal Texas Democrat and devoted so much of her life to champion Texas families and defend our progressive values."[29] Abbott appointed Ashley Wysocki of Dallas to the 254th family District Court in Dallas County to replace Darlene Ewing, replacing the loyal Democrat with a Republican. Wysocki's term is set to expire Dec. 31, 2020, and she is currently Dallas County's lone Republican district court judge.

Military Powers of the Texas Governor

On June 21, 2019, Governor Abbott acted as commander in chief of the state's National Guard units and announced that the state will deploy 1,000 Texas National Guard troops to the U.S.–Mexico border to aid the federal govern-ment in border security (Figure 7.11). An adjutant general appointed by the Texas governor heads the Texas National Guard units, and it is not unusual for the governor to deploy the National Guard. Abbott used about 12,000 Texas National Guardsmen to assist with relief and security efforts in Houston and in south Texas after devastating flooding from Hurricane Harvey.

With General Tracy Norris (the adjutant general of the Texas National Guard), Abbott said, "There is an escalating crisis at the border" during a news conference at the Texas Capitol. As the number of Central American migrants continued to surge in early 2019, Abbott said the troops will "provide assistance at temporary holding facilities" in the Rio Grande Valley and in El Paso and will help at ports of entry. National Guard deployments at the Texas—Mexico border have become relatively common in recent years. Governor Rick Perry deployed state guard units as Central American migrants began crossing illegally into the Rio Grande Valley. President Trump sent troops to the border in 2018, President Obama deployed 1,200 troops in 2010, and President George W. Bush sent about six thousand National Guard troops there in 2006.

Conclusions: The Texas Governor as a Plural System

The Texas governor clearly must share power with the Texas judicial and legislative branches and with statewide officials (elected and appointed) *within* the executive branch. On one hand, the sharing of power makes the governor weaker than most other governors in the United States. On the other hand, this shared power creates an opportunity for shared governance, compromise, and diverse opinions. As this chapter illustrates, the Texas governor's history of interest and even interference in the state's colleges and universities show the governor's powers and the multiple layers of control and policymaking.

In 2018, Governor Greg Abbott appointed Tyler businessman and former state Senator Kevin Eltife to a six-year term as the chair of the University of Texas Board of Regents.[30] On May 30, 2019, just after the end of the Texas 86th legislative session, Chairman Eltife (and UT Chancellor James B. Milliken) wrote a letter of thanks on behalf of the University of Texas System to Governor Greg Abbott, Lt. Gov. Dan Patrick, House Speaker Dennis Bonnen, and all the legislators who helped make the session successful for public higher education.

Governor Abbott and the state's leaders did not take Pa Ferguson's approach to the University of Texas. Instead, Abbott signed an appropriations bill that increased funding and provided a stable base of state support for Texas public universities.[31] The funding and support for the state's colleges and universities illustrate the complex and plural nature of the Texas executive and system of government.

Abbott did, however, use one aspect of higher education (football) in the 86th Legislative session to signal a different tone and expectations. In the November 2018 elections, Texas voters turned out in great numbers and sent a clear message to the state's political leaders. A Democrat from El Paso almost won a seat in the U.S. Senate, losing to the Republican by only three points. Texas Republican party losses (and near losses) in the 2018 elections across the state called for compromise and a more bipartisan approach to policy. Texas voters who showed up in surprising numbers in 2018 seemed to call

```
86R4363 SOS-D

By: Larson                                                      H.B. No. 412

                         A BILL TO BE ENTITLED
                              AN ACT
relating to an annual football game between The University of Texas
at Austin and Texas A&M University.
        BE IT ENACTED BY THE LEGISLATURE OF THE STATE OF TEXAS:
        SECTION 1.  Subchapter Z, Chapter 51, Education Code, is
amended by adding Section 51.9246 to read as follows:
        Sec. 51.9246.  FOOTBALL GAME BETWEEN THE UNIVERSITY OF TEXAS
AT AUSTIN AND TEXAS A&M UNIVERSITY. (a)  The intercollegiate
football teams of The University of Texas at Austin and Texas A&M
University shall play a nonconference, regular-season football
game against one another on the fourth Thursday, Friday, or
Saturday of November each year.
        (b)  If The University of Texas at Austin or Texas A&M
University refuses to play the football game required by Subsection
(a) in a year, the university may not award to any student for the
following academic year an athletic scholarship, grant, or similar
financial assistance funded by state funds and conditioned on the
student's participation on the university's intercollegiate
football team.
        SECTION 2.  Section 51.9246, Education Code, as added by
this Act, applies beginning with the intercollegiate football
season for the 2020-2021 academic year.
        SECTION 3.  This Act takes effect immediately if it receives
a vote of two-thirds of all the members elected to each house, as
provided by Section 39, Article III, Texas Constitution.  If this
Act does not receive the vote necessary for immediate effect, this
Act takes effect September 1, 2019.
```

FIGURE 7.12 State Representative Lyle Larson, a San Antonio Republican who earned a bachelor's degree from Texas A&M, filed House Bill 412, which would have required Texas A&M and The University of Texas at Austin football teams to "play a nonconference, regular-season football game against one another on the fourth Thursday, Friday, or Saturday of November each year."

for both Republicans and Democrats to produce legislative results in relevant areas—namely public and higher education, property taxes, and school safety.

While laying out his policy priorities for the legislative session in his State of the State address to lawmakers at the beginning of the session, Abbott offered an unexpected and bold compromise: reinstating an annual football game between the University of Texas at Austin and Texas A&M University. Abbott's compromise signaled to the state's leaders that he wanted to cooperate to have a successful session. He said, "I am inspired by the camaraderie and the collaboration that has already infused this session. It seems unprecedented, and I've got to tell you, I'm feeling it myself." Abbot continued, "I want to set the example. For example, I'm willing to step up and put aside past differences and work with [state Representative] Lyle Larson to reinstate the rivalry game between the Aggies and the Longhorns." (See Figure 7.12) Although Larson's bill (HB 412) never made it out of the Higher Education committee, the governor signaled his message, tone, and agenda for the session. The 86th Legislature was successful in important ways, and Texas voters' job approval numbers for the Legislature suggest that the governor's legislative strategy worked. At the end of the session, Governor Abbott's approval ratings were the highest of his governorship.[32]

Key Terms

Agriculture commissioner: elected state official who is responsible for agriculture, food, and rural matters.

Appointment power: the power of the governor to appoint people to office.

Attorney general: elected official who serves as the chief lawyer for the state.

Comptroller: elected official who directs the collection taxes and other state revenues and estimates revenue for the state budget.

Governor: elected official who is the chief executive of the state.

Impeachment: the formal charge by the Texas House of Representatives that leads to a trial in the Texas Senate and possibly removal of a state official.

Land commissioner: elected official who is in charge of Texas public lands.

Lieutenant governor: statewide elected official who presides over the Texas Senate.

Line-item veto: power of the governor to veto any specific provision (line) of an appropriations bill passed by the Texas legislature.

Plural executive system: an executive branch in which power is shared among several elected officials who are independent of the governor.

Secretary of state: state official who is responsible for overseeing elections in Texas and is appointed by the governor.

Senatorial courtesy: the practice whereby the Texas governor seeks the approval for a candidate's nomination from the senator of the candidate's home district.

Veto: the power of the Texas governor to turn down legislation and can only be overridden by a two-thirds vote of both the House and Senate.

uttyler.edu

ENDNOTES

[1] Tolleson-Rinehart, Sue, and Jeanie Ricketts Stanley. Claytie and the Lady: Ann Richards, Gender, and Politics in Texas. 1st ed. Austin: University of Texas Press, 1994.

[2] Wilson, Carol O'Keefe. In the Governor's Shadow: The True Story of Ma and Pa Ferguson. First ed. 2014.

[3] Geiger, Roger L. Perspectives on the History of Higher Education, Volume 24; Volume 2005. Routledge, 2017.

[4] Crouch, Barry A., and Donaly E. Brice. Governor's Hounds: The Texas State Police, 1870-1873. Austin: University of Texas Press, 2011.

[5] Handbook of Texas Online, James G. Dickson, Jr., "Attorney General." Retrieved from http://www.tshaonline.org/handbook/online/articles/mba03.

[6] See Texas State Board of Education Texas Permanent School Fund by David Bradley, Chairman, Committee on Finance and Permanent School Fund. Retrieved from: https://static.texastribune.org/media/documents/SBOE_Charter_School_Development_Plan_-_Draft.doc

[7] Sterken, Robert Edward Jr. Bill Ratliff: A Profile of Courage and Leadership in American Politics. Lexington Books. 2016. Pages, 71-74.

[8] The Aikin Archives. Retrieved from http://www.aikinarchives.org/index.php/main/about/about-the-aikin-archives.

[9] Agriculture Commissioner Grants Amnesty to Cupcakes in First Official Act, By Eva Hershaw, The Texas Tribune. January. 12, 2015. Retrieved from: https://www.texastribune.org/2015/01/12/commissioner-sid-miller-gives-amnesty-cupcakes.

[10] Clark, James Anthony. Three Stars for the Colonel. New York: Random House, 1954.

[11] Childs, William R. The Texas Railroad Commission: Understanding Regulation in America to the Mid-twentieth Century. 1st ed. Kenneth E. Montague Series in Oil and Business History; No. 17. College Station: Texas A & M University Press, 2005.

[12] A creek flowing to the Colorado River turned black. Now the state has sued the alleged polluter. By Carlos Anchondo, The Texas Tribune, April 17, 2019. Retrieved from https://www.texastribune.org/2019/04/17/texas-attorney-general-sues-inland-recylcling-and-remediation.

[13] Texas used money from the Help America Vote Act to help pay for its botched voter citizenship review, by Alexa Ura, The Texas Tribune, May 15, 2019. Retrieved from https://www.texastribune.org/2019/05/15/texas-used-funds-help-america-vote-act-pay-voter-roll-review.

[14] Texas Secretary of State David Whitley departs as legislative session ends, by Alexa Ura, The Texas Tribune, May 27, 2019. Retrieved from https://www.texastribune.org/2019/05/27/texas-secretary-state-david-whitley-forced-leave-office.

[15] Former Secretary of State David Whitley back at Gov. Greg Abbott's office, by Alexa Ura, The Texas Tribune, May 31, 2019. Retrieved from https://www.texastribune.org/2019/05/31/former-secretary-state-david-whitley-back-greg-abbotts-office.

[16] Valdez has $222,000 for general election, a fraction of Abbott's millions, By Patrick Svitek, The Texas Tribune, July 17, 2018. Retrieved from https://www.texastribune.org/2018/07/17/lupe-valdez-greg-abbott-millions-november-election.

[17] Sterken, Robert Edward Jr. Bill Ratliff: A Profile of Courage and Leadership in American Politics. Lexington Books. 2016.

[18] Government Disclosures Shed Light on Big Law Salaries, by Elizabeth Olson, Bloomberg Law, May 18, 2018. Retrieved from https://biglawbusiness.com/government-disclosures-shed-light-on-big-law-salaries.

[19] Source: The Texas Tribune Government Salary Explorer. Retrieved from https://salaries.texastribune.org.

[20] Sterken, Robert Edward Jr. Bill Ratliff: A Profile of Courage and Leadership in American Politics. Lexington Books. 2016. Pages 126-130.

[21] See: The Perry Legacy by Reeve Hamilton and Jay Root, The Texas Tribune. December 28, 2014. Retrieved from https://apps.texastribune.org/perry-legacy.

[22] For a complete list of appointed position see: https://gov.texas.gov/organization/appointments/positions.

[23] Six Degrees of Jeff Sandefer: Reform and Texas Higher Education, by Reeve Hamilton, The Texas Tribune, March 16, 2011. Retrieved from https://www.texastribune.org/2011/03/16/whos-behind-proposed-reforms-to-texas-higher-ed.

[24] Is Perry-Powers Tension About Rivalry or Policy? By Ross Ramsey, The Texas Tribune. April 1, 2013. Retrieved from https://www.texastribune.org/2013/04/01/reasons-wont-be-obvious-until-after-fight.

[25] Perry Issues More Than Two Dozen Vetoes, By Aman Batheja and Jay Root, The Texas Tribune, June 14, 2013. Retrieved from https://www.texastribune.org/2013/06/14/senator-perry-vetoed-equal-pay-bill.

[26]Former University of Texas at Austin President Bill Powers has died. Powers presided over the university from 2006 to 2015. By Matthew Watkins, The Texas Tribune, March 10, 2019. Retrieved from https://www.texastribune.org/2019/03/10/bill-powers-former-university-texas-president-has-died.

[27]Texas Gov. Greg Abbott signs $250 billion budget with no line-item vetoes, By Riane Roldan, The Texas Tribune, June 15, 2019. Retrieved from https://www.texastribune.org/2019/06/15/texas-gov-greg-abbott-signs-250-billion-budget.

[28]After blocking David Whitley's confirmation, Senate Democrats see bills die on Abbott's desk, By Alexa Ura and Emma Platoff, The Texas Tribune, May 29, 2019. Retrieved from https://www.texastribune.org/2019/05/29/texas-senate-democrats-block-whitley-governor-veto-bills.

[29]Darlene Ewing, who helped turn Dallas blue in a decade as Democratic Party chair, dies at 64, by Tasha Tsiaperas Gromer Jeffers Jr., The Dallas Morning News, November 16, 2018. Retrieved from https://www.dallasnews.com/news/politics/2018/11/16/darlene-ewing-helped-turn-dallas-blue-decade-democratic-party-chair-dies-64.

[30]Eltife elected chairman of The University of Texas System Board of Regents, Thursday, December 20, 2018. Retrieved from https://www.utsystem.edu/news/2018/12/20/eltife-elected-chairman-university-texas-system-board-regents.

[31]A great legislative session for higher education, By Kevin Eltife and James B. Milliken, The Texas Tribune, May 30, 2019. Retrieved from https://www.tribtalk.org/2019/05/30/a-great-legislative-session-for-higher-education.

[32]Texans' faint praise for the Legislature could get swamped by national politics. By James Henson and Joshua Blank, TribTalk, June 20, 2019. Retrieve from https://www.tribtalk.org/2019/06/20/texans-faint-praise-for-the-legislature-could-get-swamped-by-national-politics.

8

Historic architecture at the capitol building in Austin, Texas.